SEP 1 '96			
SE 8 '98			
SE 29 '98			
OC 13 '98			
JA 25 '99			
MR 22 '99			
SE 27 '99			
SE 11 '00			
JA 24 '01			
SEP 1 3 2001			
SEP 1 5 2003			

FREE SPEECH

Other Books in the Current Controversies Series:

The AIDS Crisis
Alcoholism
Drug Trafficking
Energy Alternatives
Europe
Gun Control
Illegal Immigration
Iraq
Nationalism and Ethnic Conflict
Police Brutality
Pollution
Sexual Harassment
Violence Against Women
Women in the Military
Youth Violence

FREE SPEECH

David L. Bender, *Publisher*
Bruno Leone, *Executive Editor*

Bonnie Szumski, *Managing Editor*
Katie de Koster, *Senior Editor*

Bruno Leone, *Book Editor*

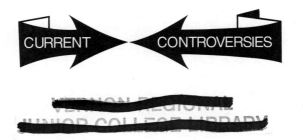

Cover photo: © R. Reinhard/Impact Visuals

Library of Congress Cataloging-in-Publication Data

Free speech / Bruno Leone, book editor.
    p. cm. — (Current controversies)
    Includes bibliographical references and index.
    Summary: A collection of articles debating issues related to free speech such as censorship, restrictions on the press, pornography, and libel.
    ISBN 1-56510-078-6 (lib. : alk. paper) — ISBN 1-56510-077-8 (pbk. : alk. paper)
    1. Freedom of speech. 2. Freedom of speech—United States. [1. Freedom of speech.] I. Leone, Bruno, 1939- . II. Series.
JC591.F77   1994
323.44'3—dc20   93-19855
                                                                   CIP
                                                                   AC

Printed on
recycled paper

© 1994 by Greenhaven Press, Inc., PO Box 289009, San Diego, CA 92198-9009
Printed in the U.S.A.
Every effort has been made to find owners of copyright material.

Contents

Chapter 1: Should Government Funding of the Arts Be Restricted?

Yes: Government Funding of the Arts Should Be Restricted

Chapter 2: Should Unrestricted Speech Be Allowed on College Campuses?

Yes: Unrestricted Speech Should Be Allowed on College Campuses

No: Unrestricted Speech Should Not Be Allowed on College Campuses

Chapter 3: Should There Be Limits to Free Speech?

Much has been made of "Cop Killer," the controversial recording by the rock performer Ice-T. Unquestionably, the song does incite and glorify violence. However, it should not be withdrawn from stores and is entitled to free speech protection.

Chapter 4: Should Pornography Be Censored?

Yes: Pornography Should Be Censored

standards, it is vital that communities loudly and clearly protest against the invasion of their homes and neighborhoods by illegal pornography."

No: Pornography Should Not Be Censored

Foreword

By definition, controversies are "discussions of questions in which opposing opinions clash" (Webster's Twentieth Century Dictionary Unabridged). Few would deny that controversies are a pervasive part of the human condition and exist on virtually every level of human enterprise. Controversies transpire between individuals and among groups, within nations and between nations. Controversies supply the grist necessary for progress by providing challenges and challengers to the status quo. They also create atmospheres where strife and warfare can flourish. A world without controversies would be a peaceful world; but it also would be, by and large, static and prosaic.

The Series' Purpose

The purpose of the Current Controversies series is to explore many of the social, political, and economic controversies dominating the national and international scenes today. Titles selected for inclusion in the series are highly focused and specific. For example, from the larger category of criminal justice, Current Controversies deals with specific topics such as police brutality, gun control, white collar crime, and others. The debates in Current Controversies also are presented in a useful, timeless fashion. Articles and book excerpts included in each title are selected if they contribute valuable, long-range ideas to the overall debate. And wherever possible, current information is enhanced with historical documents and other relevant materials. Thus, while individual titles are current in focus, every effort is made to ensure that they will not become quickly outdated. Books in the Current Controversies series will remain important resources for librarians, teachers, and students for many years.

In addition to keeping the titles focused and specific, great care is taken in the editorial format of each book in the series. Book introductions and chapter prefaces are offered to provide background material for readers. Chapters are organized around several key questions that are answered with diverse opinions representing all points on the political spectrum. Materials in each chapter include opinions in which authors clearly disagree as well as alternative opinions in which authors may agree on a broader issue but disagree on the possible solutions. In this way, the content of each volume in Current Controversies mirrors the mosaic of opinions encountered in society. Readers will quickly realize that there are many viable answers to these complex issues. By questioning each au-

11

thor's conclusions, students and casual readers can begin to develop the critical thinking skills so important to evaluating opinionated material.

Current Controversies is also ideal for controlled research. Each anthology in the series is composed of primary sources taken from a wide gamut of informational categories including periodicals, newspapers, books, United States and foreign government documents, and the publications of private and public organizations. Readers will find factual support for reports, debates, and research papers covering all areas of important issues. In addition, an annotated table of contents, an index, a book and periodical bibliography, and a list of organizations to contact are included in each book to expedite further research.

Perhaps more than ever before in history, people are confronted with diverse and contradictory information. During the Persian Gulf War, for example, the public was not only treated to minute-to-minute coverage of the war, it was also inundated with critiques of the coverage and countless analyses of the factors motivating U.S. involvement. Being able to sort through the plethora of opinions accompanying today's major issues, and to draw one's own conclusions, can be a complicated and frustrating struggle. It is the editors' hope that Current Controversies will help readers with this struggle.

"Congress shall make no law respecting an establishment of religion, or prohibiting the exercise thereof; or abridging the freedom of speech, or of the press; or the right of the people peaceably to assemble, and to petition the Government for a redress of grievances."

First Amendment to the Constitution of the United States of America

Introduction

When he was sixteen years old, a precocious Benjamin Franklin wrote that "in those wretched countries where a man cannot call his tongue his own, he can scarce call anything his own. Whoever would overthrow the liberty of a nation must begin by subduing the freeness of speech." With this statement, Franklin was expressing an opinion that a majority of Americans, both notable and obscure, would echo with conviction and regularity throughout the history of the Republic. Free thought, patterned and sheltered in the mind, is incapable of leaving its safe harbor without the vehicle of free speech to convey it. For a nation to be considered free, its people must be able to spend their thoughts, no matter how heinous or unorthodox they may seem, in the open marketplace of ideas. Conscious of these ideals, the Founding Fathers made certain that the right to free speech was incorporated into and guaranteed by the First Amendment to the Constitution of the United States.

Yet despite this guarantee, the constitutional history of the United States is a mosaic of federal legislation and prosecutions that abridge the right of free speech. The reason is that throughout the history of the nation, most judges and legal scholars have held that the Founding Fathers did not intend that the First Amendment literally and absolutely bar all limits on speech. In fact, in an article entitled "The Bill of Rights" published in 1960 in the *New York University Law Review*, U.S. Supreme Court justice Hugo Black, a widely regarded First Amendment "absolutist," wrote that the framers of the Bill of Rights (the first ten amendments) "neither said what they meant nor meant what they said" when they composed the free speech clause in the First Amendment.

Therein lies the heart of the controversy: If the Founding Fathers did not intend that all speech be accorded unequivocal protection under law, how, then, should the First Amendment be interpreted? To provide the answer, a litmus test has been furnished by which federal laws and constitutional issues called into question can be judged. The federal judiciary, which includes appellate courts and the Supreme Court, has been given the constitutional power of judicial review. That means that before the line separating freedom and restraint can be drawn on any issue, the question of intent must be reviewed by the courts. Separated from the framers of the Constitution by decades, and now even centuries, it has been incumbent upon judges and legal scholars to decide what exactly the framers intended to be protected by the free speech clause in the First Amendment. And agreement has hardly ever been uniform or arrived at easily.

For example, what constitutes "speech"? Justice Black, arguably one of America's most eminent jurists, did not believe that protest marches and other forms of nonverbal expression belonged in the category of "speech" and therefore they were not entitled to First Amendment protection. Another question involves degree. How far may one go before freedom becomes license? Justice Oliver Wendell Holmes, whose credentials in the minds of most legal scholars equaled those of Hugo Black and who, throughout his life, championed the cause of free speech, found reason to limit speech. In the Supreme Court case of Schenck v. United States, Holmes delivered the majority decision of the Court upholding the conviction of Charles T. Schenck, a socialist who mailed circulars urging draftees to refuse induction into the army during World War I. He wrote that "the character of every act depends on the circumstances in which it is done. The most stringent protection of free speech would not protect a man in falsely shouting fire in a theater and causing a panic. . . . The question in every case is whether the words are used in such circumstances and are of such a nature as to create a clear and present danger."

Finally there are those who adhere to a literal and absolutist interpretation of the First Amendment and who believe that in virtually all circumstances free speech is a right that should remain without restraints. The number of persons and organizations throughout American history dedicated to this proposition are legion. Supreme Court justice William O. Douglas spoke for this entire group when, in an address on December 3, 1952, before the Authors Guild of America, he said: "It is our attitude toward free thought and free expression that will determine our fate. There must be no limit on the range of temperate discussion, no limits on thought. No subject must be taboo. No censor must preside at our assemblies. . . . Restriction of free thought and free speech is the most dangerous of all subversions."

The question of free speech is one of the most contentious in America's history. While most persons would agree philosophically that free speech is essential in a free society, it is difficult to find agreement on what exactly constitutes protected areas of speech. *Free Speech: Current Controversies* attempts to mirror the factious nature of this issue. It has deliberately focused upon questions that have held national prominence during the decade of the 1990s. The controversies debated here include pornography, government funding of controversial art and artists, and speech codes on college campuses. In considering these seemingly disparate subjects, one can discern the principles that define the debate on freedom of speech.

Chapter 1

Should Government Funding of the Arts Be Restricted?

CURRENT CONTROVERSIES

Chapter Preface

In 1965, Congress established the National Endowment for the Arts (NEA) and its companion agency, the National Endowment for the Humanities. At the time, Congress declared that "while no government can call a great artist or scholar into existence," government can help in creating and sustaining "a climate encouraging freedom of thought, imagination, and inquiry." The congressional statement promised that the government would provide the material support necessary to facilitate "the release of this creative talent." Since 1966, the NEA has awarded approximately 100,000 grants at a cost of nearly $3 billion in federal funds (the federal monies have been more than equally matched by private sources).

During the past several years, however, government funding of the arts through the NEA has been severely criticized by both the public and key members of Congress. A series of controversial grants resulted in angry denunciations and vituperative rhetoric leveled at the NEA and its leadership. One such challenged grant, for example, was awarded in 1989 in support of an exhibition by artist Andres Serrano that included a work entitled *Piss Christ*—a plastic crucifix submerged in a jar of the artist's urine.

Conservative organizations and members of Congress raised the specter of censorship when they attempted to prevent NEA funding from going to artists such as Serrano whose works they considered offensive. Senator Jesse Helms, in July 1989, introduced a bill into the Senate designed to prevent the NEA from sponsoring "obscene or indecent" art. Although the bill died in the House of Representatives, not a year has passed since the Serrano exhibit in which Congress has not at least considered restricting funds to the NEA. Many feel that the NEA's grant-making process has become politicized in response to the intense attention focused on the conflict.

Several artists, such as author Wallace Stegner, have refused NEA medals and/or grants to protest what they perceive as government attempts to limit free speech and monitor artistic expression. Opponents of the NEA rebut that government is entitled to discriminate in the allocation of federal funds and that where obscenity is at issue, community standards should provide the yardstick against which all awards must be measured. As the following viewpoints illustrate, the controversy promises to continue as the divide separating the opposing forces broadens.

Government Funding of the Arts Should Be Restricted

by Robert H. Knight

About the author: *Robert H. Knight is a Senior Fellow, Cultural Policy Studies, at the Heritage Foundation, a conservative think tank headquartered in Washington, D.C.*

The National Endowment for the Arts remains embroiled in controversy. NEA defenders call it a battle over "censorship." But this is an attempt to divert attention from the real issues: to what extent the federal government should fund the arts; to what extent recipients must be held accountable for their grants; and to what extent American culture is affected.

That the NEA remains controversial is clear from the list of grants announced in January 1991. Tucked into $47 million worth of new awards are grants to performance artists Karen Finley and Holly Hughes. Both artists, who specialize in "shock" material, were denied grants in 1989 because of the sexually explicit nature of their performances. Karen Finley is best known for smearing her naked body with chocolate and bean sprouts, inserting yams into her vagina and saying things like: "God is death. God is dead. Forget God and religion." Holly Hughes, a self-described "man-hating lesbian," specializes in portraying "lesbian desire."

Bias and Confusion

But NEA's woes go beyond the controversy over grants to artists who delight in sexually shocking audiences. Some of the more serious problems at NEA include:

- Bias against traditional forms of art and traditional values in general;
- Bias against religion; rejecting positive portrayals of religious themes as violating the separation of church and state, but funding attacks on religion as "artistic expression";
- Elevation of "freedom of expression" and "artistic merit" as the main crite-

From Robert H. Knight, "The National Endowment for the Arts: Misusing Taxpayers' Money," the Heritage Foundation *Backgrounder*, January 18, 1991. Reprinted with permission of the Heritage Foundation.

ria for grants, ignoring the NEA's charter legislation of 1965, which set "encouragement of excellence" as the No. 1 criterion, followed by "access to the arts for all Americans";

• Confusion by upper management about how to comply with congressionally mandated standards;

• Confusion about NEA's primary mission;

• Conflicts of interest in the grant-awarding process;

• A bureaucracy openly hostile to public scrutiny. NEA officials routinely withhold information, even from Congress. And they sometimes react harshly toward NEA critics. . . .

As envisaged in its charter, the NEA is a force for excellence, education, preservation of American heritage and cultural diversity, and a means by which more Americans can appreciate and be uplifted by the best in art.

In great measure, however, particularly with regard to the visual arts (drawing, painting, and sculpting) and "performance" arts, the NEA has become a platform for attacks on religion, traditional art forms, traditional families, and traditional values. In the name of tolerance it has shown increasing intolerance toward standards of any kind. Its peer review process has become a buddy system for awarding grants to colleagues, friends, and clients of panel members, who are almost uniformly avant-garde in orientation.

Can the NEA Be Fixed?

Whether the agency can be fixed is a question that divides the agency's critics. Some want to abolish it entirely, arguing that it is beyond the government's acumen to determine which artists are worthy of sponsorship and which are not. Others want to reform it, preserving grants to certain segments of the arts community such as those museums and orchestras with widely-held reputations for excellence, like New York's Metropolitan Museum of Art or the San Francisco Opera.

Although there is no clear consensus among those who feel the agency is salvageable, suggested reforms include:

> **"Some want to abolish it [NEA] entirely."**

• *Greater oversight of the peer panel selection process.* Although current legislation prohibits the most obvious past abuse (that of artists sitting on the same panels that review their own grant applications), membership on the panels should be broadened and closely monitored for conflicts of interest.

• *Minimal content restrictions.* In 1989, NEA was prohibited from funding art depicting "sadomasochism, homoeroticism, the sexual exploitation of children" and other works deemed "obscene" by the community standards definition established by the United States Supreme Court in 1973. This year all content restrictions have been scrapped.

• *Abolishing the Inter-Arts grant category.* Inter-Arts gives money to artists who do not fit into the other grant categories, bankrolling such bizarre "performance" artists as former pornographic movie star Annie Sprinkle, who masturbates and urinates on stage.

> *"Virtually all major arts organizations in America now receive at least part of their funding from the federal government via NEA."*

• *Abolishing grants to individuals.* The original NEA charter did not provide for individual grants, focusing instead on strengthening arts institutions. Many individual grants have become bonuses for financially successful artists who do not need the money or a form of welfare for artists who produce unsalable works.

• *Increasing the emphasis on basic skills in arts education.* Most of the NEA grants to educational institutions emphasize abstract thinking, art theory, and other esoteric topics instead of practical skills such as drawing technique.

• *Promoting excellence as the prime criterion, as the NEA charter explicitly requires.* In the visual arts and theater, NEA grants consistently favor novelty rather than excellence. To be sure, experimentation is a valued part of a vibrant arts scene. This does not mean, however, that the NEA should reject artists who create traditional works of excellence just because their methods are not considered "new."

What Is the NEA?

The NEA was established in 1965 when Lyndon Johnson signed the National Foundation on the Arts and Humanities Act, which also created the National Endowment for the Humanities. With an initial budget of $2.5 million and fewer than a dozen employees, the NEA remained a small entity under Director Roger Stevens for the next four years. After Richard Nixon appointed Nancy Hanks as director in 1969, the agency grew exponentially. By 1979, the budget had reached $149,589,000 and two years later was $158,795,000. Ronald Reagan cut the NEA budget for 1982 to $143,465,000, but it soon began growing again.

The NEA's 1991 budget was $175 million, up from $171.3 million in 1990, and the agency employs about 185 full-time staffers. Including the 1991 appropriations, the NEA has spent more than $2.5 billion over its 25-year history. Virtually all major arts organizations in America now receive at least part of their funding from the federal government via NEA. This gives the agency enormous clout in shaping the art world. NEA annually awards some 4,400 grants out of approximately 18,500 applications.

Through its grants to local, state, and regional arts councils, NEA has fostered enormous growth in arts administration throughout the nation. All 50 states and six U.S. territories now have arts councils. Regional and local arts councils have mushroomed from a handful in the 1960s to 3,000, including 600 professionally staffed organizations.

The NEA distributes funds by awarding matching grants to nonprofit, tax-exempt arts organizations and fellowships to individual artists. Most of the fellowships are for $5,000 or $15,000. The largest grants are Challenge Grants, requiring matching non-federal dollars. These range from $50,000 to $1 million. The NEA also provides a minimum of 25 percent of its budget to state and regional arts agencies, which make their own grants.

NEA panels advise other federal agencies in commissioning artworks for federal buildings under the auspices of the Arts in Architecture program.

The NEA is directed by a presidentially appointed chairman and advised by the National Council on the Arts, a presidentially appointed body composed of the Endowment chairman and 26 citizens who are "recognized for their knowledge of the arts, or for their expertise or profound interest in the arts."

Expert Panels

Most of the work of approving grants is done by advisory "peer review" panels. About 800 artists or experts in the arts participate on the panels and are selected by NEA bureaucrats. The National Council reviews the panel decisions and makes final recommendations on grants and policies to the Chairman.

"The NEA should not be fostering bias toward one particular arts style over another."

In 1966 the Endowment had six active programs: Music, Dance, Literature, Visual Arts, Theater and Education. In 1967, the first full fiscal year of operation, the Endowment added Architecture, Planning and Design (now Design Arts), Public Media (now Media Arts) and the Federal-State (now State Programs), which requires a three-to-one match in non-federal to federal funds.

Over the years, more programs were added. Now the NEA operates twelve programs, plus an office for public partnership, which handles Local and State Grants Programs and Arts in Education; an Office for Private Partnership; and Office of Policy, Planning and Research, which directs a fellowship program for arts managers, international activities, and research; and an Office for Special Constituencies, which targets aid to arts programs for the disabled, the elderly, and the institutionalized.

Unlike any other arts sponsor, the federal government has unique authority and unique responsibility. Its powers derive from its claim to represent all Americans and its money comes from mandatory taxation. No matter how deftly the NEA performs, its very existence implies the imprimatur of "official art." Government subsidies connote government approval, so the NEA, unlike a private donor, must take into account public sensibilities as well as the impact of its own policies. . . .

Since its founding, the NEA consistently has favored the avant-garde—defined by Webster's Third New International Unabridged Dictionary as: "Those who create, produce or apply new, original or experimental ideas, designs, techniques . . . and sometimes: a group that is extremist, bizarre, or arty and affected." There is a place, of course, for experimental art, and for NEA to fund some of it. The trouble is, the NEA so overwhelmingly favors the avant-garde that it crowds out other forms. Artists with the traditional skills of drawing, painting, and sculpting systematically are excluded from NEA grants and NEA peer review panels, which control the grants. As Visual Arts Program Director Susan Lubowsky told *The Washington Post*: "Art is always on the cutting edge, and anything on the cutting edge is going to offend someone." By defining art solely as "cutting edge," Lubowsky reveals the pervasive NEA view that the only "real" art is avant-garde.

> *"Denying public access to such basic data is a curious way for a tax-funded agency to operate."*

Strict Guidelines

As a federal agency, the NEA should not be fostering bias toward one particular arts style over another. In fact its own grant guidelines specifically forbid it to do so: "[NEA] must not, under any circumstances, impose a single aesthetic standard or attempt to direct artistic content."

NEA's skewing of the nation's arts toward the avant-garde style has not necessarily led to higher quality art. A free market is the most reliable guarantor of excellence since it fosters competition. Government policies that hamper competition, as the NEA does, therefore, are not likely to foster excellence.

In NEA arts education programs, only a handful emphasize drawing skill—the fount of design and perspective. The 1988 NEA report on arts education *Toward Civilization* even omitted drawing from a list of "basic" skills that students should acquire. Traditional, representational artists, meanwhile, repeatedly are blackballed in the NEA grants process. The New York Academy of Art, a graduate school dedicated to teaching such traditional skills as drawing, anatomy, perspective, and composition, applied to the NEA for a Challenge Grant but was turned down by an advisory panel. The reasons, according to a December 20, 1989, NEA memo from Jeanne Hodges, director of the Challenge and Advancement Grant Programs, and Visual Arts Program director Susan Lubowsky, included:

• "Concept of the program is not reflective of current developments in the visual arts field."

• "Panel questioned the exclusive emphasis on figurative drawing and technique and its potential impact on art of our time."

• "Panel disagreed with basic philosophical impetus of the application for being too rigidly modeled on European academicism with no acknowledgement of 20th-century concepts of Modernism. It was feared that this revisionist approach would stifle creativity in young artists."

In other words, the NEA is not funding the New York Academy of Art largely because the Academy concentrates on teaching classical, technical skills. In a more detailed letter to the Academy, Ana Steele, NEA Acting Deputy Chairman for Programs, notes that the Academy's curriculum, which focuses on human figure studies, is not "balanced" with modernism. Lack of balance, however, apparently does not bother the NEA when it applies to the vast number of arts programs devoted exclusively to the modernist perspective. Says Colgate University Political Scientist Robert Kaufman, an attorney who is now a Bradley Resident Scholar at The Heritage Foundation: "Based on the language in the NEA's own statement of mission, it appears that NEA is clearly violating procedural due process."

Many other traditional artists and institutions have been denied grants. Among them is Frederick Hart, who sculpted the soldiers at the Vietnam War Memorial and the "Creation" sculptures on the facade of Washington's National Cathedral. In 1972, Hart asked the NEA for a grant to complete the design phase of the project. His application was denied. He recalls: "An NEA bureaucrat told me that they didn't do religious things. Separation of church and state and all that." To-

> *"One thrust of NEA-funded arts education is the advancement of what NEA calls a 'multicultural' agenda."*

day, the "Creation" is widely cited as one of the highlights of the National Cathedral.

NEA defenders like to point out that NEA sponsors or insures major traveling exhibitions of representational, classical art such as "Cleopatra's Egypt," "A Day in the Country: Impressionism and the French Landscape," and "Flemish Still Life Paintings from Budapest." But current artists who produce representational art are largely absent from the list of NEA grantees.

NEA "Stonewalling"

Statistics on NEA grants to representational artists are unavailable. "That's the problem," Hart says. "It's impossible to get them to give you any information. It would be interesting to find out who has been turned down."

NEA Public Affairs Director Jack Lichtenstein says that NEA will not disclose rejected applications "as a matter of privacy." Denying public access to such basic data is a curious way for a tax-funded agency to operate. Even congressmen have had difficulty obtaining information, according to Richard T. Dykema, Administrative Assistant to Representative Dana Rohrabacher, the California Republican. "That's public information," he says of grant applications. "But the NEA stonewalls it."

In November 1990, The Heritage Foundation asked NEA Museum Program Administrator Larry Rickard for permission to examine the application of artist Mike Kelley, whose grant request for a show at the Institute of Contemporary Art in Boston was vetoed by NEA Chairman John Frohnmayer in late October. In a telephone interview, Rickard said the application, complete with "visual" samples of Kelley's work, could be seen immediately. A half hour later, at NEA headquarters, Rickard told a Heritage researcher that the file was not available and was "making the rounds" of the agency because of the controversy. He said he would call when it became available. Heritage is still waiting for Rickard's call. Another file concerning another controversial grant request was also "checked out," the Heritage researcher was told.

"They're more secretive than the CIA or the Pentagon," says New York artist and arts critic James Cooper, who has tried to research NEA grant procedures.

Exaggerated Numbers

In 1975 the NEA itself conducted a study into how much money was allocated for realist art compared to modernist art. Heritage was not able to obtain the study, but Boston art consultant John Arthur said the survey greatly exaggerated the number of realist works funded, thus quieting Congressional concern. Arthur, who was helping the NEA at the time to set up the national Bicentennial arts exhibit, says he observed NEA officials openly joking about their classification methods. Works that were overwhelmingly modernist but included a tiny, recognizable object such as a feather were judged to be "representational," Arthur said.

In 1989, the General Accounting Office asked NEA to review grants in the Painting and Works on Paper categories of the Visual Arts Program. A letter written by NEA General Counsel Davis to the General Accounting Office supports Arthur's contention as to how the works are classified. NEA Visual Arts Program Director Susan Lubowsky, says the letter, reviewed 2,400 slides of work by 169 artists who applied for grants in the Painting and Works on Paper categories in 1989. Lubowsky determined that works could be "broadly categoried as representational" if they "contained identifiable imagery." She concluded that 50 percent of the images qualified as "representational" and that 33 percent of that total were "strictly representational" because their "imagery was clearly true to life."

"Few Americans want censorship, but few also want tax money funding attacks on their most deeply held values."

Art critic Cooper, who has attended hundreds of exhibitions by NEA-sponsored institutions, said he has yet to see a "strictly representational" new artwork funded by NEA. The pattern in NEA-supported visual artworks seems clearly oriented toward the avant-garde. Numerical evidence is scant, however, since, "no detailed statistics have been kept based on style of expression," NEA

Counsel Davis wrote the GAO.

The bias toward the avant-garde is not limited to the visual arts. In a January 22, 1988, memo to Members of the Professional Theater Companies Panel, Robert Marx, director of the NEA's Theater Program, outlined criteria for panel members to use in assessing grant applications. From the highest category (most likely to receive a grant) to the lowest (least likely), the salient factor was risk-taking. Theaters that indulge in too many "audience-pleasers" are to be rated lower in proportion to the number of publicly well-received productions. In other words, the more the public appreciates what is presented, the less chance the theater has of being considered worthy of NEA support. The result: NEA encourages theaters to produce works likely to be rejected in the marketplace.

The NEA's official position on art education makes sense. The 1988 NEA arts education report *Towards Civilization* states: "Trying to create or perform the nonliterary arts without skills and knowledge is like trying to write without vocabulary and syntax. The student is reduced to being the 'first artist.' . . . Arts education must include the vocabularies and basic skills which produced the great works of the past so that young people can build on those who came before."

But NEA seldom follows its own wise counsel. Its grants flow almost exclusively to modernist, avant-garde schools and multicultural laboratories; little goes to schools or artists who emphasize classical skills. In late December 1990, NEA officials told New York Academy of Art officials not to bother re-applying for a grant, even though NEA Chairman Frohnmayer visited the New York City school earlier in the year and suggested that they should re-apply, says Academy founder Stuart Pivar.

> *"The pattern of funding suggests that it mainly is elites who are subsidized by the NEA."*

According to Richard Lack, founder of Minneapolis' Richard Lack Atelier School of Classical Art: "All of us who work as representative artists consider the NEA a joke." NEA has had an avant-garde focus "since its inception," he adds. "We took some interest in it in the beginning, but watching who was appointed to policy-making positions, we decided not to bother with it." Lack's school, which had been snubbed repeatedly by the Minnesota Artists Exhibition Program, finally received a grant for 1990-1991. The MAEP, run by NEA grant recipient Minneapolis Institute of Art, is almost exclusively biased toward avant-garde art, Lack told The Heritage Foundation. Lack said he believes the unexpected funding may be NEA's attempt to blunt criticism that realists are never funded.

A Multicultural Agenda

One thrust of NEA-funded arts education is the advancement of what NEA calls a "multicultural" agenda. In practice this seems more concerned with criticizing traditional American culture than promoting understanding of other cultures. The National Arts Education Research Center, funded by a $169,420 NEA grant and $250,000 from the U.S. Department of Education, has compiled

"If censorship is being practiced, it is by the NEA."

"A Framework for Multicultural Arts Education." This 1989 study, written at the Center's New York University offices, calls for "radically different" education techniques to discredit the traditional "melting pot" view of minority assimilation into American life. . . .

Because media coverage has been largely limited to abstract concepts, a number of misconceptions have prevented meaningful debate on the NEA:

Misconception #1: Controversial works are no more objectionable than nudes seen in many major museums. NEA defenders frequently invoke images of NEA critics seeking to "censor" Michelangelo's "David" or Rubens' robust ladies.

Reality: The works in question depict explicit sex (including such practices as inserting an entire fist and wrist into an anus), human excrement and urine, various portrayals of Jesus Christ as a drug addict, a homosexual or as part of a toilet facility. In the NEA's 1991 reauthorization legislation, all content restrictions on grants were removed except for a single reference to "decency." Even this mild guideline has incensed many in the arts community. An NEA literature peer review panel resigned en masse in December 1990 over the "decency" provision, claiming they did not know what "decency" meant. NEA Chairman Frohnmayer threw in with the dissenters when he declared at a December 1 meeting of NEA's advisory council: "I am not going to be the decency czar." He said this despite his legislated mandate that "the chairman shall ensure" that grants must take into consideration "general standards of decency."

Misconception #2: Most of what NEA funds is good. The objectionable works, says Chairman Frohnmayer, constitute only a handful of the "million images" funded by NEA over the years.

Reality: Individual exhibits often contain not a handful but hundreds of images. Not only have NEA-sponsored exhibits included Andres Serrano's now-famous "Piss Christ," a crucifix submerged in the artist's own urine, but feature Serrano projects that use semen, urine, and pads soaked in menstrual blood. One work, "Piss Pope," is an image of Pope John Paul II submerged in urine. On a list of NEA-sponsored offensive images, Serrano's contributions at least number in the dozens. The NEA has also funded multiple grant recipients Karen Finley, Holly Hughes and other performance artists in dozens of performances. Finally, the list of exhibits of avant-garde images funded by NEA grants would be in the tens of thousands if not hundreds of thousands. In a typical example, the NEA in 1989 gave New York's Whitney Museum of American Art $75,000 to support the exhibit "The New Sculpture: Between Geometry and Gesture, 1965-75." The two dozen galleries in the exhibit contained hundreds of undistinguished objects such as rope, burlap, rocks and scraps of wire scattered on the floor or tacked to the walls.

Misconception #3: The arts would decline in America without federal funding.

Reality: Private support of the visual and performing arts reached $7.4 billion in 1989, compared with the NEA's annual budget of $171 million. Federal funds have generated a substantial increase in personal and corporate giving to the arts, but it is debatable whether this has resulted in better quality art or more efficient use of dollars that might have been spent on other charities. The surge in arts spending has built arts bureaucracies in all 50 states, institutionalizing the arts market. Before, artists had only to please buyers or donors. Now, they expend considerable creativity appeasing federal bureaucrats.

Misconception #4: No-strings federal funding of the arts is more consistent with "the American Way" than prudent oversight.

Reality: Polls show that few Americans want censorship, but few also want tax money funding attacks on their most deeply held values. The public seems to be able to make the distinction between privately sponsored works and those publicly funded. They resent NEA spending millions on art that the vast majority of Americans find neither uplifting, ennobling, beautiful, nor meaningful. It is understandable that Americans oppose the use of their tax dollars by Annie Sprinkle, who, at a New York City show funded by NEA, declared after purportedly achieving orgasm with a sex toy: "Usually, I get paid to do this, but tonight it's government-funded."

Misconception #5: NEA aid most benefits those who do not have access to the arts.

Reality: A significant portion of NEA funding goes to symphony orchestras, opera and other art forms patronized by those who can afford even steep ticket prices. The pattern of funding suggests that it mainly is elites who are subsidized by the NEA.

Misconception #6: NEA funds are distributed fairly across the nation.

Reality: The 1989 NEA annual report reveals that 42 percent of grants went to just six areas: New York City (23.3 percent), Minneapolis-St. Paul (5.2 percent), Washington, D.C. (3.9 percent), San Francisco (3.8 percent), Los Angeles (3.1 percent), and Chicago (2.6 percent).

> **"Before, artists had only to please buyers or donors. Now, they expend considerable creativity appeasing federal bureaucrats."**

Misconception #7: NEA primarily helps struggling artists who would not produce art without federal subsidies.

Reality: Many grants go to established artists who are anything but struggling. In 1986, NEA gave $20,000 to best-selling author Tama Janowitz (*Slaves of New York*) so she could revise her next book, *A Cannibal in Manhattan*. In 1987, NEA gave playwright/actor Wallace Shawn a $20,000 playwriting grant. He had appeared in more than a dozen films in the previous seven years and had already written several successful plays. Painter Rafael Ferrer received a $15,000 NEA grant in 1989, his third from the agency. With homes in Philadelphia and the Dominican Republic, and a biography that lists 53 one-man shows and 127 group shows over the past 25 years, Ferrer would hardly seem a deserving artistic welfare case.

Sam Gilliam, an artist whose three-dimensional canvas and aluminum works fetch from $25,000 to $45,000 in New York galleries, received a 1989 NEA grant for $15,000. It was the

> *"It is Congress's job to monitor whether taxpayers' money is being well spent."*

seventh NEA grant for the artist, whose commissioned artworks appear in Atlanta's airport terminal, a federal building in Detroit, subway stations in Boston and Buffalo, and convention centers in San Francisco and Washington, D.C.

Performance artist Karen Finley has received at least a half dozen NEA grants. Upon news that her 1990 grant application was vetoed by NEA Chairman Frohnmayer, fans sold out her $25-a-ticket performance at the NEA-supported Serious Fun Festival in July 1990 at New York's Lincoln Center, then sold out a second, added show.

Performance artist Holly Hughes, who also has collected several NEA grants, was denied a grant in 1989. Yet that year she received a $15,000 playwriting grant for a script for the show that was vetoed.

Misconception #8: Criticism of NEA grants is an infringement on the free speech guaranteed by the First Amendment.

Reality: The Bill of Rights specifically limits the government, not the populace: "Congress shall make no law. . . ." Private criticism of public policy or publicly funded artworks is protected speech.

Misconception #9: Congressional oversight of NEA grants is an infringement upon freedom of speech.

Reality: The Constitution does not prohibit Congress from setting rules for how federal money is spent. In fact, it is Congress's job to monitor whether taxpayers' money is being well spent.

Misconception #10: Recent reforms have solved NEA's most pressing problems.

Reality: There have been almost no reforms. By eliminating all content restrictions, Congress has given the green light to more funding of what NEA Acting Deputy Chairman for Programs Randolph McAusland described as "problematic grants." NEA officials proved this by issuing grants in January 1991 to Karen Finley and Holly Hughes. NEA Chairman Frohnmayer, who approved the grants, says he is "personally opposed" to federal funding of obscene art. But he has fought all restrictions on grants. On at least one occasion, he has said that NEA approval of an artwork means that, by definition, the artwork cannot possibly be obscene.

NEA defenders say that the agency aims for strict neutrality in grant awards. In truth, however, grants are approved by peer review panels, whose members are often themselves dependent to varying degrees on government handouts and on each other. The peer review process is a tightly knit buddy system, with artists taking turns giving each other grants. Until this year, artists and museum executives could even sit on panels that awarded grants to their own institutions; they merely had to leave the room when the panel voted on their grant. . . .

Saving the NEA

Although the very idea of government funding of the arts is itself questionable, a few basic reforms might end the worst abuses. Such reforms include:

• A study by Congress's General Accounting Office of allegations of conflicts of interest in the awarding of grants.

• A GAO study into charges that the NEA systematically discriminates against traditional artists and art forms. GAO, for example, should demand a list of funded artworks and inspect them to determine how NEA defines the term "representational."

• Eliminating the Inter-Arts grant division, which funds performance artists who do not fit into any other category.

• Returning to the NEA charter's demand for "excellence" as the criterion for grants.

• Reintroducing minimal content restrictions. Clearly written prohibitions on explicit sex, child pornography and attacks on religion are not inappropriate for projects funded by taxpayers. The descriptions of what is prohibited can be made very specific, leaving artists free to explore the widest array of subjects.

• Redirecting money from new works to projects that preserve the existing repertoire, such as paintings by the great masters. NEA already sponsors preservation programs for museums.

• Redirecting money to arts education programs that teach basic skills, beginning with drawing.

Chairman John E. Frohnmayer calls the NEA "critically important to the soul of this nation." Although the arts certainly flourished in America before NEA's founding in 1965, Frohnmayer has a point: NEA has an enormous amount of clout. With a budget of $175 million and 185 employees, NEA is a relatively small federal agency, but it is a giant symbolically. Indeed, the agency's stated mission is to "foster artistic excellence by helping to develop the nation's finest creative talent, to preserve our cultural heritage in all its diversity, to make the arts available to wider, more informed audiences, and to promote the overall financial stability of American arts organizations."

> *"Artists simply do not have a 'right' to money taken from taxpayers."*

Virtually every major arts institution and artist receives money from NEA. Along with the money, each grantee receives tacit approval and legitimacy from the federal government. The nation may be producing more art than in 1965, but

28

whether the taxpayers are getting better art for their money is debatable. It is a long way from the paintings of Andrew Wyeth to the antics of Annie Sprinkle.

Taxpayers' Rights

NEA defenders contend that the agency should be exempt from careful stewardship of federal spending. This shows contempt for the rights of taxpayers. Artists simply do not have a "right" to money taken from taxpayers. NEA's congressional critics are accused of advocating "censorship" of the arts, but no lawmaker has suggested that artists be prevented from creating or displaying their works.

If censorship is being practiced, it is by the NEA. In violation of its own guidelines, NEA almost exclusively favors a single artistic style, avant-garde, discriminating against artists who create traditional, representational works. Because private donors use NEA grants as indicators of worth, NEA skews the arts toward the strictly experimental.

NEA's grant approval system is rife with conflicts of interest, and 1991's reforms address only the most obvious abuses. Artists and arts administrators who sit on review panels still will have little trouble getting grants for themselves, their friends, and their own institutions through log-rolling and back-scratching. It is as simple as switching grant requests to different categories.

NEA defenders say that the reforms contained in 1991's reauthorization have solved NEA's problems. But new grants in January 1991 to sexually explicit performance artists Karen Finley and Holly Hughes show that NEA is unable to police itself. More reforms are needed, including minimal content restrictions on federally funded art and a reemphasis on excellence as the prime criterion for grant selection.

The General Accounting Office should examine charges that the NEA has violated its own prohibition against the establishment of a single arts style. The GAO also should be asked to investigate the grant-awarding process, which has been mightily abused and has potential for more of the same.

Finally, Congress should reassess its own priorities and NEA's future. In a time when already-pinched families are being asked to sacrifice more of their incomes to new taxes, Congress should ensure that every tax dollar is well spent. It does not appear that NEA, as currently constituted, is doing so.

Offensive Art Should Not Be Funded by the Government

by Irving Kristol

About the author: *Irving Kristol, an American Enterprise Institute fellow, co-edits the* Public Interest *and publishes the* National Interest, *quarterly journals that examine political science and social science issues.*

Once upon a time, when the idea of a National Endowment for the Arts was under consideration, I had some lively arguments with my conservative friends. I supported the idea, they opposed it. Their opposition was based on the simple and straightforward principle that the state had no business involving itself in this area, which should be left to private philanthropy. I argued that it would be good for our democracy if it showed an official interest in educating the tastes and refining the aesthetic sensibilities of its citizenry.

I won the argument and now wish I hadn't. They were more right than, at the time, they could know.

In retrospect, I can see that my error derived from the fact that I really had only a superficial understanding of what was happening in the arts world and no understanding of what this portended for the future evolution of what we now call "the arts community." I was raised in a generation that was taught to appreciate the virtues of modern art, from Renoir to Picasso and even to Jackson Pollock and "abstract expressionism," though I had to admit that this last stage had no appeal to me. "Pop art" and "minimalist art" I tended to dismiss as trendy fads.

Post-Modern Art

But what I was utterly unprepared for was the emergence of what is now called "post-modern art," which is a politically charged art that is utterly contemptuous of the notion of educating the tastes and refining the aesthetic sensibilities of the citizenry. Its goal, instead, is deliberately to outrage those tastes and to trash the very idea of an "aesthetic sensibility."

It is very difficult to convey to people who do not follow the weird goings-on in our culture an appreciation of the animating agenda of the "arts community" today. An ordinary American reads about a woman "performing artist" who prances nude across the stage, with chocolate smeared over her body, and though he may lament the waste of chocolate or nudity, it does

> *"Today, the destructive element has almost completely overwhelmed the creative."*

not occur to him that she is "making a statement," one that the "arts community" takes seriously indeed.

Even museum trustees in Washington, D.C., or Cincinnati—an elite, educated, and affluent group of arts philanthropists—had no idea what Mapplethorpe was up to in his photograph of a man with a bullwhip handle inserted into his rectum. All they knew is that Mapplethorpe was a very talented photographer (which he was), that no such talent could ever create an obscene work (which is false) and that any discriminating judgment on their part was a form of censorship that verged on the sacrilegious. Those trustees are there to raise money and watch the museum's balance sheet. They may or may not know what they like, but they would never presume to assert what is, or is not, "art." To qualify to become a museum trustee these days one must first suffer aesthetic castration.

To reach our current condition, it took a century of "permanent revolution" in the arts, made possible, ironically, by a capitalist economy which created affluent art collectors and entrepreneurial art dealers. "Patrons" of the arts were replaced by "consumers" of the arts, giving the artist an intoxicating freedom.

Who Is the Arbiter?

It was the artist, now, who told us what was and was not "art"—not the patron, or the philosopher, or the public. The function of the spectator was to welcome revolutions in taste by permitting himself to be intimidated and indoctrinated by the "arts community," consisting of artists themselves but also and especially (since artists are not usually articulate) art critics, art professors, art dealers, museum directors, etc. The most important spectators who were so intimidated and indoctrinated were the media, which now automatically approach anything declared to be "art" by the "arts community" with the kind of deference, even pseudo-piety, once reserved for the sphere of religion.

As with most revolutions, some impressive creative energies were released, some enduring accomplishments were achieved. But, again as with most revolutions, the longer it lasted the more the destructive impulse began to dominate over the creative. Yesteryear's creative contributions were, after all, what the latest revolutionary phase had to subvert and overthrow.

Chapter 1

After World War II, it became ever more difficult to distinguish artists from publicity-hungry pseudo-artists, from people "making statements" of one kind or other, such "statements" being the essence of pop art, minimalist art, environmental art, and now post-modern art. That practically all of this activity was infused by an anti-bourgeois ethos was unsurprising, since it was simply mirroring the literary and academic culture in this respect. The bourgeois way of coping with this situation was to purchase and "consume" this art as a commodity, to inventory it and then at some point to expel it from its system into an underground sump, usually located in the basement of museums. Cooptation, not censorship, was the strategy.

The Art of Today

But this strategy does not work with the last and, one suspects, final phase of the revolution we are now witnessing. Today the destructive element has almost completely overwhelmed the creative. What the "arts community" is engaged in is a politics of radical nihilism; it has little interest in, and will openly express contempt for, "art" in any traditional sense of the term. It is no exaggeration to say that the self-destruction of "art" is a key point in its agenda, accompanied by the "deconstruction," not only of bourgeois society, but of Western civilization itself.

"Deconstruction" is an intellectual-ideological movement that is enormously popular in the humanities departments of our universities, which seek to free themselves from the "hegemony" of Dead White Males (DWMs is the common reference) such as Shakespeare or Dante so as to justify offering a university course on, say, the TV program "The Simpsons." There are no standards of excellence other than those we improvise for ourselves, which is why members of the "arts community" can solemnly believe and assert that whatever they do is "art." The public has the right—nay, the obligation—to support it, but not to question it.

"There are no standards of excellence other than those we improvise for ourselves."

What they do, in fact, is powerfully shaped by certain radical ideological currents; radical feminism, homosexual and lesbian self-celebration and black racism are among them. This explains why, though it is *de rigeur* to insult public figures, no one in the "arts community" would ever dare insult the Rev. Louis Farrakhan. Any such painting would promptly be vandalized, to the applause of an "arts community" opposed to censorship. It also explains why there is so little pornography, in the traditional sense, in post-modern art. Such pornography evokes lust for heterosexual engagement, which post-modern art disapproves of since it is thought to debase women. Only homosexual and lesbian sex are allowed to be celebrated.

But if pornography is limited to the homosexual sphere, obscenity is unlimited. The purpose of such obscenity is to deride the Judaeo-Christian-humanist idea of "human dignity" that Western civilization has fostered. If Western civilization is itself an obscene heritage of racism, sexism and "elitist" oppression, obscenity is obviously an appropriate response.

Where will it all end? One does have the sense that we are witnessing either a final convulsion in the history of modern art (and of modern culture) or, perhaps, a final convulsion in Western civilization itself. Most of us would incline to credit the first alternative. But where does that leave the National Endowment for the Arts, founded in a different time and on quite different assumptions about the role of the arts in American life?

How to Respond?

The most obvious response would be to abolish the NEA—perhaps over a period of a few years to mitigate the financial shock. This is not going to happen, however. After all, many major institutions—symphony orchestras, for instance, and large museums—have inevitably become dependent on NEA grants. The trustees of these institutions have considerable influence with members of Congress, who are much happier opening funding spigots than closing them. And the media, it goes without saying, would be horrified at such an effort at "censorship," now redefined to include the absence of government funding.

A more limited response would be to move the NEA away from involvement with the most active and turbulent sectors of the "arts community" by requiring that it make only grants of more than $50,000 or $100,000. The institutions receiving this money will be held responsible for any regrants they make.

Most of the controversial grants one hears of are small-to-modest. But they do serve an important role in legitimating the activity that is being funded. With $10,000 from the NEA, an "experimental workshop in the arts" can approach foundations and corporations with a plausible claim to respectability. That is precisely why they will fight tooth and nail for the continuation of the small-grants program—grants made by other members of the "arts community," their "peer groups," to their friends and allies. Just how Congress will respond to such a reform . . . remains to be seen.

But one interesting and important fact has already become clear: Our politics today is so spiritually empty, so morally incoherent, that—except for a few brave souls—liberals have been quick to dismiss as "yahoos" anyone who dares to confront this

> *"The most obvious response would be to abolish the NEA."*

assault on the foundations of liberalism and conservatism alike. A great many conservatives, for their part, having long ago been ideologically disarmed, are more embarrassed than interested at having to cope with this issue at all. Something is definitely rotten in the vital areas of our body politic.

Congress Should Not Fund the NEA

by Robert K. Dornan

About the author: *Robert K. Dornan is a member of the U.S. House of Representatives from California.*

We have a full-fledged, flamboyant budget crisis going on in this Chamber and in our country. And in the midst of that crisis some in this body are attempting to reauthorize the National Endowment for the Arts.

Regardless of the social and cultural issues involved, it is simply ludicrous that this Congress continues lavishing money on special interest and corporate welfare programs that serve no essential Government function or vital national need.

Programs like the NEA are simply luxuries we cannot afford at the present time. And I don't know about your constituents, but I can tell you that the vast majority of my constituents would not choose to fund the NEA at this point in our history—controversy or not. My taxpayers will, however, sorely miss the income they will be paying for the new taxes this body is currently proposing, which will go to pay for all sorts of programs, the NEA only one of many. In reality, then, those increased tax revenues will not be going to balance the budget, but to instead pay for these interesting but low-priority programs.

An Unimportant Program

What I want to know is this: Why isn't anyone proposing program terminations? Why? Why are tax increases always the first resort? Are all Federal programs immortal? Are they? Are all Federal programs of equal worth? Is the NEA as important as national defense? Is it as important as Medicare or Social Security or highways? I do not think so. And I think the same applies to the Economic Development Administration, the Legal Services Corporation, the Export-Import Bank direct loan program and Amtrak subsidies, just to mention a few. So why are we funding them? I suppose the main question is this: Is it worth raising taxes to continue funding such programs? Is it worth risking re-

Robert K. Dornan's remarks during the floor debate on H.R. 4825, the Arts, Humanities, and Museums Amendments of 1990, 101st Cong., 2d sess., October 11, 1990.

cession to continue funding such programs?

By refusing to terminate such nonvital programs we imply that they are as important as other truly vital national functions, which is of course absurd. If we are ever going to get a handle on the deficit we are going to have to start terminating programs that have either outlived their usefulness or that provide no essential governmental service. And I say the time to start is today, right now, October 11, 1990, and the place to start is with the NEA.

Let me expand my opposition to the reauthorization of the NEA. . . . Again, two basic reasons, one economic and the other cultural.

The economic rationale for opposing the NEA reauthorization is simple. At a time when we are facing a $200 billion deficit for fiscal year 1991, we just can't afford to spend taxpayer money on special interest or corporate welfare programs that do not address a vital national need. If Congress would only start doing what it was elected to do and eliminate all unnecessary programs, however pleasant sounding, and curb waste and fraud, then a tax increase would not be necessary.

Now I would like to address the cultural aspects of my opposition to the NEA reauthorization. The problem is not the peer review process, or some other institutional flaw within the system. It is the attitude of the NEA and the arts community in general. The arts community did more than defend so-called art, they demanded that the taxpayer continue to fork over money to pay for it—with no strings attached.

> *"Is the NEA as important as national defense? . . . I do not think so."*

Take colleges and universities. Since Congress passed the Grove City bill, colleges and universities are not entitled to Federal funding if there exists "discrimination" in any of its programs. Restrictions also apply at the Defense Department. For instance, we do not allow manufacturers of jet aircraft to build and sell to the Government what they alone consider the best fighter plane. No indeed. Manufacturers are given specific design instructions concerning the number of engines, cockpit positions, speed, etc.

We always hear that Congress is not full of art critics. Well it is not full of aeronautical engineers or rocket scientists either, but that doesn't prevent Congress from exercising its duty to provide guidance and accountability for how the taxpayers' money is spent on those programs.

Public Funds, Public Purposes

Public funds, in a democracy, are to be spent for public purposes, not for the satisfaction of individuals' aesthetic impulses. And if the impulse in question produces a work which is palpably offensive to the sensibilities of a significant proportion of the public, then that work ought not to be supported by public funds.

Why does the arts community think it is somehow exempt from the strings the Federal Government attaches to all other Federal programs? We have turned some NEA recipients into nothing but a class of artistic welfare queens.

There is also a strain of thought running through this debate that obscene, blasphemous or bigoted art does us or our culture no harm. Any offensive art—as long as it is offensive to Judeo-Christian values—is excused in a headlong rush to promote "diversity," as if that were the sole goal of artistic expression.

It is clear that America is engaged in a kulturkampf, or culture war. From flag burning to abortion to capital punishment to public funding for the arts, America is struggling to define its moral and ethical foundations. On one side are the moral relativists, whose philosophy can be summed up with the credo, "If it feels good, do it." It is a philosophy based on nothing more substantial than whim and fancy. On the other side are those who find their moral direction in the Judeo-Christian tradition.

It is time to strike a blow for traditional values and economic responsibility. It is time for average Americans to take their country back from the amoral elite—in the universities, in the dominant media culture, in certain sectors of the arts community and elsewhere—who have nothing but contempt for them and their way of life. It is time to put the NEA out of business. Heaven knows we could use the money elsewhere.

> *"Any offensive art . . . is excused in a headlong rush to promote 'diversity,' as if that were the sole goal of artistic expression."*

Government Is Not Bound to Fund All Art

by Morton A. Kaplan

About the author: *Morton A. Kaplan is Distinguished Service Professor of Political Science Emeritus at the University of Chicago and editor and publisher of* The World & I, *published by the Washington Times Corporation.*

Prof. Kathleen Sullivan of Harvard University Law School has argued that governmental awards can no more be restricted to favored groups in the case of arts than in the case of political parties. Furthermore, she says, an award does not carry a seal of approval. I believe she has made her distinctions inappropriately.

Let us start with the analogy between governmental grants in the arts and those to political parties. Governmental grants to political parties obviously must be open to all legal and accredited parties. They might receive funds in relationship to, for instance, some minimum number or percentage of votes in a previous election or the amount of funds raised independently by the parties. The Nazi Party, and all other applicant political parties, not just the Republicans and the Democrats, would be entitled to legislatively specified funds if they were legal and met these standards. This would not signify approval except in a very marginal sense.

A Bad Analogy

However, the analogy to artistic grants is a bad one. The standards for the award of campaign funds, whether based on votes or monies raised, are public and objective. Except for peripheral matters such as the honesty of the vote count, for instance, the application of the standard is mechanical. The existence of the party is established by the standards for registration. All eligible applicants receive awards. Subjective preferences and hidden agendas are irrelevant to the process.

However, and much more importantly, the eligibility of any political party to governmental funding on an equal basis, dependent only upon some defining

Morton A. Kaplan, "Art 'Censorship' and Constitutionality." This article appeared in the December 1992 issue of, and is reprinted with permission from, *The World & I*, a publication of the Washington Times Corporation.

standard, follows from the requirement not to favor one legal political party over another because that would create an unfair bias with respect to access to office, a feature central to a democratic political system.

This access, dependent only upon the legality of the party, is a requirement of a democratic system. Thus, the existence of financial assistance necessarily generalizes it.

> *"Access of the arts or humanities to governmental funding is merely a privilege and not a right."*

The extent to which the government must fund expressions of opinion designed to influence legislation if it funds some is not so easy to answer. If it funds proprohibition arguments, it probably must fund antiprohibition arguments with respect to the availability of drugs. But the former conclusion would not follow with respect to the reinstitution of slavery. Public policy arguments would exclude equal treatment in the latter case. Moreover, the farther one moves from arguments designed directly to influence legislation, the greater the scope is for exclusion or inclusion on public policy grounds.

If one believes that there is a First Amendment distinction that overwhelms the prior arguments, it also would apply to the humanities in general and the social sciences. In this case, one would be obligated by their argument to fund any form or area of expression in these areas provided only that awards are available in the humanities or social sciences and that some awarding committee or peer group exists.

This reveals the inadequacy of the argument. There is no legitimate basis on which to challenge the awarding agencies' decisions to establish categories for awards or criteria for determination within these categories, provided they are reasonable. Any category of inquiry—whether the application of statistical methods to intelligence tests or inquiries into the modes of communications of mammals other than man—may be either included or excluded.

Government Funding of the Arts and Humanities

Access of the arts or humanities to governmental funding is merely a privilege and not a right, even given the existence of a National Endowment for the Arts (NEA). The provision of funds by government may be bound by categories because the government is not obligated to support all categories and forms of art if it supports some. Indeed, if there is a constitutional issue, it might affect the awards that have been made to works that by attacking religion with the assistance of federal funding might be deemed to have breached the separation between state and religion.

If the courts were to take seriously the argument that all opinions or forms of expression have equal rights to government funding if any are funded, then surely they would be overloaded with claims against public endowments that exclude proposed categories or juries that exclude some points of view or forms of artistic expression or that give preference to others.

Furthermore, if Professor Sullivan's analogy to the funding of political parties is taken seriously, then if any artistic work is funded, all legitimate works of art, assuming we know how to determine what is a "legitimate work of art," and not merely prize winners from among categories, become entitled to funding. This at least would avoid the subjective standards and hidden agendas that govern even the most distinguished awards.

Awards in many of the humanities, the arts, and the sciences, unlike political funding, are selective. The Nobel Prize, for instance, is the most prestigious of prizes, and physics is the area in which the standards for its award are most objective. Yet Max Planck, whose great work was done in 1901, did not receive the prize until 1918. And Albert Einstein, whose special theory was presented in 1905, did not receive the prize until 1921. Comparatively undistinguished physicists did receive prizes meanwhile, and it took external pressure to rectify matters with respect to two of the greatest physicists of all time.

It is well known that the Nobel awards for literature and peace are made for a variety of reasons, including political reasons. To refer to these as objective awards that are made by peer groups is to mistake process for substance. To argue that they do not signify approval is to ignore the evidence concerning the grounds on which the awards are made. Furthermore, they are so perceived by much of the public.

Any Objective Standards?

It is not at all clear that objective standards exist in the field of art. The Nobel awards in physics may misrepresent its standards, but all now acknowledge the superior status of the work of Planck and Einstein. There may be experts in the history of art or even in the authentication of a work of art, although the refusal of experts to acknowledge the faked Vermeers until the artist showed that a portrait of his own hand was in each picture casts some doubt even in this area. However, when a chance collection of objects or the wrapping of an object in cellophane is called art, it is at least the case that there are no agreed standards. Hence there are no agreed criteria to govern the choices of peer groups, in which case major weight can be given to subjective beliefs and hidden agendas.

> *"Awards in many of the humanities, the arts, and the sciences, unlike political funding, are selective."*

Furthermore, there clearly are licit denials of the use of public monies with respect to opinions or purposes that are political even when the political purposes are licit. For instance, suppose a peer panel of the National Science Foundation were to fund an institute designed to teach people to opt out of life and to go on welfare? Suppose the institute wanted to prove that some races are inferior and that the Fourteenth Amendment should be modified to take this into account?

Would anyone argue that it would be censorship to deny these grants? And almost surely the courts would uphold such a denial on public policy grounds. Yet the institutes would have political purposes that are licit and a First Amendment right to propagate their beliefs.

Suppose a group of philosophers were to form to investigate the doctrine that individual consciousness is an illusion produced by food poisons. Would the refusal to fund an award to such a group by a peer panel of the National Endowment for the Humanities (NEH) constitute an attack either on free speech or on scientific creativity? Would it be unconstitutional?

Suppose a great artist were to paint a very artistic picture of a lynched black with a sign on him that read "All niggers are rapists." Surely, the First Amendment permits the display of such an obnoxious portrait, but would even artistic greatness warrant the ideological legitimation that a government grant would accord? The Constitution may require that such beliefs be permitted expression, but there is no requirement that the government fund operations designed to undermine the principles and values upon which our constitutional system rests.

Obscenity and Community Standards

When the Court recognized that obscenity could be prevented and that community standards applied, it recognized the force of community standards in an arena in which objective standards, as that term normally is employed, are lacking. It attempted to mitigate this by its reference to redeeming artistic value. But there is no agreement on what artistic value is and, therefore, even the concept of mitigating artistic content depends upon community standards.

> "When a chance collection of objects or the wrapping of an object in cellophane is called art, it is at least the case that there are no agreed standards."

If the argument often used to support awards—for instance, the picture of Christ in a vase filled with the artist's urine or Mapplethorpe's photograph of one homosexual urinating into the mouth of another—is that their art lies in the shock value of the work, then the same argument could be made for works that the Court holds to be pornographic and that it would not permit even to be displayed. I suspect that most people when they first see pornography are shocked and that their perceptions, beliefs, and behavior are often changed if they continue to see such works. Some artists have even publicly mutilated themselves on this rationale. By these standards we would be forced to recognize de Sade's activities as great performance art rather than as lunacy and the Hellfire Club as the locale of great performance art.

The Court's qualification, however, does assist in creating a twilight zone that balances the public's interest in protecting artistic experimentation with the public's interest in preventing radical assaults on the social values and the social cohesion that are so important to the maintenance of our system of democratic government. Some works may not even be displayed. Others may be displayed, but they are not entitled to access to public funding.

> *"There is no requirement that the government fund operations designed to undermine the principles and values upon which our constitutional system rests."*

Thus, even where there are constitutional protections for the production and display of works that shock large sections of the public, it does not follow that a right to public funding is entailed. There are constitutional differences, for instance, between what can be done inside a closed building which people enter by choice and what can be done in public. For instance, nudity or intercourse that would be permitted in a movie would not be permitted in the public square no matter how artistic the performance.

The Public Square

Governmental funding is not exactly the same thing as the public square. But it resembles it in certain respects because it invokes the financial support of the general public regardless of the private opinions of individual members of the public. And denying public funding to certain types of so-called art is not analogous in any serious respect to the denial of funding to a legitimately recognized political party that meets the objective criteria for funding for reasons that have been specified earlier. There are legitimate public policy grounds for differentiations between situations merely involving display and those involving the use of public funds.

The proper constitutional balance with respect to the funding of art is quite different from that involved in production and display. The opponents of the government's placing of limits on the types of art the NEA supports would be justified in referring to this as censorship only if they referred to the peer review process as censorship. Even when peer groups take genuine—even if debatable—artistic considerations into account, they reject artists whose work is culturally or politically uncongenial and select those whose views they wish to be propagated. And sometimes this includes purposes the public would regard as evil or unnatural.

It is essential to distinguish the artist's right to use his art for cultural or political purposes from the right of the peer group without further review to use the government's money for the same purposes.

Surely the granting of tenure at a university is a more important decision than an award to an artist. Yet, the recommendation of a department is reviewed by the dean, the provost, and the president. Are such decisions based only on professional criteria? Not necessarily.

Chapter 1

A physicist of Nobel quality might receive tenure even if he belongs to the Nazi Party. But I would give odds that one of lesser stature who nonetheless meets all the other qualifications would not be given tenure at any major university in the United States. There is a legitimate question of contribution to the university community and its educational purposes that is taken into account in tenure decisions. Unfortunately, numerous departments have refused tenure to professors merely because they were conservatives (a gross misuse of discretionary authority).

The right to produce a painting that entails an effort to change the sexual standards of the public does not entail the right to public funding for that purpose. And no peer review group that represents very limited interests should have absolute authority over which works of art should be included in or excluded from funding.

When Senator Claiborne Pell put the requirement for peer groups into the funding proposal "to keep it out of politics," what he accomplished was to restrict the grants to the politics of the peer groups. Because the peer group in some cases was established to change the culture or because its members have no serious artistic standards to begin with, the subjective and illicit elements in the awards are exacerbated.

For instance, suppose a group of individuals comes up with a "theory" that the newest art form should consist of animal excrement smeared on the nude body. Their motives may range from genuine stupidity to cynical cupidity.

> *"Some works . . . may be displayed, but they are not entitled to access to public funding."*

From the attempt to change the culture to attempts to destroy it. From an intelligent evaluation of culture (although I find it exceedingly difficult to credit this) to those produced by serious personality pathologies. The peer group now would consist of artists engaged in similar activities. These individuals then become the peer groups who judge the awards. The prejudices of the long-established art establishments are bad enough. But the argument that the government is obligated to support such works demonstrates merely the outlandish arrogance of those who make such claims.

Justification of Absurd Performances

I have read many pseudo-intellectual justifications of absurd performances based on sophomoric ideas. Consider some of the slogans employed by the famous Jenny Holzer: "The breakdown comes when you stop controlling yourself and want the release of a bloodbath"; "I love my mind when it is f..king [elisions added] the cracks of events"; "Abuse of power comes as no surprise"; or "Any surplus is immoral." Although hundreds of thousands of dollars have been spent to install a single exhibit of Holzer's, somehow I think even some junior high school students would do better than this.

42

How different would the case of the artist who smeared himself with excrement be from one performer's work that was temporarily denied support by John Frohnmayer, the ex-head of the NEA, but that has regained a grant now that the furor has died down? This lady danced nude and smeared her private parts, both internal and external, with chocolate. A few years back she would have been called an exhibitionist and her audience voyeurs. But, she says, she is showing how women are degraded and this is art. By this standard, a new "Deep Throat" if performed on stage with a similar rationale would be worthy of a grant from the NEA.

Suppose an award of public funds had been made to a performance in which slogans are displayed on banners and one slogan read "Bash Homosexual Creeps." Or to choose Suzanne Fields' example, suppose the notorious Mapplethorpe photograph, instead of showing a black man urinating into the mouth of a white man, had been of a white man urinating into the mouth of a black man or into the mouth of a woman. I venture that many of the artists who defend the cited awards would be strident in their cries of outrage and that they would demand the work be banned. I would not go that far, although I would refuse to support any museum that displayed such a work.

One criterion cited at the Mapplethorpe trial by art museum directors was that placement in a museum was proof that a work was art. That arrogant claim is without merit. A number of works exhibited in museums—including chance collections of ordinary objects or the artists themselves sleeping on the floor—are proof sufficient of the contrary.

The Behavior of Establishments

How can we explain the support of the art establishment for pornography and junk? It is unreasonable to believe that the bulk of the establishment is attempting to revolutionize the culture although it is highly liberal. The answer I believe lies in the behavior of all our establishments: the scientific, military, police, educational, and political among others. And it is illustrated by the case of Dr. Margot O'Toole who was recently called a hero by the National Institutes of Health after an extensive investigation that had been demanded by Congress.

> *"Suppose an award of public funds had been made to a performance in which slogans are displayed on banners and one slogan read 'Bash Homosexual Creeps.'"*

Dr. O'Toole claimed that a colleague, Dr. Thereza Imanishi-Kari, had falsified her results. Dr. David Baltimore, a Nobel laureate in science, who was at that time president of Rockefeller University, called her "a disgruntled post-doctoral fellow." She lost her job and took work answering phones. Now that the evidence is in, Dr. Baltimore says that he was trying to keep politics out of science.

The difference among the establishments is that the scientific establishment lines up behind established members regardless of political persuasion, while the establishments in softer fields line up behind liberal deviations and against conservative ones. The brilliant Wilmoore Kendall, for instance, was fired by Yale University because of his liquor habit, which would have been fair enough if they had also fired liberal drunks, some of whom were less than brilliant.

> *"How can we explain the support of the art establishment for pornography and junk?"*

The average citizen should not be talked out of his perceptions by any establishment, and this is particularly true in the artistic field where public standards are for the most part absent. He or she should be able to understand that pornography lies in the work of the producer, not in his professional identification. By the standard asserted by art museum directors at the trial a police officer could not commit a crime. And a teacher could not propagandize a student. But, of course, both are possible and can even be carried out with professional skill. Such perversions are rampant in American society: in the arts, in academia, in business, in the media, in politics, and in religion. We have lost the ability to be shocked and that is a sad state of affairs. But it is even worse when professionals publicly defend professional perversions.

Perhaps the ideological and unreasoning character of part of the artistic and literary community is exposed by the controversy over *American Psycho*, the book that was first accepted for publication by Simon & Schuster and then rejected. There have been several op ed pieces in the *New York Times* on this issue, including one by an editor of the Beacon Press. It was not censorship to turn down the book, they say, because publishing houses have a right to take considerations of taste and public reaction into account. So far, bravo. It was surely permissible censorship.

But then they seem to suggest that no one should publish the book and attempt to distinguish this from censorship by the arts foundation. I have not read the book and I do not know if it is pornographic in the sense that Mapplethorpe's pictures are. Even if it is, I doubt that it is so far over the line that it would be legitimate to suggest that no one may publish it. If we err, we should do so on the side of liberality. But if it is pornographic in Mapplethorpe's sense, I would suggest that it certainly should not receive a grant from the government.

Funding of the Armed Forces

Let us consider a case in which funding has a much firmer constitutional foundation than in the case of the arts to explore the issue of selective funding. The Constitution specifies that the United States shall possess armed forces and that the president is their commander in chief. Yet there is no constitutional barrier to the decision to disapprove funds for the armed forces and to eliminate all officers in them. I understand that some legal theorists, and even some courts, might assert the absurd thesis that the Court could order Congress and the executive to fund the armed forces.

Suppose, for the sake of argument, we concede this thesis. Even in that case, however, there would be no barrier to legislative abandonment of the tank corps, the air forces, and the artillery. To the restriction of the services to ten thousand men and officers. And to the possession of air guns and bows and arrows.

It will be conceded that there is no constitutional duty to fund an endowment for the arts. Even if funded, however, there remains a constitutional right to determine the areas in which awards may be made. For instance, legislation may forbid awards to string quartets, folk songs, portraits of genitals, coitus, or excretory processes, nontraditional religious depictions, or whatever. Thus, the argument concerning constitutional restrictions is not merely wrong. It is without merit.

It is not true that we have no constitutional defense against the obligation to fund schlock, fraud, or attempts to set us at war with each other. It is not true that we must be a member of a peer group to be able to recognize that this is happening. Our right to make mistakes, even stupid or outrageous mistakes, in making these fallible judgments is one of the inalienable rights with which we have been endowed. It goes along with our right to make a mistake in taking a job or a partner in marriage.

The NEA Should Be Eliminated

by Philip M. Crane

About the author: *Philip M. Crane, an Illinois Republican, is a member of the U.S. House of Representatives. He is a member of the House Ways and Means Committee.*

Following what became at times a rather raucous debate in both the House and the Senate, Congress approved a "compromise" late in 1990 reauthorizing the National Endowment for the Arts (NEA) for three years with a few minor changes. They essentially were cosmetic in nature and designed to give cover to those Congressmen who did not seriously want to change the Endowment, but desired to be able to go back to their constituents and say they voted for some sort of NEA restrictions.

Ironically, while Congress was doing nothing to address the fundamental issues surrounding Federal involvement in art, a growing number of political commentators and editorial boards were reaching the following conclusions: funding art and artists is not a Federal responsibility; Federal funding of the NEA to the tune of $175,000,000 annually is not needed, considering the vast amount of money (nearly $7,500,000,000) that is spent privately to promote the arts; and the only way to get Congress out of the business of determining what is or is not art is to get the Federal government out of the art business altogether.

A Draconian Measure

The only solution to the present controversy that makes sense is to eliminate Federally funded art—that is, eliminate the NEA. Such a solution may appear to be draconian. However, when the issue honestly is assessed, it is clear that this would be in the best interest of art and the American taxpayer. Unfortunately, elements of the arts community have been unwilling to address the fundamental issue of whether the NEA should exist at all, and instead have chosen to divert attention from this question and focus instead on Congressional restrictions on

Philip M. Crane, "Eliminate the National Endowment for the Arts." Reprinted from *USA Today* magazine, July 1991, © 1991 by the Society for the Advancement of Education.

art—an issue they misleadingly characterize as one of "censorship."

The history of the NEA says a lot about why we have the maze of Federal entities we do today. The creation of the NEA would qualify as an excellent case study for a course entitled "How to Create an Unnecessary Federal Agency."

In 1964, a special House subcommittee held four days of hearings . . . which focused on the National Arts and Cultural Development Act (NACDA). In fact, these "hearings" better could be described as a love fest for the arts. Nearly everyone who testified represented some sort of arts organization, and, to no one's surprise, all those who spoke thought that injecting Federal money into the arts community was one of the best things to happen to art since the discovery of paint.

Art Lobby at Work

Although the goal of the arts supporters was to create something similar to the NEA, proponents of the endowment approach apparently thought that it was not wise initially to push for direct subsidies to artists. Instead, the arts lobby proposed creating the National Council on the Arts. With its $150,000 budget, the Council was directed to "assist in the growth and development of the arts in the United States." In August, 1964, Congress passed the NACDA, and the National Council on the Arts was created.

Those members of Congress who fought the Council in 1964 knew what was coming next. Indeed, the comments they made during the debate proved prophetic. After arguing that the Federal government had no business in the art business, opponents made some predictions of what would happen once the art community was able to get its nose in the public trough. First, they suggested that the Council was the initial step in an effort to involve the Federal government deeply in subsidizing artists. This, of course, proved correct and was accomplished even more quickly than might have been imagined—the NEA was approved by Congress one year later. Next, they predicted that Congress eventually would be spending up to $100,000,000 in direct subsidies to artists. By 1978, the total annual appropriation for the NEA exceeded that amount. Finally, concerns were expressed regarding whether it would be good for art to have the government deciding what type could or could not be funded. The cries of "censorship" we hear today are the manifestation of this feeling.

> *"The only solution . . . that makes sense is to eliminate Federally funded art."*

One of the first actions of the National Council on the Arts was to endorse the creation of the NEA. Despite the fact that the Council never did report to Congress formally on the advisability of expanding Federal involvement in the arts as it was directed to do, and even though the Education and Labor Committee spent a grand total of 15 minutes considering the bill, Congress went ahead and created the National Endowment for the Arts in 1965. Rep. Adam Clayton Powell, Jr. (D.-N.Y.) set the tone for the 1965 NEA

47

debate on the House floor: "We made a meager beginning last September by creating . . . a National Council on the Arts . . . we cannot be satisfied with merely inventing another advisory committee. Starved minds and spirits, unlike growling stomachs, may not be a very vocal lobby [sic], but failure vigorously to encourage the development of our artistic and cultural resources would be just as harmful to the quality of life in this Nation as neglect of our manpower or our natural resources." It takes little imagination to realize where the debate was going after this statement.

That funding of art is a legitimate or originally intended function of the Federal government could draw a reasonable argument perhaps—although it's doubtful. The debate over financing of the arts is as old as our nation. The Constitutional Convention addressed the matter in 1787 when South Carolina Rep. Charles Pinckney proposed that Congress "establish seminaries for the promotion of literature and the arts and sciences." His colleagues soundly defeated the motion because they reasoned that, in such matters, "The granting of patents is the extent of [our] power." John Page of Virginia argued vigorously against Federal involvement, warning that "Congress might, like many royal benefactors, misplace their munificence . . . and neglect a much greater genius of another." There would appear to be little doubt that the founders of our republic considered the question of government involvement in the arts and rejected it. I imagine the Founding Fathers would be spinning in their graves if they knew that the Federal government directly was subsidizing artists today.

> *"Art in America will continue to flourish . . . without the existence of Federal art subsidies."*

Even if it were agreed that funding art is somehow a legitimate Federal function, I do not believe it can reasonably be argued that Federal funding is needed. In 1989 alone, $7,500,000,000 was spent on the advancement of art by individuals, bequests, foundations, and corporations. There is plenty of private sector money to go around. There is no question in my mind that the arts community and its supporters could come up with the $175,000,000 currently funding the NEA and create a *private* national endowment to promote and encourage needy or blossoming artists.

Are Federal Subsidies Needed?

Art in America will continue to flourish, as it has for decades, without the existence of Federal art subsidies. For example, it was pointed out in the 1965 NEA debate that two of the greatest periods in American literature occurred when not one penny of either Federal or state money was spent in support of the arts. The middle of the 19th century boasted such giants as Mark Twain, Edgar Allan Poe, Walt Whitman, Nathaniel Hawthorne, Emily Dickinson, Henry and William James, Henry Wadsworth Longfellow, and Ralph Waldo

Emerson. Moreover, between World War I and World War II, writers such as William Faulkner, Ernest Hemingway, F. Scott Fitzgerald, Sinclair Lewis, and Theodore Dreiser emerged.

In light of our current budget woes and the extremely healthy financial condition of private contributions to the arts community, it seems difficult to justify continued Federal involvement in the arts. Although many argue that the $175,000,000 requested for the NEA in Fiscal Year 1991 is a pittance compared to the total Federal budget, few acknowledge that ongoing funding of questionable programs adds up. Although the cost for a particular weapons system over its life is often a critical element of Congressional debate on defense issues, very few members of Congress apply that same analysis when it comes to domestic spending. Since its creation in 1965, the NEA has received nearly $2,500,000,000 in taxpayer funds via Congress.

> **"I am convinced art in America will be better off without Federal involvement."**

These same sentiments were humorously expressed by Rep. H.R. Gross (R.-Iowa) in the 1965 NEA debate over whether to expand the definition of art covered by the bill to include more than paintings, literature, music, etc.: "Incidentally there is another art that is not recognized in this bill, and I believe it ought to be recognized. It is the art of picking the pockets of the taxpayers to get $20,000,000 to pay for this business, when the Federal treasury is $325,000,000,000 in debt."

All too often, we find that, once a program is established and develops a constituency, it becomes a Federal *responsibility*. Simply because an agency has existed for 25 years does not mean that it is necessary. Congress has made more than its share of mistakes in the past in expanding the role of the Federal government. Supporters of the arts would have to admit that the Federal government has more necessary and important things to do than subsidize artists. One letter I received from a senior citizens' group regarding Medicare cuts contained the following statement: "If this is to be an austerity budget, there are many 'luxuries' that can and should be cut before Medicare. For example, is the National Endowment for the Arts, regardless of the arguments on both sides, worth more than impoverished Medicare recipients?" I do not believe the supporters of the NEA can provide an adequate answer to this rhetorical question.

Congress and the Taxpayers

The NEA was a child of the Great Society—the underlying premise being that government can, should, and will do everything. Although this philosophy has proven to be a fiscal disaster and at the root of the bloated bureaucracy we have today, agencies such as the NEA continue to be reauthorized by legislators who apparently could not care less whether such involvement is necessary or is a constitutional responsibility of the Federal government.

Russell Lynes, writing in *Harper's* magazine at the time of the 1965 debate, said, "I am not worried about creeping socialism in the arts, but about creeping mediocrity. The less the arts have to do with our political process, I believe, the healthier they will be." I am convinced art in America will be better off without Federal involvement and one would think that those in the art community who are crying "censorship" when it comes to the issue of government placing restrictions on art funds would appreciate this point of view.

The term "censorship" in the context of Federal funding is inappropriate and misleading when it refers to government placing restrictions on the type of art it funds. It is not censorship for Congress to determine what type of art taxpayers' dollars will support. Rather, it is Congress' responsibility to ensure that taxpayer dollars are spent wisely. Artists can go to any private source they want in an effort to get their work marketed or displayed. With the exception of obscenity laws, no government entity in this country will restrict an artist's right to compete in the free market to display or sell his "product." If the public likes an artist's work, they will buy it. Moreover, for that artist's product which only a true art "sophisticate" can appreciate fully, there is no law preventing these connoisseurs from financially supporting such material. In addition, there is nothing to prohibit the arts community from creating a private endowment designed to accomplish the same goals as the NEA. If the arts community believes that Congress—through its funding restrictions—is acting as a straightjacket to creativity, the solution is clear.

> *"The general public, not government, should be the judge of what art will be seen."*

If placing content restrictions on the NEA is censorship, then the very existence of the NEA represents censorship. With or without them, the NEA will continue to impose government standards on art. Because the NEA cannot conceivably finance every artist who requests funding, it must be selective and establish standards of some sort. These are set by a presidentially appointed panel and naturally reflect the tastes of the appointees. As a result, in 1989, of 17,879 grant requests the NEA received, 13,507 were rejected, while 4,372 applicants were accepted. Therefore, even without any Congressional content restrictions, the NEA turns down three of every four grant requests. The government should not be the nation's art critic, but, as long as there is an NEA, it will continue to serve this role.

A Question of Fairness

It also is important to understand how important an NEA grant can be to an artist. Such funding is considered "highly important money" to artists because it attracts additional financial attention to the recipients. Consequently, it draws away potential funding from those who were not so fortunate—or so well-connected—as to be deemed worthy of NEA recognition. By advancing the career of one artist with a grant, it can be argued that the NEA conversely discourages the futures of three others.

Federal subsidies thus create two classes of artists—those who are sanctioned and supported by the government and those who are not. I have been contacted by a number of artists who tell me, for example, that if you are not connected with the "in" clique of artists in New York, you are not likely to get a Federal grant. Moreover, stories have circulated regarding ex-NEA staffers who then move on to various arts organizations—which "coincidentally" receive NEA grants or additional funding not long after the former officials arrive on the scene.

Is it fair that those who are not so fortunate as to receive a Federal grant are less likely to succeed than those who do? Should government be dictating who is successful and who is not? By funding one artist over another, isn't the government essentially dictating the type of art Americans will enjoy? In the end, the very existence of the NEA means government-sanctioned art, a concept which one would think would be anathema to the arts community.

The general public, not government, should be the judge of what art will be seen. History is replete with examples of famous artists who could not win the official blessing of a government that became involved in sanctioning art. Some have said that, if the National Gallery of Art could own the paintings of all the artists who have been snubbed by the official art authority in France, it would be the most famous museum in the world. Renoir, Cezanne, Van Gogh, and Rodin all were apparently blackballed by "official" art in France at one time or another. Indeed, it has been said that Bach and Mozart were both applicants at certain points in their careers for governmental aid by German provinces, and both were rejected. These great artists, however, overcame the official stamp of disapproval.

Yet, for many artists today, the fact that they do not have the government's stamp of approval may not bode well for their future. This is not fair and is unnecessary because it is not the government's role to endorse one artist over another or to be telling Americans what is good art.

In the debate on the floor of the U.S. House of Representatives regarding my amendment to eliminate the NEA, I unsuccessfully tried to engage its proponents in an honest discussion on the very issues described above. The NEA supporters would not or could not respond substantively to the questions of why the agency was necessary, why it was a Federal responsibility, or why the very existence of the NEA is not detrimental to the free expression of art in America. Instead, we heard from members of the New York Congressional delegation expressing their pride over the fact that their state receives 25% of the grant money, as well as countless stories of all the "nice" things the NEA has done. Basically, its supporters missed the point. The "nice" things the NEA does are not a Federal responsibility, are not necessary, and do serious damage to the concept of free and unfettered expression of art in America. Government's business is not art, and the time has come to say goodbye to the NEA.

Government Funding of the Arts Should Not Be Restricted

by E. L. Doctorow

About the author: *E. L. Doctorow is the author of* Ragtime, Billy Bathgate, *and other novels. The following is adapted from testimony submitted to a House Subcommittee in a hearing on oversight of the National Endowment for the Arts.*

I'm a working writer. I pay attention to words, to what they mean and to the meanings beneath their meaning. Underneath this question before you today as to what conditions, if any, to attach to N.E.A.'s grant-giving charter, is a very simple principle, simple but apparently elusive or beyond the tolerance of those who are so quickly and sweetly outraged, those who would punish all voices not in harmony with their own—the crucial idea that we must protect the speech of those with whom we are least comfortable. There is no First Amendment principle involved in protecting the speech of those with whom we agree, those whose hands we want to shake because they represent our own beliefs and convictions. The principle emerges in the conflict and contention with ideas that offend us and with expression perceived to be in monumentally bad taste. At that juncture we define ourselves as a civilization that is free and proud and democratic, with trust in the national community's powers of judgment and analysis and in its ability to illuminate and finally discard ideas that are foul, destructive, malevolent or simply foolish—or we are fearful and constrictive and craven and without pride in the natural self-cleansing powers of a free society through which all ideas flow. Those who would limit artists in any way, in any medium, I call craven. Those who have not the courage of their country's constitutional convictions I call cowardly.

Now you may say, and it has been said, that there is no violation of free speech in the refusal to bestow a grant; that the artist can say anything he or she damn pleases—but if it's obscene, overtly sexual, pornographic or generally indecent

From E. L. Doctorow's testimony before the House Subcommittee on Government Activities and Transportation, 102d Cong., 1st sess., Fall 1991.

by the usual standards, the artist cannot reasonably expect us to pay for making the art. This is solely a question of whether the government should pay for works of art that violate community standards of taste and decorum. This is a question of using hard-earned tax dollars to support the artist who mocks, sickens or otherwise offends the people who provide those tax dollars. That's all.

Of course, that isn't all. In the first place, as citizens we regularly see our tax dollars funding programs and policies and forms of speech we abhor—as for example when our taxes pay for presidential campaigns of candidates whose platforms are inimical to our interests and whose speeches offend our intelligence. We even see our tax dollars going to subsidize criminal enterprise, as illustrated so well by the S&L scandals. Why do we get so righteous about our tax dollars where artists are concerned? The U.S. government taxes its citizens on behalf of multitudes of services and functions it performs, some of them noble, some of them stupid, some of them destructive and shortsighted, some of them quite murderous—but in any event a hefty percentage of them in the face of the disapproval at any given time of a large segment of the tax-paying public.

Yet, this question always arises where artists are involved. Why? I suspect it is because those who would censor, those who would preen in umbrage, have no belief in the value to society of *any* kind of art, obscene or otherwise, unless it is from another age, with the artists themselves conveniently dead and gone. I suspect that behind this whole question of tax dollars is that practical man's vision of the painter, the writer, the dancer, the composer as a

> *"Those who would limit artists in any way, in any medium, I call craven."*

marginal member of society—that politician's gut sense of the artist as a luxury the society sometimes cannot and should not afford, who in most instances is something of a fraud, a sort of self-indulgent, self-aggrandizing deadbeat who performs no labor of any consequence but is nevertheless always making big claims for himself. I speak of the latent underlying jealousy we have for elevated expression that is personal, uninvited and powerful, that almost automatic anger we have for a kind of witness and truth-telling that is not endorsed or accredited by church, or corporation, or family, or other governing institution of our society.

No Rational Argument

This prejudice is profoundly in the American grain, and like all our prejudices it resists rational argument. Not all artists are good artists—very few are in fact great—but the work of independent witness, that often self-destructive willingness to articulate that which many may feel but no one dares to say, the blundering, struggling effort to connect the visible to the invisible, to find the secret meanings of places and things, to release the spirit from the clay—that rude, stubborn, squawking, self-appointed voice singing the unsingable—who we are, what we are becoming—is through all our regions and states and cities and schools and workshops and studios a natural resource as critical to us and our identity and our survival as are our oil, our coal, our timber.

> *"Why do we get so righteous about our tax dollars where artists are concerned?"*

To put restrictions on speech funded with tax dollars is itself to speak in a certain way, the way of pre-emptive state speech; it is to begin to create a realm of approved speech, an orthodoxy of discourse. To draw bounds around speech is to legislate, de facto, more speech to some than to others. And it is automatically to privilege the speech of those who would deny it to others. That is the truth that is lost in the current debate in Congress. The righteous desire to tell artists what they may and may not say is the instinct to monopolize a natural resource.

An Extreme Conservatism

This is not an isolated issue you have before you about the workings of a minor government agency. It arises in a widening context in which, for example, the Bush Administration has gotten a judicial ruling that does not permit doctors in federally funded birth-control clinics to mention the word "abortion"; a context in which the President has supported a constitutional amendment to limit free speech where the flag is concerned—a rare President in our history, to advocate a retrenchment in the Bill of Rights; a context that includes an exponential rise in the number of books banned from school libraries around the country; a context in which a self-declared neo-Nazi and former Ku Klux Klan leader has wide public support in his campaign for a governorship; a context, in short, and I say this knowing the courtesies of bipartisan inquiry may make you wince here, of racial and gender and ethnic divisiveness that proceeds directly from the ideas and values of the extreme right element of our two political parties. I ask you to consider this context—I ask you to consider these items I've mentioned as creeping increments of an official culture. I ask you to acknowledge as you think about our sinful artists that the agenda of the extreme right, just one element of our political spectrum, is what governs current political discourse—the questions we ask, the issues we raise, the problems we define—as it has for the past dozen years or so.

This issue we discuss here is created by an extreme conservatism as it wishes to organize our lives illiberally, in one mold, as a uniculture—a conservatism that has from its genuine but quite paranoid soul decided that there is no hope for this country except as all other political constituencies conform to its righteous ways. And so we have odd patterns of thought. College professors who object to racist inflammatory speech on their campuses are derided for being politically correct; at the same time, artists applying to the N.E.A. are subject to the criteria of political correctness. It is irrelevant that community standards are violated by racist speech; but it is by upholding community standards that artists are denied grants. All this is quite odd. On the other hand, the conservative movement has never let the true meaning of words interfere with its political intentions. President Bush speaks for civil rights but has repeatedly vetoed legislation that would relieve the inequities of racism. He reveres the environment but prevents laws from being enacted that would save it from despoliation. It's all very odd—and if you think I am wandering too far afield here, I remind you that we need every artist we have, every witness, just because things have become so odd, just because people in power don't mean what they say, because our public debate is so degraded, our political discourse so subject to intimidation and flimflam, do we need these strange people who go their own way, these artists. We need them. First we need to stake them to a few months' work, if they're good. And then we need to leave them alone.

No Restrictions

I point out to you, if you haven't already heard, the disbelief of the American people upon learning that in a week in which a man with a gun committed another one of our indigenous mass murders in a public place—twenty-three people dead, a new record—the Congress refused in its grim-jawed patriotic righteousness to pass a bill banning the sale of semiautomatic weapons. I want to point out to you the perception on the part of some of us of the ludicrousness of worrying at length about an artist's nudity or naughty words while granting murderous free expression to any maniac who happens to have the price of a gun and decides to walk into a restaurant and kill everyone he sees.

I'm a working writer and I dare call myself an artist. I do not feel marginal to this society but rather deeply involved in its practical working life. My work provides employment to others—editors, typesetters, publishers, binders, newspaper critics, booksellers, teachers, movie actors and directors, set designers and videotape store managers. Painters provide employment to printmakers, publishers, gallery owners and workers, art critics, TV documentarians, museum curators and museum guards. The work of artists in every medium provides jobs and stimulates the economy. The N.E.A. has generally funded younger writers at the beginning of their careers—so that they, too, presumably will be in a position one day to generate jobs for others. All artists are, economically speaking, small businesses. Perhaps we should be testifying before the Small Business Administration.

> *"Any legislative condition put on artists' speech . . . means you lay out a palette with certain colors struck from the spectrum."*

But in any event, I ask you not to accept the strange, alarmed, right-wing vision of things—it's bad not only for artists, it's bad for us all. Any legislative condition put on artists' speech, no matter how intemperate or moderate, no matter how vague or specific, means you publish a dictionary with certain words deleted from the language, it means you lay out a palette with certain colors struck from the spectrum. Do you really want to do this? Does the Congress in its wisdom really believe that bleeping out words, blacking out images, erasing portions of the tape, is what is needed to save this Republic?

I would venture to remind you by way of conclusion that if you give to Comstockery a little piece of your democratic or republican soul, it will next year demand a bigger piece. As politicians who know history you know that to appease this demon is to make it only more powerful and more voracious. It won't ever stop unless you stand up to it. For that reason, I urge you not to choose between more or less onerous grant-conditioning language. It is all censorship and I say to hell with it—it's nothing any decent American should stand for. Give the N.E.A. back its original charter, in which there is no language requiring of artists political conformity in any guise. And you'll be able to go home to your families, and especially to your children, knowing you've done them, and your country, a great service.

The Content of Art Should Not Influence Government Funding

by John E. Frohnmayer

About the author: *John E. Frohnmayer is former chairman of the National Endowment for the Arts in Washington, D.C. He received an M.A. degree in Christian ethics from the University of Chicago.*

The arts are God's gift to humanity. They help us to understand and express our deepest feelings. If, as Paul Tillich said, God is ultimate concern, then art is ultimate expression—of love, trust, alienation and hope. Art teaches us to verify our most personal experiences, to listen to intuition along with reason, and to perceive what is beyond the obvious.

Throughout history, governments and churches have understood the value of supporting their people's creativity. In the fifth century B.C. in Greece, Pericles directed the construction of the Parthenon. In Rome the statesman Maecenas supported two great Latin poets, Virgil and Horace. In the Middle Ages the Catholic Church underwrote the work of painters, architects and sculptors. Chaucer was given a government job with very little to do so he could write his poetry. During the Italian Renaissance the nobility emerged as patrons of the arts. Michelangelo painted frescoes for the city of Florence and the Sistine Chapel for the pope. King Louis XIV was the patron of French playwright Molière. Voltaire received a pension from the king's regent. Shakespeare was supported by the Earl of Southampton.

Founding Fathers' Support for the Arts

In America the Founding Fathers encouraged government support of the arts and humanities. George Washington called for the establishment of a national university. Thomas Jefferson, Alexander Hamilton and John Adams, all well versed in the arts, helped legislate funds for centers of scholarship and learning.

Adams, in fact, hoped that his grandchildren would be able to study the arts rather than war or politics. In the nation's early years, the government paid for the four paintings by John Trumbull that hang in the rotunda of the Capitol. The Smithsonian Institution, the Freer Gallery of Art and other projects demonstrate the federal government's periodic interest in the arts and culture.

> *"The works that have drawn the most vociferous complaints cost each citizen less than a penny."*

Responding to the Depression, the Works Progress Administration developed programs such as the Federal Theater Project, the Federal Art Project and the Federal Writers' Project. Over the WPA's eight-year existence it sponsored almost 10,000 works of art, including murals by Thomas Hart Benton, books and pamphlets by such writers as John Cheever and Studs Terkel, and plays and performances by the likes of John Houseman and Orson Welles.

Not until the late 1950s and early '60s, however, did Congress look for a means to regularize government support of the arts. It established the National Endowment for the Arts in 1965 with this mission statement:

> Man's need to make, experience and comprehend art is as profound as his need to speak. It is through art that we can understand ourselves and our potential. And it is through art that we will be understood and remembered by those who come after us. . . . This nation's governance is based on our people's commitment to freedom of imagination, thought, and expression. Our many aesthetic and cultural traditions are precious to us—for the rich variety of their beauty and as a symbol of the diverse nature of the U.S.

The NEA has been true to that mission for the past 27 years. Only a few grants—perhaps 30—out of 95,000 that it has awarded have stirred up any public complaint. That's a record that few federal agencies—indeed, few large organizations of any kind—can boast. Yet opponents have accused the NEA of intentionally funding offensive, antireligious, obscene and pornographic work. I deeply regret that some leaders in this vicious smear campaign have been from religious bodies.

Fundamentalist Groups

Certain groups claiming to speak for all families or all Christians have hammered away at the NEA. They remind me of Swift's maxim, "We have just enough religion to make us hate, but not enough to make us love one another." Groups such as the American Family Association have used their attacks on the NEA to attract donations and to conduct mass-mailing campaigns in an effort to influence Congress. They might take a line of poetry out of context or declare blasphemous an image of Christ without seeking to grasp the artist's message or even determining whether the NEA funded the work in the first place.

Ironically, Congress has received more mail, most of it generated by fundamentalist groups, complaining about the NEA than it has about the savings-and-loan scandal, which will cost each person more than $2,000. The arts supported by the NEA cost each person 68 cents per year for *everything* (over 4,000 grants). The works that have drawn the most vociferous complaints cost each citizen less than a penny.

It isn't that mainline churches have left the field on this issue; mainline churches have never suited up. And that's a shame. Artists are talking, writing and creating works that address social issues—war, AIDS, human cruelty. But because some images intentionally shock or cause us to rethink our positions, the NEA has been tagged as a purveyor of pornography. If an artist seeks, either gently or confrontationally, to pique our social conscience, how different is that from the example Christ set?

As chairman of the NEA, I repeatedly said to Congress and the public that the NEA never intends to support a project whose sole purpose is to offend. Obscenity and pornography are degrading, and that is not what art is about and certainly not what the National Endowment for the Arts is about. Obscenity is the antithesis of art; it has no soul.

The Necessity for Tolerance

Rather, the NEA aims to support the most excellent art and make it widely available. A certain amount of tolerance, however, is necessary. We are a diverse country with many different ethnic, social, spiritual and intellectual views, and our art will reflect that diversity. Sometimes art does not offer a pretty reflection. But art is about more than pretty pictures; it is about the truth and beauty of the human condition, the children of God in all their joy and sorrow, celebration and pain. As Willa Cather said: "Artistic growth is . . . a refining of the sense of truthfulness. The stupid believe that to be truthful is easy; only the artist, the great artist, knows how difficult it is."

Think how primitive cave paintings reflect the ideas and concerns of primitive humans—scenes depicting hunting; stylized images of humans and beasts; and works connoting the importance of early tools such as spears and arrows. Think of the idealized bodies and vacant eyes in ancient Greek and Roman statuary. Think of medieval poetry, such as the epic *Beowulf*, which dramatizes a man's confrontation with mythical beasts. Consider the sudden discovery after the Dark Ages of perspective in the visual arts. and how that changed our view of ourselves and art. Think of the glorified image of

> *"We are a diverse country with many different ethnic, social, spiritual and intellectual views, and our art will reflect that diversity."*

God and humans in Renaissance art, or the fractured self-image in the Cubist paintings of Picasso, or the existential angst in *Waiting for Godot*. Think of what the Vietnam Memorial tells us about our society, our nation, ourselves.

Art expresses our attempt to understand ourselves, which is precisely why the histories of Western art and religion are inextricably linked. Sometimes art will be controversial. So will religion. The work of an artist who has grown up in the ghetto surrounded by crime and dislocation is bound to express anger. The artist who has AIDS is bound to express frustration. If you are oppressed, your art will show it.

> *"We must not fear new ideas or different ways of expression if we are to learn and grow as a society."*

Congress has questioned the NEA about alleged blasphemy in the art it has supported because constituents, often at the urging of fundamentalist groups, have complained. Most of those constituents have not seen the works over which they are outraged. They have only been told about them—by people who also probably haven't seen the art. Two notorious cases are Andres Serrano's "Piss Christ" and David Wonorowicz's collage that shows Christ with a crown of thorns and a needle in his arm.

Wouldn't it be healthier if, rather than attacking these pieces for apparently ridiculing religion, we debated the meaning of the cross and Jesus' act of taking upon himself the sins of the world? Religious people who without inquiry or theological analysis declare these pieces blasphemous reveal the weakness of their faith. Yet these charges have influenced Congress and undermined the Arts Endowment. Where were the decent and devout of this country in this debate that concerns us all?

A List of Achievements

As I noted earlier, 99 percent of the Endowment's work is noncontroversial and enhances the lives of people all over this country. Take a quick tour with me:

• The NEA's Arts in Education Program helps put artists into schools across the country to teach children about self-expression, creativity and self-esteem through the arts. Arts education projects reach over 4 million students each year. One fourth-grader who participated in the program said he preferred art to math, because "with math you look in your head, and there is one answer, but with art, you look into your heart and there are many answers."

• The NEA funds children's television and arts education programs such as the "Wonderworks" series on public television; children's arts festivals in cities from Pittsburgh to Vancouver, Washington; numerous children's programs at art museums from Boston to New Orleans to Los Angeles; and a children's art series on PBS called "Behind the Scenes."

• The first major U.S. touring exhibit of Mexican retablo painting by Inter-Cultura, Inc., of Fort Worth, received NEA support. Retablos, which are small devotional paintings on tin depicting the Holy Family and the saints, are an important category of Mexican religious folk art from the 19th century that feature accomplished stylistic qualities of color, line and technique.

• The NEA routinely awards grants to major museums for exhibitions with religious subjects or themes. For example, it has supported the Metropolitan Museum of Art's exhibition of paintings from Renaissance Siena, which includes a large fresco of the Madonna of Mercy, and the Los Angeles County Museum of Art's exhibition of the works of 17th-century painter Guido Reni of Bologna, featuring paintings such as "St. John the Baptist," "The Coronation of the Virgin" and "The Apostles Peter and Paul."

• The Endowment funds choruses whose repertoire features religious works, including masses, passions, requiems and oratorios by Argento, Bach, Beethoven, Brahms, Mendelssohn, Verdi and many others. Gospel choruses such as the Fisk Jubilee Singers in Nashville, Tennessee; the Nashville Gospel Ministries, and the American Gospel Arts Fund for the First American Black Sacred Music Convention all receive support.

• For several years the agency awarded grants to the New Mexico Community Foundation's design study of adobe churches, which has led to the preservation of many of these historic houses of worship.

• The Endowment gave a grant to the Jewish Federation of the Greater East Bay in Oakland, California, for a festival celebrating the dance, music and culture of Yiddish-speaking people. It also helped support "The Sacred Arts of Queens," a component of the annual Queens, New York, arts festival.

• The NEA has supported smaller projects, such as Penn Community Services on St. Helena Island, South Carolina, which explains the traditional sacred music of various sites across the state; the multidisciplinary arts activities of the Franciscan Sisters of Little Falls, Minnesota; and a summer arts workshop for developmentally disabled youth at St. Norbert's College in De Pere, Wisconsin.

Fund All Projects

As this list indicates, "controversial" art is only a small part of the NEA's work. But it is an essential part. We must not fear new ideas or different ways of expression if we are to learn and grow as a society.

NEA projects are judged by citizen panels to have artistic merit, regardless of their religious content. The citizen panels are instructed to make artistic excellence their primary criterion. The NEA is not "anti" anything; it is pro-art.

The NEA has had great success in its mission. In 1965, before the NEA was started, there were 162 local arts councils; today there are over 3,000. Many of our Pulitzer prizewinners for fiction, poetry, drama and music at one time received NEA funds. Recent surveys indicate that an overwhelming majority of Americans believe that the arts play an important role in their lives.

Only good, decent and committed citizens can preserve and empower the NEA. This country has always valued freedom of expression, believing that through the vigorous and honest clash of ideas from diverse voices the truth will emerge. This is a matter of faith in democracy. Our government must be strong enough to be evenhanded. There's room in the choir of art for all Americans.

Congress Should Fund the NEA Without Restrictions

by Major R. Owens

About the author: *Major R. Owens is a U.S. representative from New York. He is a member of several congressional committees including the House Committee on Education.*

Some 80,000 projects have been funded by NEA since its inception and only 25 of those 80,000 have aroused any controversy whatsoever. This is clearly a program that benefits America. This is clearly a program that we need more of and not less of. The problem is that a few people who are very skillful at fanning the flames and leading us into diversion have commanded the media and the press and generated a stampede. . . . The stampede has been so successful that it is going to be necessary to compromise in order to keep the program alive.

While I do not question the sincerity of any Member of Congress, in total this whole stampede has been a diversion from very serious matters. It serves to divert us from the real obscenities in the Nation.

Webster defines obscenity as anything that is morally repugnant. There is a whole list of morally repugnant national matters that we ought to be concerned with. I am proud to speak this afternoon in strong support of reauthorizing the National Endowment for the Arts. One of our former Presidents once said:

"Artists stretch the limits of understanding. They express ideas that are sometimes unpopular. In an atmosphere of liberty, artists and patrons are free to think the unthinkable and create the audacious . . . where there's liberty, art succeeds. In societies that are not free, art dies."

Debating the Wrong Issues

I stress that point because the debate over the relative merits of the NEA has been centering on the wrong issues. It has been centering on what a very few artists have been doing with their grants and whether or not the works of art they have created are appropriate or decent. We are not artists. Very few of us would

Major R. Owens's remarks during the floor debate on H.R. 4825, the Arts, Humanities, and Museums Amendments of 1990, 101st Cong., 2d sess., October 11, 1990.

claim to be experts on art. So how can this body sit in judgment over the content of art and even attempt to deem it appropriate or inappropriate or good or bad?

As thousands of people who are knowledgeable about art assert, artists create art to reflect society, to explore societal ideas and concepts. They do not choose only those ideas which are comfortable and acceptable to us. If they did, art would be universally boring. There would be nothing new, nothing daring, nothing to make us think about the art itself and about what it is reflecting.

A person who grew up in the savage ghettos of an inner city, who lived in rundown housing projects and went to school in a crumbling, rat-infested school is not going to paint pretty pictures of landscapes and fruit bowls and frolicking kittens. That artist's portrayals are more likely to reflect the experiences of his or her life and the anger of being shut out from the prosperity apparently being realized elsewhere in society.

Art Reflects Society

This art reflects things that are happening in our society, and closing our eyes will not make those things go away. Such art can help us recognize other influences on our culture and even help us understand them. And if it does not help me or you specifically, you can be sure that it is helping someone, somewhere, who can relate to it.

Artistic freedom enables us to depict images and realities which may or may not be offensive but which help us explore influences in our culture that we would otherwise not experience. An image or a picture or a book can travel places and affect people all over the world. People who live in remote communities, even in the United States, may have access to a library program which contains books of stories or books of art or musical reproductions which can allow the people in that community to explore the arts and to witness the reflections of people from all corners of the world.

The NEA has financed many programs which promote access to the arts for people who otherwise would not be able to experience art. These programs may include bringing a dance troupe into rural areas on a tour, or it may include sponsoring a musical exploration program for poor students in the inner city.

In my district in central Brooklyn, the NEA has funded many small and worthwhile community programs. With such programs, restoration has become well known and attracts children and adults from throughout the city to participate in those and many other community minded programs.

> *"Art reflects things that are happening in our society, and closing our eyes will not make those things go away."*

Another cultural program funded by the NEA in my district is New Radio and Performing Arts, a pioneer in the fields of experimental documentaries, contemporary radio drama and sound experiments for the broadcast media. Endowment support over several years has helped this organization to explore new projects about women poets of color and identify new talents for underrepresented radio themes and contents.

Endowment support to another institution in my district has funded a variety of projects intended to showcase new art forms and smaller programs targeted to the local multiethnic community which seek to increase access to different art forms and encourage exploration of the arts by children.

Support the NEA

These and many other worthwhile community programs in my district have been funded by the NEA and thousands more have been funded nationwide. Of more than 80,000 grants, only 20 or 25 have been considered controversial. For this, some Members of this body are advocating that we eliminate the entire program.

Members are rising up in arms because tax dollars have been spent on funding these controversial projects. Each taxpayer is responsible for only 62 cents of the total yearly budget for the NEA. Compare that with the cost per taxpayer for each $5 billion B-2 bomber that falls from the sky, or each $20 million rocket that blows up, or the astronomical cost of the $500 billion S&L bail-out. Where is the outrage over the cost to the taxpayers of these million- and billion-dollar black holes?

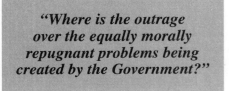

"Where is the outrage over the equally morally repugnant problems being created by the Government?"

Members are rising up in arms over supposedly morally repugnant projects being sponsored by the Government. Where is the outrage over the equally morally repugnant problems being created by the Government?

The situation with the National Endowment for the Arts has been blown way out of proportion. There are no rational reasons for restricting this program and there are no reasons at all to eliminate it altogether. This Congress has been stampeded into making wrong and potentially disastrous decisions too frequently in the recent past. We must not bow to these illogical forces. We must fight to preserve this program based not on fear and intimidation, but based on the history and good experiences of this particular program. I urge my colleagues to have courage and to vote to defend the National Endowment for the Arts reauthorization.

Government Should Fund All Art

by Eleanor L. Brilliant

About the author: *Eleanor L. Brilliant is associate professor of social work at Rutgers University. Prior to entering academia, she was associate executive director of The United Way of Westchester, NY.*

Like the situation faced by Alice In Wonderland, the controversies surrounding the Mapplethorpe Art Show seem "curiouser and curiouser" the more you ponder them. They are even more perplexing when considered as part of a long chain of events which occurred in our country in a period of about 13 months, culminating in the furor in Cincinnati when an angry sheriff attempted once again to close down the exhibit of Robert Mapplethorpe's photographs: "The Perfect Moment" (April, 1990). A brief review of the sequence of events in that year should serve to arouse concern and remind us of the emotion-laden context in which they took place and in which they seem to continue to occur.

How It Started

In a sense it started when angry voices spoke out against an exhibition at the Art Institute of Chicago where viewers were invited to tread on the American flag as part of an artistic experience (March, 1989); the Institute was subsequently punished by Illinois State legislators who reduced the Institute's grant from $70,000 to $1. In Washington the Corcoran Art Gallery cancelled the planned Mapplethorpe exhibit (June, 1989) which was thereafter moved to another less prominent place in Washington. As a result, the curator resigned, the Director of the Gallery was subject to heavy criticism, and the Board of Directors issued a public apology (September, 1989). Government support for the Andres Serrano and Mapplethorpe shows through the National Endowment for the Arts received public attention stimulating thousands of letters to Congress and the Endowment. Following the exhibit of Serrano's art with the image of a plastic cross in a container of urine in North Carolina, Jesse Helms, the conservative

Eleanor L. Brilliant, "In Whose Interest?" *Society*, September/October 1990, © 1990 by Transaction Publishers. Reprinted with permission of the publisher.

Senator from that State, succeeded in obtaining passage of the Helms Amendment prohibiting federal funds to be used for support of Art defined as obscene. In November, 1989 . . . the Chairman of the NEA withdrew funding from a controversial show about AIDS, "Witness Against Our Vanishing" at a gallery in New York, which featured erotic pictures and included a catalogue with overt political content; the NEA chairman later reinstated support for the exhibit. Finally in April 1990, the Director of the Contemporary Arts Center in the Cincinnati case already referred to actually withstood police pressure and continued the exhibit of Mapplethorpe's work, although he was indicted for doing so.

Art Politicized

It appears that we have taken Alice's adventure one step further and gone through the looking glass into an upside down world, where confusion reigns, values lack clarity, and art, which has often not been of great interest to the masses, has obtained a new visibility and salience as a subject of public concern. Although government support of the arts, and the role of the NEA in particular, has been at the center of much of the controversy, it appears that much more must be at stake to arouse such emotional outcries. What has happened is that art exhibits have now become a highly charged focus for political activity. What may be even more alarming is that the forces for binding our sense of morality have been clear in their vision of what is politically, or in their language "morally" acceptable—while the more liberal leaders, the people who have been the experts in the art world, the gallery professionals, and the philanthropists who have been proponents of free expression in art, have lacked the same kind of conviction and determination in articulating their viewpoint. While there may have been individual heroes, there has on the whole been a lack of emphatic, collective and positive argument in favor of diversity in art.

At a time when values have become so politicized, what then is the role of philanthropy? Can philanthropy support art which some critics of the art world have labelled obscene or pornographic? . . . In order to answer these questions, we need to address at least these three interrelated issues: the nature of philanthropy; the distinction, if there is one, between government support for the arts and private philanthropy; and the question of the public interest in freedom of expression in the arts. I will begin with the last of the three arguments.

Art is valued in a free society both intrinsically and extrinsically—intrinsically for the pleasure it gives the viewer and for its particular quality

"Art exhibits have now become a highly charged focus for political activity."

as a work of art; extrinsically for the functions art performs for the society, as a way of expressing our different views of reality, aspects of life, and meanings about reality as perceived and felt by the individual artist, for himself and on behalf of others. Since presentation of different views is valued by a democratic society, any attempt to curtail art through some official means, *i.e.*, public suppression, must meet strict procedural standards. Censorship and control in a democracy are abhorrent ideas, and immediately suggest an echo of totalitarian repression which not only inhibits the extrinsic function of presenting different viewpoints, but ultimately limits the intrinsic pleasures derived from aesthetic values in the art itself. Closing a show, or legal efforts which curtail significant aspects of artistic expression (*e.g.*, the Sheriff's threat against

> *"Censorship and control in a democracy are abhorrent ideas."*

works in the Mapplethorpe exhibit in Cincinnati), is not acceptable without proof of direct harm to the public, or violation of the public interest (*e.g.*, child abuse in taking the photographs or developing the artistic object), and requires explicit legal proof of the harm involved. This proof would have to compete with the overriding value of freedom of expression, which in a pluralist democratic society insures that the minority interest is protected and that Madisonian democratic principles are maintained.

Should the Government Support the Arts?

Having said that the government should not take action against an art exhibit, or prevent the showing of art which is controversial, or represents a minority, even deviant viewpoint, without proof of extreme harm, does it necessarily follow that government, and particularly the Federal government, should support that art? More explicitly, should taxpayer dollars pay for the showing of such art? Here is where a curious answer is often professed by the opponents of non-traditional art. They claim that the taxpayer dollar should not be used to promote art which is not, or cannot be, liked by most sensible people. This assumes that the majority should dictate the preferences of the few. Followed to its logical extreme, we would not use government to collect tolls on the road, nor indeed would we choose to pay income tax at all. The argument in fact goes back to the public interest. I may not want to pay for certain specific public roads or monuments and others may also share this view. But, given the impossibility of measuring individual preferences with any subtlety, we nevertheless consider taxes or tolls to be in the public interest because they pay for public goods which are deemed worthy by some representative bodies and their public agents—the agencies of government who plan and determine roadways.

The particular case of works of culture, art and literature however would seem more subtle. It may be sufficient just to remember that in this century James Joyce's masterpiece, *Ulysses*, was considered obscene; *Lady Chatterley's Lover* by D.H. Lawrence was subjected to censorship in this country; and works of Faulkner have been considered pornographic. In painting, Hilton Kramer himself notes as one example that *Dejeuner sur l'Herbe* by Manet violated acceptable social norms in France at the time.

To deal with the problem of support for new and significant exhibits in the museums of our country, the government has determined, through our process of representational voting, to create a National Endowment for the Arts (1965); and this Endowment supports artistic projects through a procedure which is meant to insure protection for such art from political pressure. Thus, panels of experts from the art world are brought in to make the selection according to appropriate artistic criteria and their professional judgement. The grant is given— in the cases above to a recognized gallery, or agent in the non-profit (independent) sector, the show is mounted—and that should be the end of the government's concern.

Is this act of granting the money, then, the same as that of a private funding source? Does it make a difference whether the grant in support of the Mapplethorpe show is given by the National Endowment or by a Ford or Rockefeller Foundation? Are both acts "philanthropy," presumably implying that the giving of money for cultural activities is the determining characteristic, with little difference whether it is supported through private or "charitable" dollars or through "tax" dollars? I must argue the opposite case even though in both situations I see no reason for withdrawing funds from the exhibits of art we have discussed above, and recognize that government funds have a notable impact on private support. It is estimated that Federal funds generate at least five dollars, primarily private dollars, for every one government dollar expended.

> *"The grant is given . . . and that should be the end of the government's concern."*

Yet there is a different principle operating in the two spheres. For even though the Ford Foundation and the Rockefeller Foundation operate in the public interest as 501 (c) (3) organizations under the Internal Revenue Code, they are part of the third sector, in which independence, individual decision making and the right of peculiar choice or preference is fiercely defended. It is indeed frequently claimed to be one of the primary reasons for the existence of the private, non-profit sector. So long as there are clear criteria, and the process is carried out fairly, with appropriate fiscal and procedural safeguards, the right to support particular pre-determined viewpoints is considered unchallengeable. Ultimately this pursuit of special interest is a unique quality of the organizations in the voluntary philanthropic sector and is part of their contribution to the public good.

Government Ecumenism

Government philanthropy, or more correctly, government funding through grants-in-aid, is required to meet a different standard. The government must be more ecumenical in approach, and it cannot pre-select its own particular point of view to uphold and support through the grants that it makes. The granting act is generally established through a third party "neutral" system: a panel of experts to whom it may give some procedural guidelines, but whose judgment the government agency should not, indeed must not control. The government cannot force a particular viewpoint through such granting; it must assure equal access for divergent viewpoints.

> *"Government must insure protection of the minority view, tolerance for the deviant, and the possibility of expression."*

According to the principles of minority protection in a democratic state, governments must go even further. Government must insure protection of the minority view, tolerance for the deviant, and the possibility of expression, whether through speech or through creativity in art, allowing for different views of the world, including criticism of the government itself and majority policies of the time. This is both theoretically necessitated by the definition of democracy and pragmatically desired. For if one reviews the events described earlier, there is certainly room for doubt as to who is actually in the majority, whether in the case of the Cincinnati show, or in other cities. . . .

We have clearly come through the looking glass and must face the need to redefine the basis for public decision making about art. In this context it is quite possible that the Mapplethorpe show presents a vision of the world which many of us find repugnant. But it is the artist's vision! He has every right to offer it to us, and we should defend and support his right to show this vision to us. It is, however, the decision of each of us individually, whether or not to see it. That is the collective principle of freedom which makes the support of such an exhibit a matter of the public interest.

Chapter 2

Should Unrestricted Speech Be Allowed on College Campuses?

CURRENT CONTROVERSIES

Political Correctness and Campus Speech: An Overview

by Paul Berman

About the author: *Paul Berman is regarded as one of America's most well known political and cultural commentators. His countless articles have appeared in such publications as the* Village Voice, *the* New Republic, *and* Dissent.

The national debate over "political correctness" began in the fall of 1990 with a small, innocuous-seeming article in *The New York Times*—and within a few months was plastered across the covers of *Newsweek*, *The Atlantic*, *New York*, *The New Republic*, and *The Village Voice*, not to mention the TV news-talk shows and the newspaper op-ed pages. George Bush himself, not otherwise known as a university intellectual or a First Amendment hard-liner, weighed in with a speech at the University of Michigan defending campus freedoms against "politically correct" censors. Dinesh D'Souza's book *Illiberal Education: The Politics of Race and Sex on Campus* rose to the best seller list. The PEN American Center in New York held a major symposium, and the intellectual journal *Partisan Review*, a conference. Every ideology known on earth, plus a few others, was invoked in this debate, which made it hard to tell exactly what was under dispute. Yet at its heart, the debate consisted of only a few main points.

A Strange Ideology

These points were by and large accusations, made at first by neoconservatives, later by liberals and a number of old-school leftists. According to the accusations, a new postmodern generation from the 1960s has come into power in the universities, mostly in the humanities departments but also in the central administrations. The postmodern professors promote a strange radical ideology that decries the United States and the West as hopelessly oppressive and that focuses on the reactionary prejudices of Western culture.

The new ideology tends toward nihilism, erasing any distinction between truth and falsity and between quality and lack of quality in art. Guided by these ideas, the postmodern professors have set out to undermine the traditional study of literature and the humanities. In the eyes of their accusers, they have reduced literary criticism to a silly obsession with political questions that don't belong to literature, and to a weird concern with sexual questions. In some cases they have gotten their students to study cheap products of Marxist and feminist propaganda instead of the masterpieces of world literature. They fan the flames of ethnic and sexual discontent among the students.

Tension on Campuses

But the worst thing they do, according to the accusations, the thing that arouses so much angry resentment, is generate an atmosphere of campus repression. In the name of "sensitivity" to others and under pain of being denounced as a sexist or racist, the postmodern radicals require everyone around them to adhere to their own codes of speech and behavior. Professors and students who remain outside the new movement have to walk on eggshells, ever reminding themselves to say "high school women" instead of "high school girls" or a hundred other politically incorrect phrases. Already the zealots of political correctness have intimidated a handful of well-respected professors into dropping courses that touch on controversial topics. They have succeeded in imposing official speech codes on a large number of campuses. And the resulting atmosphere—the prissiness of it, the air of caution that many people in academic settings have adopted, the new habit of using one language in private and a different and euphemistic one in public—has finally come to resemble, according to the accusers, the odious McCarthy era of the 1950s. Except this time the intimidation originates on the left.

The main accusation is summed up by the title of a 1986 article from *Commentary* magazine: "The Campus: 'An Island of Repression in a Sea of Freedom'" (by Chester E. Finn, Jr.). But there are secondary accusations too. The repression, bad enough in the universities, is said to be spreading to the museums, where the political slant of the new ideas has a disastrous effect on art, and to the cultural journalism of a beleaguered politically correct city like Boston. And still worse, the same trends have made the fatal leap to the curriculum committees of public school education.

"They have succeeded in imposing official speech codes on a large number of campuses."

New curricular developments emphasizing hyperethnicity, Afrocentrism, and other notions of the avant-garde have been adopted in quite a few school districts around the country and are on the verge of being adopted in some of the major states, with effects that, in the view of the critics, can be predicted to be calamitous. There is going to be a deliberate miseducation of children from impoverished backgrounds. The educational emphasis on ethnic distinctions and the suspicion of American democratic institutions are going to wear down the bonds that hold the country together. And sooner or later, according to these accusations, problems that are political and social, not just educational, will come of all this, and the United States will break up into a swarm of warring Croatias and Serbias. "Deculturation prefigures disintegration," in James Atlas's sardonic phrase.

A Widening Debate

All in all, these were very exotic accusations, which made them interesting—but also easy to doubt, as some of P.C.'s severest critics have frankly acknowledged. Any number of liberal and left wing professors instantly stood up to challenge the entire complaint and to scoff at the alarmist tone. . . . Yet the accusations were not without a historical background. In some respects they have been with us for a decade or longer—ever since the engagé art critic Hilton Kramer used to scandalize the readers of *The New York Times* with his thunderings against the radical counterculture and the left. Elements of the argument surfaced in the national political discussion as early as 1984, when William Bennett, at that time the chairman of the National Endowment for the Humanities, criticized the universities in a pamphlet called *To Reclaim a Legacy*.

> *"Aspects of the debate turned up in other countries too."*

Allan Bloom's oddball best seller of 1987, *The Closing of the American Mind*, brought the debate to a wider public. Bennett's conservative successor at the National Endowment for the Humanities, Lynne V. Cheney, produced a pamphlet of her own called *Humanities in America*—which was answered by the liberal members of the American Council of Learned Societies in their own pamphlet, *Speaking for the Humanities*. There was a national debate in 1988 about the curriculum at Stanford University and the merits of substituting "multiculturalism" for the traditional study of Western Civ. And the same argument took other forms—the debates over artists like Andres Serrano and Robert Mapplethorpe (accused respectively of blasphemy and obscenity) and over Yale University's literary theorist, the late Paul de Man, whose secret life turned out postmortem to include a stint as a pro-Nazi book critic in German-occupied Belgium.

Aspects of the debate turned up in other countries too. There was a battle at Cambridge University in 1981 when university authorities more or less declined to make room for some of the new literary theories. France saw the biggest arguments of all—measured in ink spilled and probable influence (once the news of these arguments begins to spread into other languages), with the subjects ranging from the influence and politics of the German philosopher Martin Heidegger to the new glass pyramid at the Louvre to the meaning of Third World revolution.

What was new, then, in the American controversy over political correctness in the early 1990s? A few things, certainly. The name was new. "Politically correct" was originally an approving phrase on the Leninist left to denote someone who steadfastly toed the party line. Then it evolved into "P.C.," an ironic phrase among wised-up leftists to denote someone whose line-toeing fervor was too much to bear. Only in conjunction with the P.C. debate itself did the phrase get picked up by people who had no fidelity to radicalism at all, but who relished the nasty syllables for their twist of irony. Apart from this phrase, some of the particulars had a fresh aspect: the focus on campus speech codes, and the amusing experience of watching people on the right argue for the First Amendment and people on the left against it. The way that certain liberals and old-school leftists joined the neoconservatives in making several of the arguments was also new, and perhaps quite significant, since previous debates tended to observe a chaste division of left and right.

A New Name for an Old Argument

Yet at bottom, the P.C. debate was just a continuation of an argument that is more than a decade old. And the longevity of this argument, the way it keeps reappearing in different forms, growing instead of shrinking, producing best-selling books about university education every couple of years, its international dimension, the heat and fury—all this should tell us that something big and important is under discussion. How to specify that big and important thing is not so easy, though. The closer you examine the argument over political correctness, the more it begins to look like one of Paul de Man's literary interpretations, where everything is a puzzle without a solution. No three people agree about the meaning of central terms like "deconstruction," "difference," "multiculturalism," or "poststructuralism." Every participant carries around his own definitions, the way that on certain American streets every person packs his own gun. And when you take these numberless definitions into consideration, the entire argument begins to look like . . . what?

> *"Yet at bottom, the P.C. debate was just a continuation of an argument that is more than a decade old."*

I would say it looks like the Battle of Waterloo as described by Stendhal. A murky fog hangs over the field. Now and then a line of soldiers marches past. Who are they? Which army do they represent? They may be Belgian deconstructionists from Yale, or perhaps the followers of Lionel Trilling in exile from Columbia. Perhaps they are French mercenaries. It is impossible to tell. The fog thickens. Shots go off. The debate is unintelligible. But it is noisy!

All Speech Should Be Unrestricted on College Campuses

by Gerald Gunther

About the author: *Gerald Gunther is William Nelson Cromwell Professor of Law at California's Stanford University. He is regarded as one of the nation's leading authorities on constitutional law.*

I am deeply troubled by current efforts—however well-intentioned—to place new limits on freedom of expression at Stanford and other campuses. Such limits are not only incompatible with the mission and meaning of a university; they also send exactly the wrong message from academia to society as a whole. University campuses should exhibit greater, not less, freedom of expression than prevails in society at large.

Proponents of new limits argue that historic First Amendment rights must be balanced against "Stanford's commitment to the diversity of ideas and persons." Clearly, there is ample room and need for vigorous university action to combat racial and other discrimination. But curbing freedom of speech is the wrong way to do so. The proper answer to bad speech is usually more and better speech—not new laws, litigation and repression.

Lest it be thought that I am insensitive to the pain imposed by expressions of racial or religious hatred, let me say that I have suffered that pain and empathize with others under similar verbal assault. My deep belief in the principles of the First Amendment arises in part from my own experiences.

Lesson from the Nazis

I received my elementary education in a public school in a very small town in Nazi Germany. There I was subjected to vehement anti-Semitic remarks from my teacher, classmates and others—"*Judensau*" (Jew pig) was far from the harshest. I can assure you that they hurt. More generally, I lived in a country where ideologi-

Gerald Gunther, "Is There Ever a Good Reason to Restrict Free Speech on a College Campus?—No," *This World*, September 9, 1990. Copyright 1990, Leland Stanford Junior University. Reprinted with permission of *The Stanford Lawyer*.

cal orthodoxy reigned and where the opportunity for dissent was severely limited.

The lesson I have drawn from my childhood in Nazi Germany and my happier adult life in this country is the need to walk the sometimes difficult path of denouncing the bigot's hateful ideas with all my power, yet at the same time challenging any community's attempt to suppress hateful ideas by force of law.

Obviously, given my own experience, I do *not* quarrel with the claim that words *can* do harm. But I firmly disagree that a showing of harm suffices to deny First Amendment protection, and I insist on the elementary First Amendment principle that our Constitution usually protects even offensive, harmful expression.

That is why—at the risk of being thought callous or doctrinaire—I feel compelled to speak out against the attempt by some members of the Stanford community to enlarge the area of forbidden speech under the Fundamental Standard [for student conduct]. Such proposals, in my view seriously undervalue the First Amendment and far too readily endanger its precious content.

In explaining my position, I will avoid extensive legal arguments. Instead, I want to speak from the heart, on the basis of my own background and of my understanding of First Amendment principles—principles supported by an ever larger number of scholars and Supreme Court justices especially since the days of the Warren Court.

> *"University campuses should exhibit greater, not less, freedom of expression than prevails in society at large."*

Among the core principles is that any official effort to suppress expression must be viewed with the greatest skepticism and suspicion. Only in very narrow, urgent circumstances should government or similar institutions be permitted to inhibit speech. True, there are certain categories of speech that may be prohibited; but the number and scope of these categories has steadily shrunk over the last 50 years. Face-to-face insults are one such category; incitement to immediate illegal action is another. But opinions expressed in debates and arguments about a wide range of political and social issues should not be suppressed simply because of disagreement with the content of the expression.

Similarly, speech should not and cannot be banned simply because it is "offensive" to substantial parts of, or a majority of, a community. The refusal to suppress offensive speech is one of the most difficult obligations the free-speech principle imposes upon all of us; yet it is also one of the First Amendment's greatest glories—indeed it is a central test of a community's commitment to a free speech.

"Fighting Words" Doesn't Apply

The Supreme Court's 1989 decision to allow flag-burning as a form of political protest, in *Texas vs. Johnson*, warrants careful pondering by all those who continue to advocate campus restraints on "racist speech." As Justice William J.

Brennan's majority opinion in the *Johnson* case reminded, "If there is a bedrock principle underlying the First Amendment it is that the Government may not prohibit the expression of an idea simply because society finds the idea itself offensive or disagreeable." In refusing to place flag-burning outside the First Amendment, moreover, the *Johnson* majority insisted (in words especially apt for the "racist speech" debate): "The First Amendment does not guarantee that other concepts virtually sacred to our Nation as a whole—*such as the principle that discrimination on the basis of race is odious and destructive*—will go un-questioned in the marketplace of ideas. We decline, therefore, to create for the flag an exception to the joust of principles protected by the First Amendment." (Italics added.)

Campus proponents of restricting offensive speech are currently relying for justification on the Supreme Court's allegedly repeated opinion that "fighting words" constitute an exception to the First Amendment. Such an exception has indeed been recognized in a number of lower-court cases. However, there has been only one case in the history of the Supreme Court in which a majority of the justices has ever found a statement to be a punishable resort to "fighting words." That was *Chaplinsky vs. New Hampshire*, a 50-year-old case involving words that would very likely not be found punishable today.

An Exception in Theory, Not in Practice

More significant is what has happened in the half-century since: Despite re-peated appeals to the Supreme Court to recognize the applicability of the "fight-ing words" exception by affirming challenged convictions, the court has in every instance refused. One must wonder about the strength of an exception that, while theoretically recognized, has for so long not been found apt in practice. (More-over, the proposed Stanford rules are not limited to face-to-face insults, and thus go well beyond the traditional, albeit fragile, "fighting words" exception.)

In recent decades, well-meaning but in my view misguided majorities have sought to suppress not only racist speech but also antiwar and antidraft speech, civil rights demonstrators, Nazis, the Ku Klux Klan and left-wing groups.

Typically, it is people on the extremes of the political spectrum (including those who advocate overthrow of our constitutional system and those who would not protect their opponents' right to dissent were they the major-ity) who feel the brunt of repression and have found protection in the First Amendment; it is well-meaning peo-

> *"Opinions expressed in debates . . . about a wide range of . . . issues should not be suppressed."*

ple in the majority who believe that their "community standards," their sensibili-ties, their sense of outrage, justify restraints.

Those in power in a community recurrently seek to repress speech they find abhorrent; their efforts are understandable human impulses. Yet freedom of expression—and especially the protection of dissident speech, the most important function of the First Amendment—is an anti-majoritarian principle. Is it too much to hope, especially of a university campus, that a majority can be persuaded of the value of freedom of expression and of the resultant need to curb our impulses to repress dissident views?

Eminent Jurists Agree

The principles to which I appeal are not new. They have been expressed, for example, by the most distinguished Supreme Court justices ever since the beginning of the court's confrontations with First Amendment issues nearly 70 years ago. These principles are reflected in the words of so imperfect a First Amendment defender as Justice Oliver Wendell Holmes: "If there is any principle of the Constitution that more imperatively calls for attachment than any other it is the principle of free thought—not free thought for those who agree with us but freedom for the thought that we hate."

This is the principle most elaborately and eloquently addressed by Justice Louis D. Brandeis, who reminded us that the First Amendment rests on a belief "in the power of reason as applied through public discussion" and therefore bars "silence coerced by law—the argument of force in its worst form."

This theme, first articulated in dissents, has repeatedly been voiced in majority opinions in more recent decades. It underlies Justice William O. Douglas's remark in striking down a conviction under a law banning

> *"Constitutional protection 'does not turn upon the truth, popularity or social utility of the ideas and beliefs which are offered.'"*

speech that "stirs the public to anger": "A function of free speech [is] to invite dispute. . . . Speech is often provocative and challenging. That is why freedom of speech [is ordinarily] protected against censorship or punishment."

It also underlies Brennan's comment about our "profound national commitment to the principle that debate on public issues should be uninhibited, robust and wide-open, and that it may well include vehement, caustic and sometimes unpleasantly sharp attacks"—a comment he followed with a reminder that constitutional protection "does not turn upon the truth, popularity or social utility of the ideas and beliefs which are offered."

These principles underlie as well the repeated insistence by Justice John Marshall Harlan, again in majority opinions, that the mere "inutility or immorality" of a message cannot justify its repression and that the state may not punish because of "the underlying content of the message." Moreover, Harlan, in one of the finest First Amendment opinions on the books, noted in words that Stanford would ignore at its peril at this time:

> The constitutional right of free expression is powerful medicine in a society as
> diverse and populous as ours. . . . To many, the immediate consequence of this

freedom may often appear to be only verbal tumult, discord and even offensive utterance. These are, however, within established limits, in truth necessary side effects of the broader enduring values which the process of open debate permits us to achieve. That the air may at times seem filled with verbal cacophony is, in this sense, not a sign of weakness but of strength.

In this same passage, Harlan warned that a power to ban speech merely because it is offensive is an "inherently boundless" notion, and added that "we think it is largely because governmental officials cannot make principled distinctions in this area that the Constitution leaves matters of taste and style so largely to the individual." (The justice made these comments while overturning the conviction of an antiwar protester for "offensive conduct." The defendant had worn, in a courthouse corridor, a jacket bearing the words "F--- the Draft." It bears noting, in light of the ongoing campus debate, that Harlan's majority opinion also warned that "we cannot indulge in the facile assumption that one can forbid particular words without also running the substantial risk of suppressing ideas in the process.")

I restate these principles and repeat these words for reasons going far beyond the fact that they are familiar to me as a First Amendment scholar. I believe—in my heart as well as my mind—that these principles and ideals are not only established but right. I hope that the entire Stanford community will seriously reflect upon the risks to free expression, lest we weaken hard-won liberties at Stanford and, by example, in this nation.

Campus Speech Codes Are Incompatible with Free Speech

by Nat Hentoff

About the author: *Nat Hentoff, a staunch defender of free speech, is a columnist at the* Village Voice *and the* Washington Post *and a staff writer at the* New Yorker.

During three years of reporting on anti-free-speech tendencies in higher education, I've been at more than twenty colleges and universities—from Washington and Lee and Columbia to Mesa State in Colorado and Stanford.

On this voyage of initially reverse expectations—with liberals fiercely advocating censorship of "offensive" speech and conservatives merrily taking the moral high ground as champions of free expression—the most dismaying moment of revelation took place at Stanford.

An Ecumenical Call for a Harsh Code

In the course of a two-year debate on whether Stanford, like many other universities, should have a speech code punishing language that might wound minorities, women, and gays, a letter appeared in the *Stanford Daily*. Signed by the African-American Law Students Association, the Asian-American Law Students Association, and the Jewish Law Students Association, the letter called for a harsh code. It reflected the letter and the spirit of an earlier declaration by Canetta Ivy, a black leader of student government at Stanford during the period of the grand debate. "We don't put as many restrictions on freedom of speech," she said, "as we should."

Reading the letter by this rare ecumenical body of law students (so pressing was the situation that even Jews were allowed in), I thought of twenty, thirty years from now. From so bright a cadre of graduates, from so prestigious a law school would come some of the law professors, civic leaders, college presi-

Nat Hentoff, " 'Speech Codes' on the Campus and Problems of Free Speech," *Dissent*, Fall 1991,

dents, and even maybe a Supreme Court justice of the future. And many of them would have learned—like so many other university students in the land—that censorship is okay provided your motives are okay.

The debate at Stanford ended when the president, Donald Kennedy, following the prevailing winds, surrendered his previous position that once you start telling people what they can't say, you will end up telling them what they can't think. Stanford now has a speech code.

This is not to say that these gags on speech—every one of them so overboard and vague that a student can violate a code without knowing he or she has done so—are invariably imposed by student demand. At most colleges, it is the administration that sets up the code. Because there have been racist or sexist or homophobic taunts, anonymous notes or graffiti, the administration feels it must *do something*. The cheapest, quickest way to demonstrate that it cares is to appear to suppress racist, sexist, homophobic speech.

"The Pall of Orthodoxy"

Usually, the leading opposition among the faculty consists of conservatives—when there is opposition. An exception at Stanford was law professor Gerald Gunther, arguably the nation's leading authority on constitutional law. But Gunther did not have much support among other faculty members, conservative or liberal.

At the University of Buffalo Law School, which has a code restricting speech, I could find just one faculty member who was against it. A liberal, he spoke only on condition that I not use his name. He did not want to be categorized as a racist.

On another campus, a political science professor, for whom I had great respect after meeting and talking with him years ago, has been silent—students told me—on what Justice William Brennan once called "the pall of orthodoxy" that has fallen on his campus.

When I talked to him, the professor said, "It doesn't happen in my class. There's no 'politically correct' orthodoxy here. It may happen in other places at this university, but I don't know about that." He said no more.

One of the myths about the rise of P.C. (politically correct) is that, coming from the left, it is primarily intimidating conservatives on campus. Quite the contrary. At almost every college I've been, conservative students have their own newspaper, usually quite lively and fired by a muckraking glee at exposing "politically correct" follies on campus.

> *"At most colleges, it is the administration that sets up the code."*

By and large, those most intimidated—not so much by the speech codes themselves but by the Madame Defarge-like spirit behind them—are liberal students and those who can be called politically moderate.

I've talked to many of them, and they no longer get involved in class discussions where their views would go against the grain of P.C. righteousness. Many, for instance, have questions about certain kinds of affirmative action. They are not partisans of Jesse Helms or David Duke, but they wonder whether progeny of middle-class black families should get scholarship preference. Others have a question about abortion. Most are not pro-life, but they believe that fathers should have a say in whether the fetus should be sent off into eternity.

Self-Censorship

Jeff Shesol, a recent graduate of Brown and now a Rhodes scholar at Oxford, became nationally known while at Brown because of his comic strip, "Thatch," which, not too kindly, parodied P.C. students. At a forum on free speech at Brown before he left, Shesol said he wished he could tell the new students at Brown to have no fear of speaking freely. But he couldn't tell them that, he said, advising the new students to stay clear of talking critically about affirmative action or abortion, among other things, in public.

At that forum, Shesol told me, he said that those members of the left who regard dissent from their views as racist and sexist should realize that they are discrediting their goals. "They're honorable goals," said Shesol, "and I agree with them. I'm against racism and sexism. But these people's tactics are obscuring the goals. And they've resulted in Brown's no longer being an open-minded place." There were hisses from the audience.

> *"Those members of the left who regard dissent from their views as racist and sexist should realize that they are discrediting their goals."*

Students at New York University Law School have also told me that they censor themselves in class. The kind of chilling atmosphere they describe was exemplified as a case assigned for a moot court competition became subject to denunciation when a sizable number of law students said it was too "offensive" and would hurt the feelings of gay and lesbian students. The case concerned a divorced father's attempt to gain custody of his children on the grounds that their mother had become a lesbian. It was against P.C. to represent the father.

Although some of the faculty responded by insisting that you learn to be a lawyer by dealing with all kinds of cases, including those you personally find offensive, other faculty members supported the rebellious students, praising them for their sensitivity. There was little public opposition from the other students to the attempt to suppress the case. A leading dissenter was a member of the conservative Federalist Society.

What is P.C. to white students is not necessarily P.C. to black students. Most of the latter did not get involved in the N.Y.U. protest, but throughout the country many black students do support speech codes. A vigorous exception was a black Harvard law school student during a debate on whether the law school should start punishing speech. A white student got up and said that the codes are necessary because without them, black students would be driven away from colleges and thereby deprived of the equal opportunity to get an education.

A black student rose and said that the white student had a hell of a nerve to assume that he—in the face of racist speech—would pack up his books and go home. He's been familiar with that kind of speech all his life, and he had never felt the need to run away from it. He'd handled it before and he could again.

> *"Students are to be punished . . . if they use 'fighting words'—derogatory references to 'race, sex, sexual orientation, or disability.'"*

The black student then looked at his white colleague and said that it was condescending to say that blacks have to be "protected" from racist speech. "It is more racist and insulting," he emphasized, "to say that to me than to call me a nigger."

But that would appear to be a minority view among black students. Most are convinced they do need to be protected from wounding language. On the other hand, a good many black student organizations on campus do not feel that Jews have to be protected from wounding language.

Presence of Anti-Semitism

Though it's not much written about in reports of the language wars on campuses, there is a strong strain of anti-Semitism among some—not all, by any means—black students. They invite such speakers as Louis Farrakhan, the former Stokely Carmichael (now Kwame Touré), and such lesser but still burning bushes as Steve Cokely, the Chicago commentator who has declared that Jewish doctors inject the AIDS virus into black babies. That distinguished leader was invited to speak at the University of Michigan.

The black student organization at Columbia University brought to the campus Dr. Khallid Abdul Muhammad. He began his address by saying: "My leader, my teacher, my guide is the honorable Louis Farrakhan. I thought that should be said at Columbia Jewniversity."

Many Jewish students have not censored themselves in reacting to this form of political correctness among some blacks. A Columbia student, Rachel Stoll, wrote a letter to the *Columbia Spectator*: "I have an idea. As a white Jewish American, I'll just stand in the middle of a circle comprising . . . Khallid Abdul Muhammad and assorted members of the Black Students Organization and let them all hurl large stones at me. From recent events and statements made on this campus, I gather this will be a good cheap method of making these people feel good."

At UCLA, a black student magazine printed an article indicating there is considerable truth to the *Protocols of the Elders of Zion* [a document forged c. 1897 alleging that an international Jewish conspiracy was plotting the overthrow of Christian civilization]. For months, the black faculty, when asked their reactions, preferred not to comment. One of them did say that the black students already considered the black faculty to be insufficiently militant, and the professors didn't want to make the gap any wider. Like white liberal faculty members on other campuses, they want to be liked—or at least not too disliked.

Along with quiet white liberal faculty members, most black professors have not opposed the speech codes. But unlike the white liberals, many honestly do believe that minority students have to be insulated from barbed language. They do not believe—as I have found out in a number of conversations—that an essential part of an education is to learn to demystify language, to strip it of its ability to demonize and stigmatize you. They do not believe that the way to deal with bigoted language is to answer it with more and better language of your own. This seems very elementary to me, but not to the defenders, black and white, of the speech codes.

"Fighting Words"

Consider University of California president David Gardner. He has imposed a speech code on all the campuses in his university system. Students are to be punished—and this is characteristic of the other codes around the country—if they use "fighting words"—derogatory references to "race, sex, sexual orientation, or disability."

The term "fighting words" comes from a 1942 Supreme Court decision, *Chaplinsky v. New Hampshire*, which ruled that "fighting words" are not protected by the First Amendment. That decision, however, has been in disuse at the High Court for many years. But it is thriving on college campuses.

In the California code, a word becomes "fighting" if it is directly addressed to "any ordinary person" (presumably, extraordinary people are above all this). These are the kinds of words that are "inherently likely to provoke a violent reaction, *whether or not they actually do*." (Emphasis added.)

Moreover, he or she who fires a fighting word at any ordinary person can be reprimanded or dismissed from the university because the perpetrator should "reasonably know" that what he or she has said will interfere with the "victim's ability to pursue effectively his or her education or otherwise participate fully in university programs and activities."

> *"A precedent has been set . . . that the principle of free speech is merely situational."*

Asked Gary Murikami, chairman of the Gay and Lesbian Association at the University of California, Berkeley: "What does it mean?"

Among those—faculty, law professors, college administrators—who insist such codes are essential to the university's purpose of making *all* students feel at home and thereby able to concentrate on their work, there has been a celebratory resort to the Fourteenth Amendment.

That amendment guarantees "equal protection of the laws" to all, and that means to all students on campus. Accordingly, when the First Amendment rights of those engaging in offensive speech clash with the equality rights of their targets under the Fourteenth Amendment, the First Amendment must give way.

> *"Universities cannot censor or suppress speech, no matter how obnoxious in content, without violating their justification for existence."*

This is the thesis, by the way, of John Powell, legal director of the American Civil Liberties Union, even though that organization has now formally opposed all college speech codes—after a considerable civil war among and within its affiliates.

The battle of the amendments continues, and when harsher codes are called for at some campuses, you can expect the Fourteenth Amendment—which was not intended to censor *speech*—will rise again.

A precedent has been set at, of all places, colleges and universities, that the principle of free speech is merely situational. As college administrators change, so will the extent of free speech on campus. And invariably, permissible speech will become more and more narrowly defined. Once speech can be limited in such subjective ways, more and more expression will be included in what is forbidden.

Freedom of Thought

One of the exceedingly few college presidents who speaks out on the consequences of the anti-free-speech movement is Yale University's Benno Schmidt:

> Freedom of thought must be Yale's central commitment. It is not easy to embrace. It is, indeed, the effort of a lifetime. . . . Much expression that is free may deserve our contempt. We may well be moved to exercise our own freedom to counter it or to ignore it. But universities cannot censor or suppress speech, no matter how obnoxious in content, without violating their justification for existence. . . .

> On some other campuses in this country, values of civility and community have been offered by some as paramount values of the university, even to the extent of superseding freedom of expression.

> Such a view is wrong in principle and, if extended, is disastrous to freedom of thought. . . . The chilling effects on speech of the vagueness and open-ended nature of many universities' prohibitions . . . are compounded by the fact that these codes are typically enforced by faculty and students who commonly assert that vague notions of community are more important to the academy than freedom of thought and expression. . . .

> This is a flabby and uncertain time for freedom in the United States.

On the Public Broadcasting System in June 1991, I was part of a Fred Friendly panel at Stanford University in a debate on speech codes versus free-

85

dom of expression. The three black panelists strongly supported the codes. So did the one Asian-American on the panel. But then so did Stanford law professor Thomas Grey, who wrote the Stanford code, and Stanford president Donald Kennedy, who first opposed and then embraced the code. We have a new ecumenicism of those who would control speech for the greater good. It is hardly a new idea, but the mix of advocates is rather new.

But there are other voices. In the national board debate at the ACLU on college speech codes, the first speaker—and I think she had a lot to do with making the final vote against codes unanimous—was Gwen Thomas.

A black community college administrator from Colorado, she is a fiercely persistent exposer of racial discrimination.

She started by saying, "I have always felt as a minority person that we have to protect the rights of all because if we infringe on the rights of any persons, we'll be next.

"As for providing a nonintimidating educational environment, our young people have to learn to grow up on college campuses. We have to teach them how to deal with adversarial situations. They have to learn how to survive offensive speech they find wounding and hurtful." Gwen Thomas is an educator—an endangered species in higher education.

Free Speech Is Necessary on College Campuses

by Barbara Dority

About the author: *Barbara Dority is president of the Humanists of Washington, executive director of the Washington Coalition Against Censorship, and co-chair of the Northwest Feminist Anti-Censorship Taskforce.*

The dogma of PCism advocates the suppression of anything that might give offense "on the grounds of gender, sexual orientation, race, ethnicity, religion, creed, national origin, ancestry, age, or handicap." Offense is determined by the affronted person; truth is no defense. The aim is to protect minorities and women and enforce awareness of their dignity and worth. This can include enforced separatism—but only when blacks, gays, or women choose it.

Imposing "Tolerance"

When the form of language takes precedence over its meaning, rationalists must take heed. Notwithstanding that the *intent* of PC speech is usually humane and progressive, civil libertarians are justifiably concerned when universities (of all places) become enforcers of imposed "tolerance" through speech-restrictive codes. What are we teaching students about the guarantee of equal protection under the law? Federal courts and the Supreme Court have consistently held that restrictive speech codes are unconstitutional.

Certainly no one would argue that racist, sexist, ageist, and homophobic beliefs do not persist in this country. But the way to ensure that their toxic influence will multiply is to sweep them into a dark corner and pretend they don't exist.

There is no question that certain non European and feminist views have been squeezed out of university studies for too long. But now proponents have gone to the other extreme, censoring ideas they dislike just as their own ideas were censored in the past. Surely women and minorities should have learned that suppression is an admission of weakness and fear—a diversion from dealing with the real social issues at the root of intolerance.

"The PC Speech Police" by Barbara Dority first appeared in the March/April 1992 issue of *The Humanist* and is reprinted with permission.

The climate created by PC promoters has led to an appalling level of academic self-censorship. For instance, many professors are taping their lectures in case they have a future need to defend themselves from charges of sexism, racism, homophobia, and so on. Professors, most notably at Princeton University and Carleton College, have dropped some courses entirely under pressure from PC forces. Even Nadine Strossen, new president of the American Civil Liberties Union and a professor at New York University Law School, has resorted to allowing students to make their "non-PC" feelings and questions known through anonymous notes which she reads and addresses in class—a culture of forbidden questions.

> *"Civil libertarians are justifiably concerned when universities . . . become enforcers of imposed 'tolerance' through speech-restrictive codes."*

The Carnegie Foundation for the Advancement of Teaching, in its report *Campus Life: In Search of Community*, states that "restrictive codes, for practical as well as legal reasons, do not provide a satisfactory response to offensive language. They may be expedient, even grounded in conviction, but the university cannot submit the cherished ideals of freedom and equality to the legal system and expect them to be returned intact."

Benno Schmidt, president of Yale University, makes the same point. "Universities cannot censor or suppress speech," he says, "no matter how obnoxious in content, without violating their justification for existence. It is to elevate fear over the capacity for a liberated and humane mind and will loose an utterly open-ended engine of censorship." In other words, universities, above all, must not permit "sensitivity" to stifle the free discourse they are supposed to represent and encourage. The PC mindset is too rigid and reactionary for careful thought or objective analysis.

A 1990 study by the American Council on Education and the National Association of Student Personnel Administrators found that 60 percent of the colleges and universities they surveyed already had written policies on bigotry and verbal intimidation, including such schools as the University of Pennsylvania, the University of California, Columbia, Tufts, Emory, and Stanford. Another 11 percent reported that such policies were being formulated.

The University of Connecticut's policy bans "inappropriately directed laughter" and "conspicuous exclusion of students from conversations." The University of Wisconsin has become a model of PC decorum since the Wisconsin state legislature stiffened the student conduct code to ban by state law "discriminatory comments, name calling, racial slurs, or 'jokes.'"

Examples of the Problem

Numerous documented examples of the enforcement of such policies include an incident in which a University of Michigan student asserted in class that he felt homosexuality was treatable through therapy. The administration has charged him with violating the university's speech code and is seeking his expulsion. This student is black. So is another Michigan student who was punished under the same rules for using the term *white trash* in class.

In March 1991, the social science department at Santa Monica College censured economics professor Eugene Buchholz for arguing that ethnic- and gender-based studies "sidetrack students who could otherwise gain useful disciplines or skills."

At the University of Washington in early 1990, a student was removed from a course with a nonpassing grade and threatened with expulsion because he questioned an assertion by a women's studies professor that lesbians make the best mothers.

Nina Wu, a sophomore at the University of Connecticut, was brought up on charges of violating the student-behavior code, which prohibits "posting or advertising publicly offensive, indecent, or abusive matter concerning persons. . . ." She allegedly put a poster on her dorm room door listing "people who should be shot on sight"—among them "preppies, bimboes, men without chest hair, and homos." Wu was ordered to move off campus and forbidden to set foot in any university dormitory or cafeteria. Under pressure from a federal lawsuit, the university administration allowed her to move back onto campus.

> *"The climate created by PC promoters has led to an appalling level of academic self-censorship."*

Certainly drunks shouting racial epithets in dormitory halls should be disciplined for disturbing the peace, and people who spray-paint public or private property should be disciplined for vandalism regardless of the message. But when a Brown University student was expelled after a wee-hours drunken tirade, it was because he was found guilty not only of public inebriation and disruption but of violating the university's speech code prohibiting "racial, homophobic, and anti Semitic slurs." (These slurs were not accompanied by verbal or physical threats.)

"Gross Insensitivity"?

Linda Chavez, a Hispanic Reagan administration official, was asked to speak at the University of Colorado. Upon learning that she opposed affirmative action and thought Hispanics should learn English as soon as possible, PC students protested and the university president, apologizing for his "gross insensitivity," withdrew his invitation to Chavez.

Students have been suspended not only for using "epithets" toward blacks, gays, and other minorities in the classroom but also in dormitories, at sporting events, and off-campus entirely.

Jean Bethke Elshtain, a political-science professor at Vanderbilt, says, "It's reached the point that, if you make any judgment or assessment as to the quality of a work, somehow you aren't being an 'intellectual egalitarian.'" At a recent conference, she referred to Czeslaw Milosz's *The Captive Mind* as a "classic," to which another female professor exclaimed in dismay that the word classic made her "feel oppressed."

> ***"If one wishes to preserve one's own freedom, one must be equally prepared to defend the freedom of those who express views one abhors."***

Some who should know better trivialize the problem, rationalizing that incidents have been few and far between and that the accused do have legal recourse. After all, they say, violators aren't shot or sent to the gulag. Amazing. Are these to be the new standards by which we measure the seriousness of First Amendment violations?

It has even been stated that Jewish organizations are "placating" a bigot like [former Ku Klux Klan leader] David Duke when they uncategorically defend his right to speak. It is suggested that they believe that, by doing this, they'll "be spared."

Spared what? The suspension of their own free speech rights? Jewish organizations defend the rights of people like Duke because they understand the First Amendment. They understand that, if one wishes to preserve one's own freedom, one must be equally prepared to defend the freedom of those who express views one abhors. They know that no one was ever won over to a more inclusive view of life via bullying and coercion, and that suppression merely allows insupportable views to become stronger. In short, they know the difference between genuine social change and enforced verbal purification.

First Amendment Protection

In its publication *Bigotry on Campus: A Planned Response*, the American Jewish Committee states:

> Universities work best when students and faculty are free to say whatever they think. Whereas students should be aware that their words can hurt others, they should not be forced to weigh their thoughts against administration-imposed limits of political correctness. Higher education is at its best when the clash between ideas is heated, not chilled. . . . No lawyer can draft language precise enough to punish the person who says "nigger" only when he or she really means it. . . . Punishing a student for using bigoted words or printing bigoted articles drapes the bigot, instead of the university, in the First Amendment. Thus, the bigot becomes the victim, even the martyr. . . .

What do the courts say? The Supreme Court ruled in *Near* v. *Minnesota* that racist speech is protected by the First Amendment. In 1991, a federal court judge in Wisconsin ruled that a University of Wisconsin rule forbidding racist and sexist speech violated the First Amendment. The university's Board of Regents adopted the rule in 1989 after a series of incidents described as racist, including a fraternity's "Fiji Island" party which included some caricatures of blacks. The university has appealed.

Black students should remember that Malcolm X was censored on campuses 25 years ago. What is to save outspoken black rappers from the same fate today? How much better to expose hateful and bigoted ideas to the light of reason!

The underlying issues are much more complicated, and educational institutions are reluctant to tackle them. Some suggestions have been proposed: offering courses on racism; upgrading and expanding black studies; addressing the issues in orientation sessions; welcoming speakers and artists of every sort to contribute their perspective; and broadening the undergraduate curriculum so that no graduating student has failed to be exposed to other cultures and histories.

Truth cannot be determined by government fiat or popular opinion. It is particularly noxious to define truth according to those who are in political power at the moment. Bring on the neo-Nazis, the skinheads, the misogynists, the racists, the hateful, and the angry and let them speak. As always, the answer to a bad idea is a good idea; the answer to the "problem" of free speech is *more* speech.

Ray Bradbury, in a 1979 afterword to *Fahrenheit 451*, wrote:

> I have always maintained that there is more than one way to burn a book—and the world is full of people running about with lit matches. Every minority . . . feels it has the will, the right, and the duty to douse the kerosene and light the fuse. Fahrenheit 451 describes how books were burned first by minorities, each ripping a page or a paragraph from this book, then that, until the day when the books were empty and the minds shut and the libraries closed forever.

Exaggeration? Alarmism? Not to those who understand the First Amendment.

Speech Codes Should Not Be Permitted on Campuses

by Jennifer Kelley

About the author: *When she wrote the following article, Jennifer Kelley was a junior majoring in English and philosophy at Columbia University. She was on the staff of the Freedom Forum Media Studies Center at Columbia.*

Over the last few years, the issue of restricting offensive speech has mushroomed into a ferocious and long-winded debate that has taken on a variety of forms and names—from "political correctness" to "fighting words" to "hate speech." On one side of the debate are those who favor limited or extensive restrictions on speech; on the other, those who believe the First Amendment guaranteeing the right to freedom of expression should be protected without qualification.

Issues of biased expression and speech restrictions on college and university campuses have been at the forefront of this debate. Although there is a growing reluctance to prolong what many view as a superficial and stalemated discussion of bias at the university, I would argue that the issue of free speech must continue to receive attention in the campus setting. The issue provides the opportunity to examine the appropriateness and effectiveness of efforts to curb intolerance and hatred through speech codes. With racism, sexism, sexual harassment, and homophobia on the rise on American college campuses, the academic community must continue to seek effective means of dealing with these and other forms of prejudice.

The Principles Behind the Codes

It is important to note that bias-related incidents on campuses have *increased* since the implementation of speech and civility codes, raising questions about the effectiveness of such codes. Universities, therefore, need to focus not on the wording of speech codes, the kinds of speech and conduct they target, or their enforcement, but rather on the validity of the principles behind the codes. This

Jennifer Kelley, "Free Speech/Hate Speech: A Student's View," *Peace & Democracy News*, Winter 1992/1993. Reprinted by permission of the publisher.

basic investigation of the philosophical justification for speech and civility codes is too often forgotten in the frantic effort to revise and perfect the wording of campus speech codes.

The fact of the matter is that controlling speech does not work; nor will it ever be an effective weapon against hatred and prejudice. It is ridiculous to suggest that anti-Semitism and homophobia, for instance, are simply forms of speech. Yet that is the implicit mentality behind policies that seek to eradicate prejudice by targeting individual acts of expression. Hatred is not simply a matter of semantics. It is a matter of ignorance and of violent, intolerant attitudes and practices.

> *"The fact of the matter is that controlling speech does not work."*

We are facing a pivotal moment in the debate over free speech on campus. On June 22, 1991, the Supreme Court held a St. Paul, Minnesota, ordinance used to prosecute a teenager for burning a cross on the lawn of a black family to be an unconstitutional restriction of the right to free expression. At the same time, the Court's ruling left open the possibility that some restrictions on expression are valid. On campuses, the ruling has already inspired renewed efforts to re-word campus speech codes to make them less vulnerable to constitutional challenges.

Speech Codes Undermine Progress Toward Tolerance

It is my belief that, rather than leading us to revive old strategies, the St. Paul decision should push us in a different direction—toward the far more difficult task of understanding the origins of hate and prejudice, and exploring more effective alternatives to speech and conduct restrictions. From my involvement with issues of free speech on campus, I have come to realize that speech codes are not only ineffective, but that they actually undermine progress toward greater tolerance. I have seen nothing as effective in the fight against hatred on campus as free, open, unrestricted expression and discussion of the issues—the kind of discussion speech codes seek to suppress. In the attempt to overcome narrow and hateful attitudes, and to develop tolerance for diversity, it is essential that differences among people are openly discussed and understood. Because ignorance helps to feed intolerance, protecting ignorance through censorship serves only to feed intolerance. Speech codes tend to create an atmosphere in which many issues are considered taboo and off-limits because of the sensitivity that surrounds them.

The most productive and worthwhile (if sometimes tense) discussions I have observed in the classroom have been those in which sensitive issues relating to social attitudes were directly confronted. Through these discussions, students revealed and challenged each others' assumptions. Many of my classmates and I left these conversations with a greater appreciation and acceptance of fellow-students' differences in race, religion, gender, or sexual orientation. Considering the value of the experiences, it would be unthinkable to consider restricting this free interchange of feelings and ideas.

While free expression is not a panacea that will eradicate prejudice and hatred, it can help to dispel ignorance. In addition to inculcating a tolerance of diversity, free expression tends to encourage personal empowerment, another important weapon in the fight against bias. Unfortunately, one cannot always count on being able to convince others that their intolerance is misguided. Those who are sometimes the objects of prejudice, however, become better equipped by open debate to combat the feelings of intimidation, oppression, and victimization that hateful words and acts engender. "Protecting" people from intolerant views through speech restrictions can do them a disservice by preventing them from confronting these views.

Free Expression Offers Hope

I have seen people strengthened by the experience of unrestricted expression at events like the annual "Take Back the Night" march for rape victims sponsored by students at Barnard College and Columbia University, and the huge yearly Gay Pride March on Fifth Avenue in New York City. At the "Take Back the Night" event, women as well as men are able to find an alternative to fear, oppression, and hate through the sharing of experiences and feelings of solidarity and support. At this year's Gay Pride march, there were a number of protesters holding signs with messages objecting to homosexual lifestyles. The marchers did not call for restricting the expression of these biased views. Instead, as they passed the protesters, they confidently chanted "Shame, shame, shame." Witnessing and participating in such events make one highly conscious of the empowering nature of expression.

Free expression on campus (and in the rest of society) offers hope for changing intolerant attitudes, and provides an important means for overcoming the paralyzing sense of victimization these attitudes can create. Institutions of higher learning are theoretically supposed to provide an open and unrestricted marketplace of ideas. What is the purpose, then, of spending endless hours reading and discussing the forms in Plato's *Republic*, but ignoring his conception of the innate, caste-like differences between people, or understanding Augustine's faith, but denying his references to homosexuality and his view of women, or contemplating Wagner's influence on twentieth-century music, but not his anti-

> *"While free expression is not a panacea that will eradicate prejudice and hatred, it can help to dispel ignorance."*

Semitism and his influence on the National Socialist movement in Germany, and so on, just because these topics are deemed by some to be too touchy, too sensitive, too potentially offensive? What is to be gained from completely sterile studies that avoid controversy at all costs? The answer is nothing; furthermore, there is a lot to be lost. We must not sacrifice the integrity and value of institutions of higher education to hasty and ineffective efforts to discourage prejudice. It is therefore crucial that we stop the dangerous and counterproductive attacks on free speech, and re-focus our efforts on developing real solutions to the problems of hatred and intolerance.

College Speech Codes Endanger Freedom of Speech

by Thomas L. Jipping

About the author: *Thomas L. Jipping is director of the Free Congress Founda-tion Center for Law and Democracy.*

Freedom of speech is under attack in America. This has nothing to do with ei-ther 2 Live Crew or the National Endowment for the Arts. No, there is a gen-uine and overt attack on intellectual freedom and tolerance that threatens to subvert the Bill of Rights. . . .

The First Amendment to the U.S. Constitution states that "Congress shall make no law . . . abridging the freedom of speech." This concept has certainly been expanded since those words were penned. "Speech" has become "expres-sion." The Supreme Court [in 1990] decided whether the First Amendment pro-tects flag burning (it said yes) and begging (it said no). On January 8, 1991, the Court considered whether that lofty provision protects "nude dancing" by women selling drinks in bars.

One Fundamental Principle

Despite debate at the margins, however, this clause stands for at least one fun-damental principle. Supreme Court Justice William Brennan put it this way: "If there is a bedrock principle underlying the First Amendment, it is that the Gov-ernment may not prohibit the expression of an idea simply because society finds the idea itself offensive or disagreeable" (*Texas v. Johnson*, 1989). Chief Justice William Rehnquist quoted a 1978 Supreme Court decision holding that "the fact that society may find speech offensive is not a sufficient reason for suppressing it" (*Hustler Magazine v. Falwell*, 1988).

Justice Sandra Day O'Connor wrote for the Court that giving this First Amendment freedom sufficient "breathing space" requires that "our citizens

Thomas L. Jipping, "Shedding Rights on the American Campus." This article appeared in the March 1991 issue of, and is reprinted with permission from, *The World & I*, a publication of the Washington Times Corporation, copyright 1991.

must tolerate insulting, and even outrageous, speech" (*Boos v. Barry*, 1988). In one of the most oft-quoted expressions of this principle, Justice Oliver Wendell Holmes wrote more than 70 years ago that "the ultimate good desired is better reached by free trade in ideas. . . . The best test of truth is the power of the thought to get itself accepted in the competition of the market" (dissenting in *Abrams v. United States*, 1919).

> *"Free trade in ideas is central to the mission of higher education in America."*

Free trade in ideas is central to the mission of higher education in America, particularly in the public school arena. Not long ago no one questioned that intellectual freedom and tolerance of alternative views and opinions must be especially protected in that context. The Supreme Court stated the obvious more than 30 years ago, that "the essentiality of freedom in the community of American universities is almost self-evident" (*Sweezy v. New Hampshire*, 1957). The Court soon after repeated this principle: "The vigilant protection of constitutional freedoms is nowhere more vital than in the community of American schools" (*Shelton v. Tucker*, 1960).

Nearly a decade later, Justice Brennan wrote for the Court that "the classroom is particularly the 'marketplace of ideas.' The Nation's future depends upon leaders trained through wide exposure to that robust exchange of ideas which discovers truth 'out of a multitude of tongues [rather] than through any kind of authoritative selection'" (*Keyishian v. Board of Regents*, 1967).

The Supreme Court has even applied this principle at the junior and senior high school level, stating clearly that students do not "shed their constitutional rights to freedom of speech or expression at the schoolhouse gate" (*Tinker v. Des Moines Ind. Comm. School Dist.*, 1969). School officials may, of course, prevent conduct that interferes with school discipline—a concern present in the elementary and secondary school environment that disappears at higher levels. The bottom line is that "First Amendment rights, applied in light of the special characteristics of the school environment, are available to . . . students" (*Board of Education v. Pico*, 1982).

Prohibited Speech

Despite all this, colleges and universities across America are adopting and enforcing codes prohibiting undesirable or politically incorrect speech, aggressively imposing the very kind of "authoritative selection" that the Supreme Court once considered the antithesis of the marketplace of ideas. Typically, these speech codes are classified as "antiharassment" policies designed to shield selected groups from hearing insensitive or unwelcome words.

The list of prohibited speech categories in each of these codes varies in length (State University of New York (SUNY)-Buffalo has 5 plus a catchall, Stanford has 7, Michigan has 11), depending on which groups have used their freedom of speech to complain the loudest that the same freedom exercised by others should be curtailed. A few examples:

• The law school faculty at SUNY-Buffalo unanimously adopted a policy in 1987 warning that "racist, sexist, homophobic and anti-lesbian, ageist and ethnically derogatory statements, as well as other remarks based on prejudice and group stereotype, will generate . . . swift, open condemnation by the faculty, wherever and however they occur."

• Stanford University forbids speech intended to "stigmatize an individual or a small number of individuals on the basis of their sex, race, color, handicap, religion, sexual orientation or national and ethnic origin."

• An early version of the University of Connecticut's speech code, changed following a lawsuit, banned "inappropriately directed laughter, inconsiderate jokes, anonymous notes or phone calls and the conspicuous exclusion of another student from conversation."

• Before a federal court found it unconstitutional, the University of Michigan's "Policy on Discrimination and Discriminatory Harassment" prohibited speech that stigmatizes individuals "on the basis of race, ethnicity, sex, sexual orientation, creed, national origin, ancestry, age, marital status, handicap or Vietnam-era veteran status."

> *"Seventy percent of the nation's colleges and universities have adopted some form of censorship."*

• The California affiliate of the American Civil Liberties Union has drafted a model speech code. It would punish a student whose speech "creates a hostile and intimidating environment which the speaker knows or reasonably should know will seriously and directly impede the educational opportunities of the individual or individuals to whom it is addressed."

• At Smith College, the Office of Student Affairs warns students against 10 kinds of oppression. "Heterosexism," defined as "oppression of those of sexual orientations other than heterosexual," can even occur "by not acknowledging their existence." The form or manner of this apparent mandatory affirmation is unclear.

Seventy percent of the nation's colleges and universities have adopted some form of censorship. In addition to the examples above, these include Wisconsin, Brown, Emory, Tufts, Penn State, Smith, and Berkeley.

No Need to Explain?

Why do these speech codes exist? The Buffalo policy—ironically titled the "Faculty Statement Regarding Intellectual Freedom, Tolerance, and Prohibited Harassment"—stated that "by entering law school . . . each student's absolute right to liberty of speech must also become tempered . . . by the responsibility to promote equality and justice. Therefore, it should be understood that" the faculty would search out and destroy the listed categories of "badspeak."

There apparently exists no need to explain the source for this supposed responsibility, whose version of equality and justice is to be promoted by it, or how students will know what constitutes the particular remarks this responsibility demands they suppress. Author Charles Sykes quotes sociology professor Paul Hollander as saying of the Buffalo policy: "It would be interesting to know who will be authorized to define what constitutes equality and justice and just how they are to be promoted. In any event, no totalitarian could have put it better."

Free inquiry and the exchange of ideas were once the essence of higher education. Whether or not the First Amendment formally applies, its spirit of respect and tolerance should prevail at every educational institution. Voltaire once said, "I disapprove of what you say, but I will defend to the death your right to say it." No more. Today, if what you say does not promote "equality and justice," you simply may not say it.

A Sample of Results

These policies do, indeed, have concrete results. A few examples follow:

• At the University of Michigan, a graduate student in the School of Social Work expressed his opinion that homosexuality was a disease and his intention to develop a counseling plan based on that perspective. He was unanimously found guilty of sexual harassment by a panel of university administrators.

• Also at Michigan, a graduate student in the School of Business Administration read an allegedly homophobic limerick during a public speaking exercise. He was required to apologize to his class, apologize to the university community through the student newspaper, and attend a "gay rap session."

• Sykes reports that when a Yale student posted a notice of a debate about whether the CIA's policy of discriminating against homosexuals was legitimate, he was kicked off campus and barred from graduation ceremonies.

• At Buffalo, administrators attempted to invoke their speech policy against a student who had uttered a racial remark following a bad call during an intramural basketball game and against a student who made an insensitive remark to a cashier at a university cafeteria.

• Brown University banned ethnic theme parties because a fraternity's "South of the Border" party was considered insensitive to Mexicans.

An interpretive guide issued to explain Michigan's speech codes offered examples of sanctionable conduct, including: "A male student makes remarks in class like 'Women just aren't as good in this field as men,' thus creating a hostile learning atmosphere for female classmates."

> *"In addition to being unconstitutional, these speech codes are simply bad educational policy."*

Opposition to this censorship movement comes from across the political spectrum. At Buffalo, conservative students have been joined in condemning the policy by an attorney affiliated with the New York Civil Liberties Union and by liberal columnist Nat Hentoff. Hentoff blasted the policy as "a revision of the First Amendment," stating that "the First Amendment has been suspended by the law school faculty of a public university."

Stanford law professor Gerald Gunther, one of the nation's leading constitutional scholars, stated that his university "will be on record as adopting an anti-speech regulation—a hideous precedent for a university that boasts of the winds of freedom and claims to be bound [though a private institution] by the principles of the First Amendment."

> *"Freedom of speech is clearly under attack on America's college and university campuses."*

Columnist Suzanne Fields exposes the "Super Sensitive Speech Patrol" this way: "In the 1960s, campus rebels rallied against the paternalism of the university. The New Puritans encourage paternalism, to 'save' students from themselves." Another columnist, John Leo, denounced "the academy's new ayatollahs," who seek only to enforce politically correct (P.C.) speech: "P.C.-ers favor the Orwellian language of freedom, tolerance and diversity. But the reality is a good deal different."

Are Speech Codes Constitutional?

The 82-member national board of the ACLU voted unanimously to "oppose all campus regulations which interfere with the freedom of professors, students and administrators to teach, learn, discuss and debate or to express ideas, opinions or feelings in classroom, public or private discourse . . . that others may find repugnant, offensive or emotionally distressing." People for the American Way opposes them also. Its report on campus intolerance concludes that "schools looking for a shortcut through the First Amendment toward the difficult goal of fighting intolerance forget the obligation to foster a climate of acceptance and open debate. In fact, such a shortcut is an abdication of this responsibility."

In public university settings, these speech codes are unconstitutional. The Supreme Court has consistently held that content-based restrictions on pure speech must receive the highest scrutiny. Justice Brennan, who is said to believe these speech codes should be abolished, wrote for the Court that "because First Amendment freedoms need breathing space to survive, government may regulate in the area only with narrow specificity" (*NAACP v. Button*, 1963).

A federal judge found that the University of Michigan policy violated the First Amendment. In doing so, Judge Avern Cohn wrote that the school could not

> establish an anti-discrimination policy which had the effect of prohibiting certain speech because it disagreed with ideas or messages sought to be conveyed. . . . Nor could the University proscribe speech simply because it was found to be offensive, even grossly so, by large numbers of people. . . . These principles acquire a special significance in the university setting, where the free and unfettered interplay of competing ideas is essential to the institution's educational mission. (*Doe v. University of Michigan*, 1989)

In addition to being unconstitutional, these speech codes are simply bad educational policy. They restrict, rather than expand, the educational environment. Give-and-take, exposure to new ideas, and an incentive to think through and evaluate one's cherished views all suffer in an atmosphere of "authoritative selection." Even if a particular university's speech code does not threaten formal discipline, how can anyone doubt that the message will be no less loud and clear: Watch what you say, certain views are not welcome in this school!

It is certainly a radically new approach to education in America when those in power begin picking and choosing which speech, views, and opinions are acceptable and which amount to nothing but "harassment."

Another objection to speech codes is their inherent elitist paternalism. No longer is "the best test of truth . . . the power of the thought to get itself accepted in the competition of the market." No longer do people need to compete in that market. Rather, the liberal elite looks out for its constituencies and authoritatively selects appropriate or acceptable categories of speech. As if this were not bad enough, it does so by speech codes that assume that women, minorities, or members of other "protected" groups can do nothing but sit idly by in oppressed silence and need the strong arm of Big Brother to protect them from insensitivity.

> *"The catch-22 is that the very freedom necessary to [debate this issue] is under attack."*

Apparently, some special interest groups now have a "right" to an educational environment free from words they do not want to hear, and this right is sufficient to overcome the Constitution itself. Yale University president Benno Schmidt, himself a First Amendment expert, said in his 1986 inaugural address that "there is no speech so horrendous in content that it does not in principle serve our purposes."

What Can Be Done?

Freedom of speech is clearly under attack on America's college and university campuses. What can concerned citizens do? One approach is to debate this issue openly and vigorously, engaging students, faculty, administrators, and trustees. The catch-22 is that the very freedom necessary to do this is under attack.

A second approach is litigation. Students whose speech is suppressed or chilled must go to court to vindicate their rights. The policies at Buffalo and the University of Wisconsin [have been] challenged in federal court. In addition to the U.S. Constitution, state constitutions specifically protect freedom of speech and can be used to invalidate speech codes.

A third approach is for Congress or state legislatures to use the carrot/stick of public funds and withhold education dollars from schools that suppress speech on campus. No school pursuing this brave new path of "authoritative selection" deserves tax money to do it. A draft proposal titled the Freedom of Speech on Campus Act is being discussed among members of Congress and representatives of interest groups.

This discussion comes on the heels of the debate over funding for the National Endowment for the Arts. Most members of Congress voted against any restrictions on that funding, arguing that artists have the right not only to produce what they want but to receive a government subsidy to produce it, no matter who may be offended in the process. It remains to be seen whether they feel the same way about college students. Some highlights of the legislation follow:

• It states that "no student attending any institution of higher education shall, on the basis of protected speech, be excluded from participation in, be denied the benefits of, or be subjected to discrimination or official sanction under any higher education program or activity receiving Federal financial assistance."

• It contains appropriate exceptions for institutions training individuals for military service and for private institutions controlled by or affiliated with religious organizations when application of the statute would violate those organizations' religious tenets.

• It would still allow educational institutions to prevent disruption of classes, speeches, performances, or other activities conducted under official auspices.

• It would not prevent reasonable institutional actions to ensure safety of individuals or property, or the continuation of the academic and administrative process.

• It defines "protected speech" as speech protected under the First and Fourteenth amendments to the U.S. Constitution or speech that would be protected if the institution were subject to those amendments, thereby including private schools receiving federal funds.

Change Standards for Accreditation

Finally, accreditation of educational institutions can be made contingent upon assurance that students will not be subjected to official sanction because of the content of protected speech. Accrediting agencies such as the Middle States Association of Colleges and Schools hinge accreditation on questionable factors such as the racial or gender composition of student bodies or faculties. Accreditation can more properly hinge on a climate of intellectual freedom, something relating directly to the educational process.

Free speech is under attack in America. The kind of individual liberty introduced by the experiment called the United States of America is unmatched by anything in world history. The antispeech movement in American higher education threatens this foundation of liberty. We will all suffer if our future citizens and leaders are educated in an environment of authoritative selection rather than in a marketplace of ideas.

Racist Speech Should Be Restricted on College Campuses

by Charles Lawrence

About the author: *Charles Lawrence is professor of law at Stanford University in Palo Alto, California.*

I have spent the better part of my life as a dissenter. As a high school student, I was threatened with suspension for refusing to participate in a civil defense drill, and I have been a conspicuous consumer of my First Amendment liberties ever since. There are very strong reasons for protecting even speech that is racist. Perhaps the most important is that such protection reinforces our society's commitment to tolerance as a value. By protecting bad speech from government regulation, we are forced to combat it as a community.

The Resurgence of Racial Violence

I am, however, deeply apprehensive about the resurgence of racial violence and the corresponding increase in the incidence of verbal and symbolic assault and harassment to which blacks and other traditionally excluded groups are subjected. I am troubled by the way the debate has been framed in response to the recent surge of racist incidents on college and university campuses and in response to some universities' attempts to regulate harassing speech. The problem has been framed as one in which the liberty of free speech is in conflict with the elimination of racism. I believe this has placed the bigot on the moral high ground and fanned the rising flames of racism.

Above all, I am troubled that we have not listened to the real victims—that we have shown so little understanding of their injury, and that we have abandoned those whose race, gender or sexual orientation continues to make them second-class citizens. It seems to me a very sad irony that the first instinct of civil libertarians has been to challenge even the smallest, most narrowly framed

103

efforts by universities to provide minority students with the protection that the Constitution, in my opinion, guarantees them.

The landmark 1954 case of *Brown vs. Board of Education* is not about speech. But *Brown* can be broadly read as articulating the principle of equal citizenship. *Brown* held that segregated schools were inherently unequal because of the message that segregation conveyed: that black children were an untouchable caste, unfit to go to school with white children. If we understand the necessity of eliminating the system of signs and symbols that signal the inferiority of blacks, then we should hesitate before proclaiming that all racist speech that stops short of physical violence must be defended.

University officials who have formulated policies to respond to incidents of racial harassment have been characterized in the press as "thought police," even though such policies generally do nothing more than impose sanctions against intentional face-to-face insults. Racist speech that takes the form of such insults, catcalls or other assaultive speech aimed at an individual or small group of persons falls directly within the "fighting words" exception to First Amendment protection. The Supreme Court has held in *Chaplinsky vs. New Hampshire* that words which "by their very utterance inflict injury or tend to incite an immediate breach of the peace" are not protected by the First Amendment.

A Pre-Emptive Strike

If the purpose of the First Amendment is to foster the greatest amount of speech, racial insults disserve that purpose. Assaultive racist speech functions as a pre-emptive strike. The invective is experienced as a blow, not as a proffered idea. And once the blow is struck, a dialogue is unlikely to follow. Racial insults are particularly undeserving of First Amendment protection, because the perpetrator's intention is not to discover truth or initiate dialogue but to injure the victim. In most situations, members of minority groups realize that they are likely to lose if they fight back, and are forced to remain silent and submissive.

Courts have held that offensive speech may not be regulated in public forums (such as streets, where the listener may avoid the speech by moving on). But the regulation of otherwise protected speech has been permitted when the speech invades the privacy of the unwilling listener's home, or when the unwilling listener cannot avoid the speech. Racist posters, flyers and graffiti in dormitories, bathrooms and other common living spaces would seem to fall within the reasoning of these cases. Minority students should not be required to remain in their rooms in order to avoid racial insult. Minimally, they should find a safe haven in their dorms and in all other common rooms that are a part of their daily routine.

> *"Racial insults are particularly undeserving of First Amendment protection."*

I would also argue that the university's responsibility to give these students an equal educational opportunity provides a compelling justification for regulations that ensure them safe passage in all common areas. A minority student should not have to risk becoming the target of racially assaulting speech every time he or she chooses to walk across campus. Regulating vilifying speech that cannot be anticipated or avoided need not preclude announced speeches and rallies—situations that would give minority group members and their allies the opportunity to organize counterdemonstrations or avoid the speech altogether.

Racist Speech Inflicts Harm

The most commonly advanced argument against the regulation of racist speech proceeds something like this: We recognize that minority groups suffer pain and injury as the result of racist speech, but we must allow this hatemongering for the benefit of society as a whole. Freedom of speech is the life blood of our democratic system. It is especially important for minorities, because often it is their only vehicle for rallying support for the redress of their grievances. It will be impossible to formulate a prohibition so precise that it will prevent the racist speech you want to suppress, without catching in the same net all kinds of speech that it would be unconscionable for a democratic society to suppress.

Such arguments seek to strike a balance between our concern, on the one hand, for the continued free flow of ideas and the democratic process dependent on that flow, and, on the

> *"Racist speech inflicts real harm, and . . . this harm is far from trivial."*

other, our desire to further the cause of equality. There can, however, be no meaningful discussion of reconciling these two values until it is acknowledged that racist speech inflicts real harm, and that this harm is far from trivial.

To engage in a debate about the First Amendment and racist speech without a full understanding of the nature and extent of that harm is to risk making the First Amendment an instrument of domination rather than a vehicle of liberation. We have not all known the experience of victimization by racist, misogynist and homophobic speech, nor do we equally share the burden of the harm it inflicts. We are often quick to say that we have heard the cry of the victims when we have not.

The *Brown* case is again instructive, because it speaks directly to the psychic injury inflicted by racist speech by noting that the symbolic message of segregation affected "the hearts and minds" of Negro children "in a way unlikely ever to be undone." Racial epithets and harassment often cause deep emotional scarring and feelings of anxiety and fear that pervade every aspect of a victim's life.

Brown also recognized that black children did not have an equal opportunity to learn and participate in the school community when they were subjected to the humiliation and psychic assault contained in the message of segregation. University students bear an analogous burden when they are forced to live and work in an environment where at any moment they may be subjected to denigrating verbal harassment and assault. The same injury was addressed by the Supreme Court when it held that, under Title VII of the Civil Rights Act of 1964, sexual harassment that creates a hostile or abusive work environment violates the ban on sex discrimination in employment.

> *"We must think hard about how best to launch legal attacks against the most indefensible forms of hate speech."*

Carefully drafted university regulations could bar the use of words as assault weapons while leaving unregulated even the most heinous of ideas, provided those ideas are presented at times and places and in manners that leave an opportunity for reasoned rebuttal or escape from immediate insult. The history of the development of the right to free speech has been one of carefully evaluating the importance of free expression and its effects on other important societal interests. We have drawn the line between protected and unprotected speech before without dire results. (Courts have, for example, exempted from the protection of the First Amendment obscene speech and speech that disseminates official secrets, defames or libels another person, or is used to form a conspiracy or monopoly.)

Too Many Demagogues

Blacks and other people of color are skeptical about the argument that even the most injurious speech must remain unregulated because, in an unregulated marketplace of ideas, the best ideas will rise to the top and gain acceptance. Experience tells quite the opposite. People of color have seen too many demagogues elected by appealing to America's racism, and too many sympathetic politicians shy away from issues that might brand them as too closely allied with disparaged groups.

Whenever we decide that the racist speech must be tolerated because of the importance of maintaining societal tolerance for all unpopular speech, we are asking blacks and other subordinated groups to bear the burden for the good of all. We must be careful that the ease with which we strike the balance against the regulation of racist speech is in no way influenced by the fact that the cost will be borne by others. We must be certain that those who will pay that price are fairly represented in our deliberations and that they are heard.

At the core of the argument that we should resist all government regulation of speech is the ideal that the best cure for bad speech is good—that ideas that affirm equality and the worth of all individuals will ultimately prevail. This is an empty ideal unless those of us who would fight racism are vigilant and unequivocal in that fight. We must look for ways to assist students whose speech and political participation are chilled in a climate of racial harassment.

Civil rights lawyers might consider suing on behalf of blacks whose right to an equal education is denied by a university's failure to ensure a nondiscriminatory educational climate or conditions of employment. We must develop a First Amendment jurisprudence grounded in the reality of our history and our contemporary experience. We must think hard about how best to launch legal attacks against the most indefensible forms of hate speech. Good lawyers can create exceptions and narrow interpretations that limit the harm of hate speech without opening the floodgates of censorship.

Everyone concerned with these issues must find ways to engage actively in actions that resist and counter the racist ideas that we would have the First Amendment protect. If we fail in this, the victims of hate speech must rightly assume that we are on the bigots' side.

Political Correctness Necessitates Some Restrictions on Speech

by John E. Van de Wetering

About the author: *John E. Van de Wetering is president of the State University of New York at Brockport.*

Some of you may be wondering, what is this political correctness, and what does it have to do with us who are in business or the professions? It appears to be an issue on college campuses, and not one of corporate or governmental or professional significance. As I explain the history and essentials of political correctness, I'll also address the connection of it to business and professional people, for it is vitally important to all of us. . . .

Slavishly Neutral Language

Political correctness is a pejorative term. In its very modern usage, to be politically correct is to slavishly adhere to language that is neutral of any sexist, racist, ageist, or any other "ist" connotations. The politically correct person is one who is so sensitive to the feelings of minority groups that he or she exhibits no attitudes and uses no speech that may in any way insinuate offense upon any minority group. And the correct speech is very specific, to be used slavishly, and to fail to use it is to be a bigot. The definition of the politically correct is meant to be absurd; it is meant to carry with it the baggage of unwarranted and excessive sensitivity. It also bears with it the suggestion of sanctimoniousness and smug self-righteousness. As it has come to be used today, it is itself an epithet of conformity which nobody wishes to claim. It is meant to be a mockery of certain constricted behavior, usually by people who are perceived to be the most knee-jerk of liberals. This definition is unfortunate. It is unfortunate because it has a history which has led to attacks on some of the most fundamentally positive changes that have occurred socially in this country over the past

From "Political Correctness: The Insult and the Injury," a speech by John E. Van de Wetering delivered to the Rotary Club of Rochester, New York, September 3, 1991. Reprinted with the author's permission.

three decades. The charge of politically correct is more specifically an attack upon certain campus policies of civil intercourse promoted by administrators like me who wish to make the campus community a community of civil exchanges of ideas, a community in which, despite debate, all people are encouraged and comfortable in their differences.

Beginnings of "Politically Correct"

The politically correct, or rather the modern version of the politically correct, began, then, as a mockery of what was perceived by certain people to be the excesses of affirmative action programs on campus. It was affirmative action programs, after all, that engendered the spirit of careful, civil speech with respect to minority groups. Notions of the politically correct spread, especially in this state, to become not only a satire on affirmative action programs, but more seriously a grave attack on programs of multiculturalism. Several events coalesced . . . to bring political correctness satire to the forefront of *serious* discourse.

First was the series of articles in such magazines as *Newsweek*, *Time*, and *U.S. News & World Report* in which certain campus administrations of affirmative action were satirized for going overboard in their advocacy of civil behavior on campus. Students were told in handbooks what terms were considered offensive or taboo by minority groups, how these groups preferred to be addressed, what bodily terms were taken as disrespectful to women. Accordingly, we learned that both "black" and "African American" were acceptable, but "colored" was not; that "Asian" was preferred to "Oriental"; that women of thirty who worked as clerks in offices were not "the girls." These directives, obviously, are not without merit. Young men at college need to know, for their own sakes, what is acceptable behavior, for example, to women and what is not. People who have had no contact with African Americans or Asians were made aware not only of their preferences in names, but also of the history behind such preferences. It is not simple etiquette that requires that we not call Jewish people by a derisive name, but a long and dreadful history of rock-pelting, derision, and segregation that recommends it. Blacks remember lynch mobs as well. Asians remember the Yellow Peril associated with the word "Oriental." Nomenclature, in short, is not devoid of significant history and education.

In any case, politically correct language *began* to become part of the general public consciousness with these satires in widely published magazines. At the same time, as the public has come to perceive it, political correctness is not simply saying and writing about and doing the civil or "nice" thing in order to show respect for minorities. Political correctness has, today, become confused with issues of censorship and totalitarianism.

> *"It was affirmative action programs . . . that engendered the spirit of careful, civil speech with respect to minority groups."*

This occurrence is a strange twist of history. As far back as we can judge, the term was used first by Marxists and left progressives as a way of offering criticism to themselves for their own overbearing preachiness. It was to them a label for a person who mindlessly adhered to the party line, no matter how inappropriate the policy might be for the given occasion. Marxists, thus, who preached to tough and practical-minded American auto workers about the class revolution were called by their comrades "politically correct." What was left unsaid was "politically correct" but absolutely inappropriate. It wasn't until the late 1980s that politically correct was applied to a set of beliefs that sprang from campus policies of multiculturalism. PC, starting first as a satire of the excesses of the language of affirmative action and multiculturalism, became later, in the hands of frightened scholars and laymen, a convenient label for curricular changes which seemed threatening to the traditional and established structure of the white, masculine-dominated educational system. I've read headlines in publications that could be called anything from conservative to liberal equating politically correct with "Sensitivity Fascism," or the "New McCarthyism," or "Academic Thought Control." For the most part, the fears emanating from the suggestion of restrictions on freedom of speech, I believe, have been overblown and lack an historical foundation or perspective. The academy infrequently mandates anything, let alone restrictions on free speech.

> *"The best ethic is the one which seeks to do the least harm to others while preserving individual prerogative."*

But there is an almost universal search among campuses for an enlightened and invigorating ethos, a code of behavior following the straightforward precepts of some of the more noteworthy members of the law faculty at Harvard University. They argue that the best ethic is the one which seeks to do the least harm to others while preserving individual prerogative. We on the campus realize, without pretensions to great knowledge or insight, that although sticks and stones do break bones, words do, in fact, hurt as well.

Damage Inflicted on the Deprived

We must remember that this so-called politically correct language did not breed itself; it did not start in a vacuum. The rule that we now mock, that we now fear for its restraint on free speech, did not come as an invention of some bored bureaucrat. It came because damage was inflicted by the language of the advantaged upon the spirits of the deprived. My good friend and colleague, the president of St. John Fisher College, Bill Pickett, has perhaps put it best for all of us. He has outlined his defense of policies that answer to the slurs and mockeries of those who satirize serious attempts to construct an ethos of civility on our campuses. He reported thus:

110

A student hangs a swastika on a banner out of a residence hall window; he is disciplined by college authorities. A student loudly and repeatedly uses racial epithets to refer to Jewish students but takes no overt action against them; she is expelled from her university. A female campus minister is subjected to harassment and those responsible must publicly apologize.

These are not peculiar or isolated incidents. Racial tensions have grown immeasurably in the past several years.

Necessary Code of Conduct

As another author, this time one of our students at SUNY Brockport, has documented:

> Eight Asian students at the University of Connecticut were harassed by a group of white students who hurled racial epithets and spit on them. At the University of San Diego a group of students burned a cross in May 1989 in front of a Black Student Union. At the University of Pennsylvania, a young black student, a woman, was harassed by racial slurs coming from two white men as she passed their dormitory. They then poured jars of urine on her. At the University of Montana several male athletes mercilessly harassed an admitted gay student until he moved out of his dormitory saying he feared for his life.

This is in addition to a rising incidence of date rape on campuses throughout the country. An ethic, a code of decent social behavior among peoples, is sorely needed on our campuses and communities. Politically correct did not emerge for no reason at all.

In this environment, intolerance and the *test* of all kinds of freedoms of speech have proliferated on campuses as though student and/or professor and/or reporter and/or editor are all daring administrators to lay down rules and damning them if they do.

Simple humane rules of decent conduct have thus become targets for tests of free speech, under the mocking aegis of politically correct. It is almost as though one were saying, "If I cannot speak exactly what is on my mind at the moment it occurs to me, in exactly the terms I wish, expressing honest hatred, then my First Amendment rights have been violated." Let us not play games about this. Those who have made politically correct a political issue of free speech are saying just that. Perhaps they are right. There is much legal doctrine recommending this position. The protectionist view in opposition to campus regulations governing hate speech is represented

> *"Simple humane rules of decent conduct have thus become targets for tests of free speech, under the mocking aegis of politically correct."*

best by those like Robert O'Neil, president of the Virginia School of Law, who has said, "The worthiest motives prompt efforts to restrict speech that may wound, or embarrass, or offend." Yet, the "enduring precepts of free expression that compel Americans to tolerate such speech" are legally upheld by the Supreme Court, even in its decision to strike down the flag desecration rulings that had been attempted in local jurisdictions.

On the other hand, we have legal precedents that argue for the 14th Amendment on the grounds that certain kinds of speech are harmful in its creation of an atmosphere in which equality is compromised. In *Brown vs. the Board of Education*, it was held that the fact of segregation affected the "hearts and minds" of black children, and that "racial epithets" similarly caused "deep emotional scarring" that rendered the atmosphere of the schoolroom of black children unequal to the atmosphere of the schoolroom of white children.

Perhaps the protectionists of unrestricted free speech are right. Perhaps we will once again have to say, "I hate what you are saying, but I will defend your right to say it." And perhaps it is right to defend the immunity that the Nazis enjoyed, when they marched down the streets of Skokie, Illinois, as a warrantable price for the pleasures of our freedom. If the issue of free speech surrounding politically correct had resolved itself simply into speaking the unpopular, speaking the hated, then that is probably the way I would have resolved the question myself. Let them speak without sensitivity in the hope that an ultimately educated population will reject them.

> *"Certain kinds of speech are harmful in [their] creation of an atmosphere in which equality is compromised."*

But that was not the whole story. There is more. Especially in New York there is more. The juxtaposition of the Board of Regents recommendation on multiculturalism in the classroom with the publicity surrounding the "politically correct" has brought a grave connection with politically correct and multiculturalism to the foreground. Let me illustrate this by referring to a popular column in our daily newspaper to point out just how clearly the juxtaposition between politically correct and campus attempts at multiculturalism are perceived by the public as coterminous.

The Demise of the Ethnic Joke?

In the "Speaking Out" in the *Democrat & Chronicle* of June 23, 1991, a writer named Bill Kauffman gave voice to his real fears on this issue. His concern, and it may be a typical one, is that the mounting attempts to create regulations on campus and habituate students to a language of civility and super-sensitivity to diverse ethnic groups will lead, he cried, "by decade's end, to an attempt by speech-controllers to outlaw harmful speech, for example, ethnic jokes." He said, without embarrassment, that an example of the "general deterioration of American political debate" would result in the demise of "ancient vaudevillians," who, in "telling the one about the Pole, the Italian, and the Irishman, will be hauled into court and subjected to grim harangue about Sensitivity and Diversity and the Trojan Horse concept of the year, multiculturalism."

In his angry diatribe over the potential loss of such Americanisms as the ethnic joke, the right to describe a woman's body as "cheesecake," and what he
called the "frank speech" of personal insult, Kauffman rightly named his enemy: the advancing ethos of mul-ticultural sensitivity. Kauffman is right. The so-called "politically cor-rect" derives from the push on aca-

> *"We have always been a nation of states, not a unified, univocal people."*

demic campuses to recognize the reality of a multicultural world in which their
students will eventually live and earn their keep. It recognizes that it is necessary to understand and even to accommodate Asian conventions of correct intercourse and Middle Eastern conventions of correct intercourse, if for no other
reason than we must live and do business with them. Campuses, of course, go
further. They actually suggest it is ethical to behave in such accommodating
ways, even if the result is a restriction on one's speech. Multiculturalism was
born and bred, first, by political reality and, second, by a need to define a work-
able and honorable ethic for an ethics-hungry America. Those among the scholars of America, those like the revered Arthur Schlesinger, who fear that an emphasis on multicultural diversity will Balkanize America as it seems to be doing
in central Europe, strangely ignore the straightforward truth that America, unlike homogeneous pockets of Europe, never was unified into a homogeneity, always was a squabbling, vocal, insistent bunch of haranguers. We were always
diverse in this country; our attempts to carve unity have always come self-con-
sciously because of the truth of our inherent differences. Before there were
Asians and blacks to speak of, did not the Puritan deliberately separate himself
from Anglican, from Methodist, from Roman Catholic? Did not the Virginian
claim superiority over the Pennsylvanian and vice versa? We have always been
a nation of states, not a unified, univocal people. Is that not our strength, our
great strength historically? That we failed at homogeneity?

Multiculturalism and the School Curriculum

Finally, there is the last concern with respect to multiculturalism and the politically correct. It is articulately presented by several historians in criticism of
the new multicultural public school curriculum.

They want to prevent the change. A quick look at American history will make
the point. When we were growing up, we certainly knew about Washington's
crossing the Delaware and his refusal to be a king; monumental events without
a doubt. We learned about a revolution of brave men for the privileges of independence. We learned about the battles of the Civil War. We chuckled over Ben
Franklin's journals and autobiography if we were really educated. What we did
not find on the pages of these works was anything that women were doing; or
blacks were doing; or, indeed, what day laborers, school teachers, or volunteers

were doing. But the critics say the new approach goes too far and is not accurate history.

I disagree. Our concern with multiculturalism is not to promote patriotism, or any particular ethnic position, but a true picture of who we are. We are not Puritan Pilgrim Nordic churchmen who transformed themselves into pioneers, cowboys, Indian fighters forever chanting democratic slogans and itching to go to war. We are diverse people struggling, groping to reach each other; not to fight but to recognize; not to defeat but to accommodate. That is what we were before, too; but only recently, through multiculturalism, are we beginning to recognize this. Multiculturalism is not a clever invention by college folk to appease ethnic sensibilities. It is an acknowledgement, not an invention, of who we are, who we have always been, and what makes us both strong and unique. Both extremes tend to ignore this in the debate.

Political Correctness and Change

I hope what I have said today has provided you with a context for abandoning the term politically correct because it is a pejorative that has been too closely associated with attacking change—change in the language we use, change in the curriculum our students and your children study, and change in the way we go about doing business day-to-day.

I think it's important to keep in mind that the development of sensitivity to people of color and women and those who are physically challenged isn't limited to campus life. We're going to need that sensitivity in the business world, too.

Speech Codes Are Sometimes Necessary on Campuses

by Richard Perry and Patricia Williams

About the authors: *Richard Perry is a researcher in linguistics at the University of Louvain, Belgium. Patricia Williams is an associate professor of law and women's studies at the University of Wisconsin at Madison.*

Until well after the Second World War, American institutions of higher education were bastions of a sort of cheery and thoughtlessly jingoistic nativism (isn't this some part of what we've always meant when we spoke of "that old college spirit"?). Except for the historically black and women's colleges and a couple of schools serving immigrant populations (such as the City College of New York), the vast majority of the student bodies of America's hundreds of colleges were overwhelmingly U.S.-born, male, Christian, and of Northern European descent, and their faculties were even more so. The structure of the core liberal arts curriculum suggested that the university understood itself as an umpire of timeless values, high above the rough and tumble of mere politics, standing at the summit of Western civilization, which from this vantage point could be seen to have risen in an unbroken crescendo from Plato to NATO.

An Arbiter of "Universal Values"?

However, the assumptions that made the university an arbiter of "universal values" have been questioned, as multinational business and research institutions have evolved into ever more global and ethnically diverse enterprises. On the home front, meanwhile, the hard-won material gains of women and ethnic minorities have produced halting progress toward the goal of making American universities truly representative of the country's population as a whole. Responding to these historical developments, many have sought to make the core curriculum a more effective preparation for the diverse, multicultural environ-

Richard Perry and Patricia Williams, "Freedom of Hate Speech." Reprinted from *Tikkun* (July/August 1991), *a Bimonthly Jewish Critique of Politics, Culture, and Society.* Subscriptions: $31/yr. 1-800-846-8575.

ments of both the contemporary United States and the world. There have also been efforts to make the campus itself a more hospitable place for its newly heterogeneous population, most notably amendments to the campus conduct rules intended to discourage harassment on the basis of race, religion, ethnicity, gender, and sexual orientation.

These reform efforts have been met with a virulent backlash. This backlash has recently been fueled by a series of often scurrilous stories in the most visible national magazines and by fervent denunciations from the Left, Right, and center of political debate.

Multiculturalism and the First Amendment

This confusion stems largely from the dishonest manner in which the debates have been reported. Most accounts of this campus dispute have been characterized by repeated distortions of fact and a profound bad faith with history. First, it is preposterous to claim, as many opponents of multiculturalism have, that these debates are about some supposed new infringement of the First Amendment rights of American citizens. No position seriously advocated by multiculturalists would have the slightest effect upon our right as Americans to be nativist, racist, anti-Semitic, sexist, homophobic, or just as narrowly monocultural-as-we-wanna-be in our personal lives. So too it remains entirely possible to stand in the public arena and call one another any of the whole litany of terms with which we

> *"It is preposterous to claim . . . that these debates are about some supposed new infringement of the First Amendment rights of American citizens."*

as Americans have learned throughout our history to abuse one another. One might instructively compare this situation with the Canadian constitution, which specifically limits the protection of certain kinds of hate speech, without much evidence that this provision has started Canada down that slippery slope toward being a Stalinist police state.

Nor do the multiculturalist reforms pose any institutional threat to the many securely tenured professors on the most prestigious faculties who teach doctrines (such as sociobiology and kindred theories on the margins of intellectual respectability) that are patently demeaning to members of the most long-abused groups. And the debate over multiculturalism scarcely disturbs the work of eminent scholars who regularly contrive to put a revisionist happy face upon the history of slavery, the Czarist pogroms, the Nazi genocides, the colonial subjugation of indigenous peoples, or the oppression of women.

What has *never* been true is that one member of an institution has an unrestrained legal right to harass another member and remain in the good graces of the institution.

Yet the barrage of media coverage would have us believe that some *novel* restriction is being imposed in multiculturalist speech and behavior codes. This misinformation has been conveyed by those who are apparently unable to distinguish between a liberty interest on the one hand and, on the other, a quite specific interest in being able to spout racist, sexist, and homophobic epithets completely unchallenged—without, in other words, the terrible inconvenience of feeling bad about it.

There is a sharp paradox at the heart of all this, a contradiction whose effective message is: "I have the right to express as much hatred as I want, so you shut up about it." It may be appropriate to defend the First Amendment rights of students who, for example, openly advocate Nazi policies. However, there has been a good deal of unacknowledged power-brokering that has informed the refusal even to think about the effect of relentless racist propagandizing on educational institutions in particular. Now those who even criticize this selective invocation of the First Amendment on the behalf of one social group over another are themselves called Nazis.

This fundamental paradox has bred a host of others. Conservatives such as George Will hurriedly discard their hallowed distinction between the public and private spheres when expediency beckons. Not long ago right-wingers were asserting that the evangelical Bob Jones University should be allowed to practice segregation and still be given a tax exemption—because it was a *private* institution. Where were these free-speech patriots in 1986 when Captain Goldman, a U.S. Air Force officer and an Orthodox Jew, was denied by the [Ronald] Reagan Supreme Court the right to wear a yarmulke at his desk job? And where were they when the new Supreme Court of our new world order asserted that the government *can* control speech between doctor and patient—heretofore one of the most sacred of privacy privileges—when the clinic receives federal funds and the topic of conversation is reproductive choice?

A Double Standard

These ironies of free-speech opportunism have been accompanied by a breathtaking effort to rewrite our history. The multiculturalist reforms on campus have been characterized as being at odds with the two moral touchstones of recent political memory: the World War II-era fight against Nazi theory of Aryan supremacy and the American anti-slavery and civil rights movements. Both of these struggles were in fact fought over—among other things—the sort of contested social meanings that can be traced directly to the present university discussions. The new interpretation of these two contests, however, rewrites them as triumphs of the inevitable, forward-marching progress of modern liberal individualism. Commentators from George Will

> *"Media coverage would have us believe that some novel restriction is being imposed in multiculturalist speech and behavior codes."*

to Shelby Steele have consistently depicted Martin Luther King, Jr., for example, as having pursued the higher moral ground of individual achievement rather than the validation of African-American collective social identity—as though these notions were inherently in opposition to one another. We are to imagine, for example, that the brave people who faced fire hoses and police dogs and who sat-in at lunch counters in the 1950s and 1960s were after nothing more than, say, the market freedom of an individual black American to eat a grilled cheese sandwich in the company of raving bigots. Conservative opponents of multiculturalism would have us forget about the other part of that struggle: the fight to expand the social space of all blacks and to re-articulate the political semantics of the collective identity of the descendants of slaves.

Another striking paradox is the way that much of this backlash proceeds in the name of democratic values, while mounting a sustained assault precisely on the democratic process of academic self-governance. The academic Right devotes itself to attacks on changes in curricula and conduct codes that have been adopted only after lengthy deliberation and votes by the faculty senates (such as in the Stanford Western civilization reforms or the Berkeley ethnic studies requirement), administrative committees, or student bodies. More curiously still, these assaults are typically said to be conducted in defense of something like "a free marketplace of ideas." Yet the recent multiculturalist changes might accurately be viewed as shifts in an intellectual marketplace where several positions have been rising in value, while another, older position, adamantly refusing to innovate, has been steadily losing its market share. There is a certain irony, therefore, in the spectacle of [former director of the Office of National Drug Policy] William Bennett and company engaged in a kind of status brokerage, trading on their appointed positions of authority for advantage they cannot gain via democratic votes in faculty senates or in the governing bodies of professional organizations.

True Multiculturalism

Such distortions of the debate have worked to obscure what could be a genuine opportunity. The market idea, considered not simply as the nineteenth-century social-Darwinist mechanism whereby big fish eat little fish for the greater good, might serve as a multidimensional matrix for the representation of certain types of social information. If, for example, we could ever get to the point where we can honestly speak of having achieved a level playing-field in the marketplace of ideas (for this is precisely what is at stake in the present debates), then we might begin to understand the market as one means of representing multicentered networks of social interaction. Just as the American monetary system went off the gold standard in 1934, it is now time to get off the traditional *rational man* standard (the straight, white, male, Christian, English-speaking, middle-class individualist) as the universal measure of humanity. It is time to initiate a *perestroika* of personhood—to make a world in which all of us, in our multiple, overlapping, individual and collective identities can come to terms.

Campus Speech Should Be Subject to Proper Etiquette

by Judith Martin and Gunther Stent

About the authors: *Judith Martin writes the* Miss Manners *syndicated column. Gunther Stent is chairman of the department of molecular and cell biology at the University of California at Berkeley.*

Can the university, with its special trust of protecting free speech, be hampered by the restrictions of civility? What kind of a frill is etiquette, anyway, for those in the noble pursuit of truth?

These questions are raised whenever a loose-tongued student turns publicly nasty. When Brown University expelled such a student, many argued that all restrictions of free speech are intolerable in the university. Brown's president, Vartan Gregorian, agreed with that premise and neatly reclassified the offensive speech as behavior.

But the premise is wrong.

The special trust of a university is not to foster unlimited speech: It is to foster unlimited inquiry. And totally free speech inhibits rather than enhances the free exchange of ideas.

Etiquette and the Law

The law cannot restrict such speech without violating our constitutional rights. But etiquette, the extra legal regulative system that seeks to avert conflict before it becomes serious enough to call in the law, can and does. You may have a legal right to call your mother an idiot, or somebody else's mother a slut, but you won't if you know what's good for you.

Nor could you convince many people that the controversy that such remarks are likely to provoke will lead to advances in knowledge.

The university needs to enforce rules banning speech that interferes with the free exchange of ideas. It must protect the discussion of offensive topics but not the use of offensive manners. It must enable people freely to attack ideas but not one another.

Education is impossible without the order that prevents intimidation and mayhem. When children first enter school, they must be taught to sit still, refrain from taunting their classmates, show respect for their teacher and wait their turn to talk, or they will never be able to learn.

> *"The special trust of a university is not to foster unlimited speech."*

To those who find it horrifying that the university should allow a lesser degree of free speech than the law permits, it might be pointed out that the law itself restricts free speech in its pursuit of juridical truth. Try saying some of the things in a courtroom that the law will protect your right to say in a barroom.

Jurisprudence uses etiquette in courtroom procedure, not only to restrict speech but to impose standards of dress, comportment and forms of address—matters over which universities have long since abandoned authority.

The Need for Manners

Legislators and diplomats also know the value of keeping speech within the bounds of civility. The parliamentary etiquette book, "Robert's Rules of Order," proscribes "disorderly words" and forbids speakers "to arraign the motives of a member" during strongly worded debate. "It is not the man, but the measure, that is the subject of debate," decrees its section on "Decorum."

The rougher the conflict, the more manners are needed. Only when insults, harassment, disrespect and obscenity are banned can people engage in truly substantive argument.

Of course it is also a personal insult to call someone a racist or a sexist. Incivility is no more acceptable in defense than in attack.

Rebuttal, however, is a staple of open debate. Members of the university community should always have the opportunity to attack ideas—but not to attack people. The university should be obliged to provide a forum for anyone who wants to argue for or against an idea, provided the argument is made in good faith and a polite manner.

This standard of academic etiquette must be required not only in the classroom and lecture hall but wherever the community of scholars gathers—residence halls, dining commons, recreational facilities. Invective, whether spoken or conveyed through posters or graffiti, in the classroom or in the community, is detrimental to rational debate, to which universities are dedicated.

Chapter 3

Should There Be Limits to Free Speech?

Chapter Preface

The question of free speech is arguably one of the most complex of all constitutional issues. If speech were legally regarded only as expressions of verbal and written opinions, the establishment of constitutional standards and precedents regarding its use or denial of its use would be much less involved. However, this is not the case. The legal history of the free speech clause of the First Amendment is a miscellany of disparate and seemingly unrelated issues.

This chapter focuses on the multifaceted nature of the free speech question by offering debates on several diverse issues. The topics covered include song lyrics, regulation of the press, panhandling, and flag burning. Each topic, in its own way, is illustrative of the problems inherent in evaluating First Amendment issues. For example, deciding whether free speech limits should be placed on song lyrics requires determining if a distinction exists between pure entertainment and the communication of ideas. Regarding flag burning, the following question must be addressed: Is the act itself a nonverbal and legitimate form of expression or an overt and illegal gesture of defiance in which a cherished national symbol is defiled? More than two hundred years of Supreme Court and appellate court decisions involving these and similar issues have not led to any final or definitive answers. The Constitution leaves it to each generation to provide answers appropriate to its own age.

Song Lyrics Should Be Subject to Free Speech Limitations

by Charlton Heston

About the author: *Charlton Heston is an Oscar-winning movie actor and past president of the Academy of Motion Picture Arts and Sciences. The following remarks were delivered by Heston, a shareholder, to the 1992 Time-Warner corporation shareholders' meeting.*

I'm here as a shareholder, but I speak as a private citizen and as the public artist I've been most of my life. I think I understand the rights and responsibilities of both identities.

I'm here to condemn this company's response to the growing clamor across the country against *Body Count*, the CD Time-Warner released [in 1992]. I'm not talking about Ice-T, the young black performer trying for his 15 minutes of fame. The little he's said about his lyrics has been contradictory. "Aw, that's just black street talk. It don't mean the same to whites." Then again, "I ain't never killed no cop. . . . I felt like it a lot."

"A Promotional Gimmick"

I condemn the responsible officials in this company. Long after police groups across the country, the President of the United States, members of Congress, and major religious and media figures protested *Body Count*, Time-Warner began to ship CDs to disc jockeys in miniature black plastic body bags. Isn't that cute? A Time-Warner spokesman called this "a promotional gimmick." Is this the same clever executive who proposed as the cover art on another upcoming album a gunman lurking with an Uzi near the White House, waiting for President Bush?

In the end, of course, the buck stops at the top. At Gerald Levin [Time-Warner chief executive officer and president]. In the beginning, he could, prob-

Charlton Heston, "Just a Song?" *The National Review*, August 17, 1992. Reprinted with the author's permission.

ably honestly, have said, "Look, I don't have time to listen to rap lyrics. If some clown in the record division screwed up, we'll deal with it." Instead, since the CD was already successful, he tried to claim the moral high ground with protestations of Time-Warner's respect for the artist's creative freedom. Mr. Levin—come on. I've been doing this for a living all my life. I know, at least as well as you do, that an artist's creative freedom depends on the success of his last work and the demand for his next. All entertainment companies reject, alter, and cancel hundreds of artists' projects each year.

You also claimed the lyrics in *Body Count* were protected by the First Amendment. I know, at least as well as you do, that the right to free speech is not without limits, both public and private. I'm exercising my right of free speech this very moment, but I know, at least as well as you do, that it'll be a cold day in Hell before I'm offered another picture at Warner's, or get another good review in *Time* magazine.

Supreme Court Justice [Oliver Wendell] Holmes said it: Free speech does not include the right to yell "Fire!" in a crowded theater. The lyrics of "Cop Killer" go a lot further than that. They celebrate the murder of police officers. A year ago, you pulled country singer Holly Dunn's song,

> *"The right to free speech is not without limits, both public and private."*

"Maybe I Mean Yes," out of release because some groups felt it might encourage date rape. Where was your concern for the rights of artists then, sir? Rape is a terrible crime. So is murder, Mr. Levin.

Let's take a close look at what *Body Count* really is. You may have read the only quote from the lyrics of "Cop Killer" published so far: "I got my 12-gauge sawed-off; I'm 'bout to bust some shots off; I'm 'bout to dust some cops off." Well, you can handle that right?

Let me give you a taste of what they can't publish, though Time-Warner did, in this booklet they enclose with the *Body Count* CD. The song goes on: "I got my brain on hype—tonight'll be your night. Die, die, die pig, die. F--k the police! I know your family's grievin'. F--k 'em!" Catchy little number, isn't it?

Mr. Levin, you say, "Well, that's just fantasy. He never murdered a police officer." Jews and homosexuals are also often attacked, though of course not as frequently as police officers. Let me ask you: If that song were titled "Fag Killer," or if the lyrics went, "Die, die, die kike, die," would you still sell it? It's often been said that if Adolf Hitler came back with a hot movie synopsis, every studio in town would be after it. Would Warner's be among them?

Collection of Vile Songs

I know, ladies and gentlemen, this is painful. As the dentist says, "Just one more time, it'll hurt a bit, then we're through. Ready?" There's another song on this CD, called "KKK Bitch." It's about girls in a Southern town the *Body Count* group visited. Here's a taste of the lyrics:"I love my KKK bitch, love it when she s---s me. I love my KKK bitch, love it when she f---s me. I love my KKK bitch, she loves it when I treat her bad, you know what I'm sayin'. So we was down South . . . fallin' in love. D-Roc had this Nazi girl, my man Mooseman had a skinhead . . . I fell in love with Tipper Gore's two 12-year-old nieces. It was *wild*, it got even worse. She pushed her butt up against my d--k . . . my d--k got hard, entered in her a-s. She said, 'O, my God!' So what we really tryin' to say is *Body Count* loves everybody . . . Mexican, black, Oriental girls, it really don't matter. If you from Mars and you got a p---y, we will f--k you."

There, I'm through now. This is the material Time-Warner is defending. Not out of principle, but out of greed. Mr. Levin, I ask you to stop selling *Body Count*. Donate the money you have made from it to the families of murdered police officers. In the name of decency, sir. And one more thing, Mr. Levin. The next time a police officer is murdered, would you please go to the bereaved family, look them in the eye, and repeat to them what you have said for the record: "'Cop Killer' doesn't incite murder, any more than 'Frankie and Johnny' does. It's just a song."

Regulation of the Press Is Needed

by Claudia Mills

About the author: *Claudia Mills teaches at the University of Maryland, Balti-more. From 1980 to 1989 she was editor of* OO: Report from the Institute for Philosophy and Public Policy *at the University of Maryland.*

Freedom of the press is the cornerstone of America's image of itself. . . . Of late, however, the shining armor of the press has become tarnished. The increasing number of libel suits and the size of punitive judgments against the press show public wariness about its trustworthiness. Critics charge that reporters are not, indeed cannot be, impartial spokespersons for the Truth, but necessarily represent the interests of entrenched power groups, inspiring the quip that the only way to have freedom of the press is to own one.

According to philosopher Judith Lichtenberg, the growing power of the mass media means that we need protections *from* the press as well as protections *for* it, and both, she argues, are consistent with the ideal of freedom of speech. Our commitment to freedom of speech has two different strands: The first is an opposition to censorship, based on a belief that "one should not be prevented from thinking, speaking, reading, writing, or listening as one sees fit"; the second, equally fundamental, is our conviction that "the purposes of freedom of speech are realized when expression and diversity of expression flourish." We want no voice to be silenced; we also want many voices to be heard. While "government intervention seems to intrude upon the first principle, . . . it may advance the second."

Two Landmark Cases

Both principles are codified in landmark Supreme Court cases. In *Miami Herald* v. *Tornillo* the Court struck down a Florida statute requiring newspapers to provide politicians, attacked in the course of an electoral campaign, with a free opportunity to reply. Freedom of the press here was equated with editorial au-

Claudia Mills, "Freedom and Fairness: Regulating the Mass Media," *OO: Report from the Institute for Philosophy and Public Policy*, Fall 1986. Reprinted by permission of the publisher.

tonomy. But the second strand in our commitment to free speech is represented by *Red Lion Broadcasting* v. *FCC*, in which the Court upheld the Federal Communications Commission's (FCC) requirements that radio and television stations provide free reply time to those attacked in station broadcasts. Unlike their print counterparts, the broadcast media, which are federally licensed, were required (until 1987) by the "fairness doctrine" to devote a reasonable amount of time to the coverage of controversial issues of public importance and to do so fairly. While the asymmetrical treatment of the print and broadcast media is troubling to many, it is not clear whether the discrepancy should be resolved by treating the press more like broadcasting or treating broadcasting more like the press.

> "Of late, . . . the shining armor of the press has become tarnished."

Proposals for heightened regulation of the press raise goosebumps in many, however, who view governmental intervention in the mass media as a last resort. They would rather implement the goals of broadening access to the press and stimulating robust wide-open debate of public issues by allowing the press itself to exercise professional responsibility, or by relying on market forces. Only if these fail can government regulation be considered—and even then perhaps not. Whether or not we turn to the state to implement our commitment to a diversity of voices may depend crucially on how well it has been shown to work—what kinds of regulation work best, what kinds work at all.

Self-Regulation of the Press

Many journalists maintain that external regulation of the press is unnecessary, because the press itself is its own severest critic. Reporters, at least in popular imagery, are by nature independent and skeptical, delighting in controversy and muckraking, even when some of the muck to be raked lies close to home. In numerous ways the various organs of print and broadcast journalism bend over backwards to achieve fair and balanced coverage of thorny issues. A casual reading of the ombudsman's column in the *Washington Post* and of a week's worth of letters to the editor shows the willingness of a major paper to print inside accounts of its own failures and hostile outside criticism. Thus journalism professor Carl Sessions Stepp argues that "journalism is a craft peculiarly suited to internal reform. . . . Journalists are propelled by the First Amendment syndrome, a set of beliefs (maybe even a mythology) that, via broad acceptance, assumes a self-fulfilling power that can drive the profession."

Several recent trends, however, which Stepp himself notes, undermine the journalistic heritage on which his hopes for reform are founded. The first of these is intensified concentration of media ownership. Twenty corporations control more than half the 61 million daily newspapers sold every day; twenty corporations control more than half the revenues of the country's 11,000 magazines;

three corporations control most of the revenues and audience in television, ten corporations in radio, eleven corporations in all kinds of books, and four corporations in motion pictures. Continuing concentration drastically centralizes control over the forum in which voices are heard and likely limits access to it.

A second troubling development is the increasing intrusion of nonnews corporations into the news enterprise. As Stepp points out, "The press is part of big business, and increasingly it is owned and operated by big business corporations that may have only incidental interest in journalism and that may be controlled by individuals without grounding in journalistic principles." Finally, the proliferation of broadcast and cable outlets forces the news media to compete incessantly for consumer time, thus driving public-affairs coverage further toward entertainment.

Even in the face of these challenges, Stepp still calls for a renewed commitment to professional responsibility on the part of the media themselves, rather than government regulation. In his view, regulation would only make matters worse: "The system is animated by the ideal of First Amendment freedom from government interference; government intrusion would necessarily subvert that ideal and demolish the fundamental assumption on which the press operates. It is hard to imagine that the ensuing system would be an improvement."

> *"Critics charge that reporters are not, indeed cannot be, impartial spokespersons for the Truth."*

But legal scholar Owen Fiss fails to see an inevitable tension between government regulation and professional accountability: "Why is it assumed that state regulation of the media and professional independence are necessarily inconsistent? It seems to me that it all depends on the nature of the regulation. Indeed, the fairness doctrine can be seen as strengthening and perhaps even generating the resolve of reporters and editors to act in a way that furthers the democratic aspirations of the First Amendment. As we saw from *Brown* v. *Board of Education* and the civil rights movement of the sixties, exemplary 'folkways' can sometimes be nourished—and maybe even created or legitimated—by strong exercise of state power." He concludes that professional norms alone are "frail and weak, compared to the challenge."

Let the Market Do It

If self-regulation cannot give us the kind of media we require in a democracy, what about letting the people themselves decide what kind of media they want by what kind of media they watch and read? Let them vote, so to speak, with their remote control buttons. Originally, regulation of broadcasting was justified by appeal to scarcity of broadcast frequencies; the fairness doctrine was devised to correct the "market failure" produced by the physical limitations of the electromagnetic spectrum. Now, with the advent of cable and satellite technology, scarcity has given way to abundance, oligopoly to cornucopia. With this imped-iment to a freely functioning market removed, market forces should ensure that if people in fact want a certain kind of news coverage, it will be provided; if in fact they do not, then in one view of democracy the loss is not to be regretted. By allowing the media to be driven by ratings and advertising, we will at least be giving the people the media they want, indeed the media they deserve. By accurately mirroring the state of popular tastes, ratings are a way of empower-ing the people to have the final say on television programming.

What Do We Watch?

We might find ourselves appalled, however, at what popular sovereignty in this context really means. Fewer people watch the news every night than watch *Wheel of Fortune*. The ratings wars among network news programs have been blamed for further crumbling of the time-honored wall of separation between news and entertainment and the resulting replacement of hard news coverage with fluffier "lifestyle" stories. (As one network news executive asked, "Do people in Lubbock, Texas, really need to know about the latest vote in Ways and Means?") Unless the nation is faced with a war or major disaster, interest in events of the day gives way to interest in what sweater Dan Rather is wearing and what sign-off phrase he uses.

According to Jeffrey Abramson, a political scientist, the "democratic" de-fense of ratings-driven news misunderstands what democracy really requires; it assumes that "the only news democratic citizens need is news that pleases them—news that they watch for the same reasons that they watch a situation comedy. But this is to treat viewers not as democratic citizens at all but only as consumers tuning in to be amused. . . . [Such news] can flatter the culture but not examine it; it can please viewers but not make them think."

Abramson also objects that the only audience that matters to Nielsen ratings is the mass audience, measured in forty or sixty million persons. "All power goes to that audience and even a show that attracts, say, thirty million persons in a time slot where competitors are bringing in forty million persons is in danger of cancellation. A television documentary such as PBS's history of the civil rights movement is expected to hold an audience of 1 million persons per segment; but this is a virtual no-show as far as commercial television is concerned."

Each network thus pursues the same mass audience with the same fare in each time slot. As a result, Abramson concludes, "The nation

> "**We need protections from the press as well as protections for it.**"

can for the most part conduct its business on television only on borrowed time; the economics of commercial television are pushed solely by the imperative to capture the largest possible audience for advertisers. This imperative typically stands against the realization of democratic ideals we commonly associate with diversity in programming or access to the marketplace of ideas for the widest possible array of contending voices."

Is Regulation the Answer?

Considerations such as these lead us to turn to the state for a remedy, for government, via such provisions as the fairness doctrine, can mandate broader access to the media and enhance the quality and breadth of public debate. But now the question arises: How can we trust the government to be a watchdog of the media when a chief function of the media is to be a watchdog of the government? If the government is empowered to tell the media how to run their business, won't this compromise the fundamental adversary relationship between the two?

The appropriate response here, according to Lichtenberg, "is not that we can trust government more than opponents of regulation believe, but that we can trust others less. Regulation is needed just because private power poses a grave threat to the independence and integrity of the press." Lee Bollinger, a law professor, states simply: "Our concern is with power—that is, the ability to command an audience more or less exclusively—and that is a concern that is not diminished by the way in which that power is achieved. It should make no difference to us, in other words, whether the power is the consequence of physical limitations associated with the use of that medium. . . or the result of limitations of the economic system (concentrations of economic power) or the result of clear market success in solidly appealing to a segment or majority of the community. It is the risks associated with power over access to the marketplace that raise the sense of alarm and not the source of that power."

> *"The press is part of big business, and . . . may be controlled by individuals without grounding in journalistic principles."*

But isn't the state equally subject to the influences of social and economic power that it would seek to control? A democratic government is responsive to the public will, which often means to private money, and hence to privileged power groups. Stepp argues, "If one defines the problem of access and diversity as seeking voice for perspectives other than those of a privileged and powerful minority, then government seems an ironic place to turn for help. Government is by definition integrated with the power class in American society and it is axiomatic that the press already gives greater voice to the 'outs' than the government does or is likely to."

Fiss concedes the danger that the state "will be the victim of the very same forces that dominate public debate and not counteract the skew of the market but rather reinforce it." He maintains nonetheless that "there is still a difference worth observing between a public official and a program manager of one of the networks (or an editor of a newspaper). However imperfect the systems of accountability are in the public sphere, at least they exist." Fiss concludes, "We turn to the state because it is the most public of institutions and because it alone has the power . . . to counteract, or modulate, the influence of the market and the constraint that it imposes on our politics."

Does Regulation Work?

The final question is a pragmatic one: Does regulation work? If no objections arise in principle, objections still may occur in practice. Does regulation in reality enhance or stifle robust, wide-open debate? Does it foster or chill discussion of public issues?

How successful—and how intrusive—regulation is depends on the form it takes. Two broad approaches to regulation of the media are usually distinguished. *Content regulation* makes specific demands of press institutions to cover certain kinds of issues, to cover them in a certain way, or to provide access to certain points of view. (The fairness doctrine is the most prominent example.) *Structural regulation* instead builds rules and constraints into the structure and organization of the media taken as a whole.

Most press resistance has been mounted against content regulation, as both dangerous and ineffective. Sara Engram, deputy editorial page editor for the Baltimore *Evening Sun*, reflects the sentiments of many journalists in arguing that the fairness doctrine ended up working against the goals it was designed to achieve: "Instead of encouraging enlightening discussion of matters of public interest, the fairness doctrine provides a crutch for the kind of journalism that can be described as, at best, terminally bland." In her view, the fairness doctrine "can—and does—encourage a constricted notion of fairness that ultimately limits the public debate. . . . I suspect that in practice 'each side' quickly becomes 'both sides' and the broadcaster can move on to the next 'issue' satisfied that he has gotten the FCC off his back."

Bollinger replies, however, that evidence for the alleged "chilling effect" of the fairness doctrine rests largely on broadcasters' own testimonial claims, which are likely to be self-serving. He points out that the often overlooked first provision of the fairness doctrine, which requires broadcasters to provide coverage of public issues, could be used to overcome any chilling tendencies of the requirement of fairness. Finally, he insists that any amount of chilling must be balanced against the enhancement of speech provided by the expanded number of voices heard.

> *"Regulation is needed just because private power poses a grave threat to the independence and integrity of the press."*

But did the fairness doctrine, as it was enforced, enhance public debate significantly? Henry Geller, director of the Washington Center for Public Policy Research, charges that the FCC "failed miserably" in requiring broadcasters to devote a reasonable amount of time to issues of public concern: "In a half-century of regulation, it has never denied a license for failure to deliver sufficient news or public affairs. . . . The comparative renewal process is just as great a charade. The incumbent always wins, no matter what its past record." The fairness doctrine shaped broadcasters' concern more by the shadow it cast than by the stick it wielded.

What Kind of Regulation?

We might do better, then, to rely on structural approaches to regulation, such as rules prohibiting multiple ownership of news organizations or designating certain cable channels for public access. Economic incentives can be offered to news organizations to promote diversity or provide services unlikely to be offered in the unrestricted marketplace. Instead of returning to the concept of broadcasters as public trustees, bound by a fairness doctrine, Geller proposes exacting from station owners a modest "spectrum fee," to be used to subsidize public affairs and similar programming by public radio and television stations, who are willing and able to provide the high-quality broadcasting other stations eschew. This proposal faces the objection that only a miniscule proportion of the population tunes in to public stations and so the majority would still lack exposure to thorough, thoughtful treatment of the issues of the day. But at least their deprivation would be self-chosen.

The press has had a long history of resisting governmental regulation and defines itself by its adversary role to government. But as the media grow more powerful, the government may be needed as an adversary to them, and, in the late twentieth century, both government and media may be needed as adversaries to powerful economic interests. The question we should be asking, then, is not whether regulation of the press is permissible, but what kinds of regulation work most effectively to enhance the diversity and quality of public debate in our democracy.

Speech That Causes Clear Danger Should Be Limited

by James E. Leahy

About the author: *James E. Leahy is a former law professor at California Western School of Law in San Diego. He is retired and has authored several books.*

"Speech . . . is . . . protected . . . unless shown to . . . produce a clear and present danger of a . . . substantive evil that rises far above public inconvenience, annoyance or unrest." [Terminiello v. Chicago, 1949]

U.S. Supreme Court Justice William O. Douglas once declared that "a function of free speech under our system of government is to invite dispute." Even though inviting dispute is an acceptable objective of speech, when speech passes beyond dispute and creates danger of a breach of the peace, it is no longer protected and can be punished. Determining when a speaker has passed the bounds of acceptable speech and crossed into the area of punishable speech is sometimes very difficult.

Generally, before speech can be punished, there must be some rule, regulation, or law that defines the kind of utterances that are prohibited. Such laws, regulations, or rules must be carefully drafted so that maximum protection is given to the right of free speech. The case of *Terminiello v. Chicago* illustrates the importance of careful draftsmanship.

A Critical Speech

Arthur W. Terminiello was a Catholic priest under suspension by his bishop, who was brought from Alabama to Chicago to speak under the auspices of the Christian Veterans of America. The year was 1946. The conditions under which the meeting was held were described by Justice Robert H. Jackson.

> The crowd [estimated to be 1,500] constituted "a surging, howling mob hurling epithets" at those who would enter and "tried to tear their clothes off." One young woman's coat was torn off and she had to be assisted into the meeting by policemen. Those inside the hall could hear the loud noises and hear those on the outside yell, "Fascists," "Hitlers" and curse words like "damn Fascists."

From *The First Amendment, 1791-1991: Two Hundred Years of Freedom*, © 1991 James E. Leahy, McFarland & Company, Inc., Publishers, Jefferson, NC 28640. Reprinted with permission.

Bricks were thrown through the windowpanes before and during the speaking. . . . The street was black with people on both sides for at least a block either way; bottles, stink bombs and brickbats were thrown. Police were unable to control the mob, which kept breaking the windows at the meeting hall, drowning out the speaker's voice at times and breaking in through the back door of the auditorium. About 17 of the group outside were arrested by the police.

In spite of the disturbance outside, Terminiello made a speech critical of Russia, communism, Jews, and the government under president Franklin D. Roosevelt. He referred to Eleanor Roosevelt as Queen Eleanor and to Secretary of Agriculture Henry Wallace as Henry Adolph Wallace.

Terminiello was arrested for disorderly conduct, which was described by a city ordinance as making "any improper noise, riot, disturbance, (or) breach of peace. . . ." At the trial, the testimony with regard to the reaction of those inside the hall was contradictory. One witness testified that "the people were disturbed and angry." Another said that "when [Terminiello] said there was no crime too great for the Jews to commit, the woman next to her said, 'Yes the Jews are all killers, murderers. If we don't kill them first, they will kill us. . . .'"

A witness for the defendant testified that the audience was quiet and attentive at all times.

The trial judge charged the jury that "misbehavior may constitute a breach of the peace if it stirs the public to anger, invites dispute, brings about a condition of unrest, or creates a disturbance. . . ."

Following his conviction, Terminiello appealed to the Illinois Supreme Court, which sustained the jury's decision. The U.S. Supreme Court granted review "because of the importance of the question presented." The question presented was whether it was a violation of the First Amendment to convict someone whose speech "stirs the public to anger, invites dispute, brings about a condition of unrest, or creates a disturbance. . . ."

Reverse the Conviction

Six justices held that such a conviction was an infringement on freedom of speech and voted to reverse Terminiello's conviction. Justice Douglas, after noting that "a function of free speech under our system of government is to invite dispute," continued, "it may indeed best serve its high purpose when it induces a condition of unrest, creates dissatisfaction with conditions as they are, or even stirs people to anger. Speech is often provocative

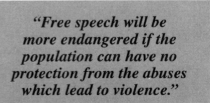

"Free speech will be more endangered if the population can have no protection from the abuses which lead to violence."

and challenging. It may strike at prejudices and preconceptions and have profound unsettling effect as it presses for acceptance of an idea." Only when speech is "shown likely to produce a clear and present danger of a serious substantive evil that rises far above public inconvenience, annoyance or unrest" can it be punished.

While the situation surrounding Terminiello's speech could reasonably have been considered to have produced a "clear and present danger," the possibility that the jury may have convicted him only for "inviting dispute" was enough to require the conviction to be set aside. Allowing Terminiello to go free did not sit well with Justices Jackson and Harold H. Burton. Rather than focus on the judge's instructions, Justice Jackson discussed at length the volatile situation that existed outside and inside the hall, and argued that in "the long run, maintenance of free speech will be more endangered if the population can have no protection from the abuses which lead to violence."

Whether a speaker has created a "clear and present danger" by his or her speech is a question upon which people may differ. And this is true whether the person called upon to make the decision serves as a juror, judge, or justice of the Supreme Court.

A Different Case

In *Feiner v. New York*, the trial judge, after hearing testimony about a speech by Irving Feiner on a street in Syracuse, New York, decided the police were

> *"There was a clear and present danger that a riot or disturbance would break out."*

justified in arresting him to "prevent a breach of the peace." There wasn't much dispute over whether Feiner's statements were controversial. For example, he said: "Mayor Costello (of Syracuse) is a champagne-sipping bum; he does not speak for the Negro people." "President Truman is a bum." "Mayor O'Dwyer is a bum." "The American Legion is a Nazi Gestapo." "The Negroes don't have equal rights; they should rise up in arms and fight for their rights."

Nor was there much disagreement over what happened as Feiner was speaking. The police officers who were on the scene testified that the gathering had spilled over into the street. They moved the people back to the sidewalk. The crowd was "restless and there was some pushing, shoving and milling around," and "some of the onlookers made remarks to the police about their inability to handle the crowd, and at least one threatened violence if the police did not act. There were others who appeared to be favoring the [speaker's] arguments."

After observing the situation for a while, the police stepped in and requested Feiner to stop, but he refused. After waiting a short while and again asking him to stop, a request which Feiner ignored, the officers arrested him. The speaker's final words were: "The law has arrived, and I suppose they will take over now."

Feiner was charged with "ignoring and refusing to heed and obey reasonable police orders issued at the time and place mentioned in the Information to regulate and control said crowd and to prevent a breach or breaches of the peace and to prevent injury to pedestrians attempting to use said walk, and being forced into the highway adjacent to the place in question, and prevent injury to the public generally."

The speaker was tried before a judge who agreed that there was danger of a breach of the peace from the listeners reacting to the speech and therefore found Feiner guilty. This decision was upheld by two New York appellate courts and by the Supreme Court.

> *"The New Hampshire statute did no more than punish 'fighting words.'"*

The majority's opinion acknowledges "that the ordinary murmurings and objections of a hostile audience cannot be allowed to silence a speaker. . . ."

> But we are not faced with such a situation. It is one thing to say that the police cannot be used as an instrument for the suppression of unpopular views, and another to say that, when as here the speaker passes the bounds of argument or persuasion and undertakes incitement to riot, they are powerless to prevent a breach of the peace.

Justice Hugo L. Black's view of this case was substantially different. "The record before us," he explained, "convinces me that petitioner, a young college student, has been sentenced to the penitentiary for the unpopular views he expressed on matters of public interest while lawfully making a street-corner speech in Syracuse, New York." Justice Black was joined in dissent by Justice Douglas, who declared that "one high function of the police is to protect these lawful gatherings so that speakers may exercise their constitutional rights." He saw no danger of a riot or breach of the peace in the record of the case. "It shows an unsympathetic audience and the threat of one man to haul the speaker from the stage. It is against that kind of threat that speakers need police protection."

A Clear and Present Danger

In *Feiner*, it should be noted, no breach of the peace occurred. Feiner did not breach the peace, nor did the grumbling, pushing, and threats by one man constitute such a breach. His conviction was upheld because the majority agreed that there was a clear and present danger that a riot or disturbance would break out.

The principle that speech that creates a danger of disorderly conduct may be punished applies even though the audience is only one person. That lesson was brought home to Walter Chaplinsky, a Jehovah's Witness, while he was distributing literature on the streets of Rochester, New Hampshire. Some of the people on the streets did not like what he was doing and complained to the city marshal, who "told them that Chaplinsky was lawfully engaged and that he must be left alone." The marshal then warned Chaplinsky, but "some hours later, the crowd got out of hand and treated Chaplinsky with some violence. He was then led towards the police station, though apparently more for his protection than for arrest. . . ." On the way to the station, Chaplinsky said to the marshal, "You are a God damned racketeer" and "a damned Fascist and the whole government of Rochester are Fascists or agents of Fascists. . . ." He was charged with violating the following New Hampshire statute:

> No person shall address any offensive, derisive or annoying word to any other person who is lawfully in any street . . . nor call him by any offensive or derisive name.

Chaplinsky's version of the incident is somewhat different than the marshal's. He claimed that "when he met Bowering [the marshal], he asked him to arrest the ones responsible for the disturbance. In reply, Bowering cursed him and told him to come along." Chaplinsky also denied that he had used the "name of the Deity." He was found guilty, and the conviction was affirmed by the New Hampshire Supreme Court.

"Fighting Words"

In discussing the meaning of the statute, that court explained that "the statute's purpose was to preserve the public peace, no words being 'forbidden except such as have a direct tendency to cause acts of violence by the persons to whom, individually, the remark is addressed.'" Further, the court said, "the word 'offensive' [as used in the statute] is not to be defined in terms of what a particular addressee thinks. . . . The test is what men of common intelligence would understand would be words likely to cause an average addressee to fight." In other words, what the statute condemned was speech, in this case Chaplinsky's, directed at an individual, the marshal, "likely to cause an average addressee to fight."

"The laws under which a speaker is arrested must be drawn with precision."

When the case reached the Supreme Court, Chaplinsky's conviction was sustained because "there are certain well-defined and narrowly limited classes of speech, the prevention and punishment of which has never thought to raise any Constitutional problem. These include the lewd and obscene, the profane, the libelous, and the insulting or 'fighting' words—those which by their very utterance inflict injury or tend to incite an immediate breach of the peace."

The New Hampshire statute did no more than punish "fighting words," according to the majority, and the only question that remained was whether Chaplinsky's words were within the statute. The justices said they were. "Argument is unnecessary to demonstrate that the appellations 'damn racketeer' and 'damned Fascist' are epithets likely to provoke the average person to retaliation, and thereby cause a breach of the peace."

Here again, no breach of the peace occurred. But that was not the question before the Court. The question to be decided was "what men of common intelligence would understand would be words likely to cause an average addressee to fight." In the early 1940s, "men of common intelligence" might agree that "damn racketeer" and "damned Fascist" would "likely" cause a fight.

As the *Terminiello* and *Chaplinsky* cases illustrate, the laws under which a speaker is arrested must be drawn with precision so that there is no infringement of speech protected by the First Amendment. These cases stand for the proposition that speech that presents a "clear and present danger" and speech that includes "fighting words" may be punished without violating the First Amendment.

New Orleans Law Found Unconstitutional

Section 49-7 of the ordinances of the city of New Orleans is an example of an attempt to draft a valid "fighting words" law but which was not drawn carefully enough to accomplish that result. Section 49-7 reads as follows:

> It shall be unlawful and a breach of the peace for any person wantonly to curse or revile or to use obscene or opprobrious language toward or with reference to any member of the city police while in the actual performance of his duty.

Mallie Lewis was arrested for violating Section 49-7, but the evidence concerning the arrest was conflicting. Lewis and her husband were following a police car in which their son, who had been arrested, was being taken to the police station. Officer Berner, who was driving another police car, stopped the Lewis truck, and "words were exchanged between Berner and [Lewis], and Berner arrested" her.

> The parties' respective versions of the words exchanged were in sharp contradiction. Berner testified that [Lewis] left the truck and "started yelling and screaming that I had her son or did something to her son and she wanted to know where he was. . . . She said, "you god damn m.f. police—I am going to [the superintendent of police] about this.". . . [Lewis'] husband testified that Berner's first words were "let me see your god damned license. I'll show you that you can't follow the police all over the streets. . . ." After . . . [Lewis] got out and said "Officer I want to find out about my son." He said "you get in the car woman. Get your black ass in the god damned car or I will show you something. . . ." [Lewis] denied that she used "any profanity toward the officer."

The municipal judge who heard the case believed the officer and found Lewis guilty of violating Section 49-7. If the officer's testimony is taken as true, then certainly Lewis did "wantonly . . . curse or revile or use obscene . . . language toward . . . a member of the city police while in the actual performance of his duty." Believing that to be the case, the Louisiana Supreme Court upheld the conviction.

Without being concerned with the facts, the Supreme Court reversed. A majority of the justices found the ordinance not to be a narrowly drawn "fighting words" law. "At least," Justice William J. Brennan Jr. wrote, "the proscription of the use of 'opprobrious language,' embraces words that do not 'by their very utterance inflict injury or

> *"Because [a New Orleans] law embraced more than 'fighting words,' it was unconstitutional as an infringement on free speech."*

tend to incite an immediate breach of the peace.'" Because the law embraced more than "fighting words," it was unconstitutional as an infringement on free speech.

Although Justice Lewis F. Powell Jr. did not agree with all that the majority said, he did agree that the conviction should be overturned. His concern was that the law conferred upon the police almost "unrestrained power to arrest and charge persons with a violation." "Many arrests are made," he noted, "in 'one-on-one' situations where the only witnesses are the arresting officer and the person charged." That makes it too easy to convict.

Aggressive Begging Should Not Receive Free Speech Protection

by Roger Conner

About the author: *Roger Conner is director of the American Alliance for Rights and Responsibilities, the legal arm of the Communitarian movement.*

Aggressive begging laws are being advanced by some of our most progressive urban politicians—like Mayors Maynard Jackson in Atlanta and Norman Rice in Seattle. For them, this issue is not about homelessness. It is, rather, about staving off urban decline, about dealing with the latest reason citizens are avoiding downtowns: aggressive panhandlers, not all of them homeless, who use verbal and physical intimidation in place of the passive palm.

Not Common Panhandling

This point cannot be overemphasized: Aggressive begging is not common panhandling. It is uncommon panhandling, a type of harassment bordering on extortion that is practiced by a minority of street people. Mumbling "spare change?" or squatting on the curb with a sign is not aggressive begging. Chasing down vulnerable people is.

Some civil libertarians object that these laws are inherently vague, impinge on free speech, or deal with acts already covered by current law. Not so on all counts.

Aggressive begging laws are aimed at behavior that a reasonable person would interpret as threatening or intimidating. Examples from recently enacted statutes include: following before, after, or during the course of asking for money; touching people or screaming at them while asking for money; accosting or blocking the passage of someone while asking for money; asking for money in a confined space such as a bank lobby or a subway tunnel; or asking for money in a clearly inappropriate, threatening or intimidating setting, such as in front of an automated teller machine.

The Supreme Court is likely to accept these statutes as reasonable time, place, and manner restrictions. A majority of the justices are agreed that "in-person solicitations of funds, when combined with immediate receipt of that money, creates a risk of fraud and duress which is well recognized, and which is different in kind from other forms of expression or conduct." (*Krishna Consciousness v. Lee* (1992).) Justice [Sandra Day] O'Connor added, "As residents of metropolitan areas know from daily experience, confrontation by a person asking for money . . . is more intrusive and intimidating than an encounter with a person giving out information."

Even Krishna dissenters agreed that bans could be justified to facilitate pedestrian traffic at "choke points," or upon "evidence of coercive conduct."

A Sense of Violation

Finally, aggressive begging behavior is not covered by other, more general statutes. Most intimidating panhandlers never cross the line into formal assault or sustain their threatening barrage long enough to qualify under harassment statutes (which have themselves come under ACLU attack).

Yet their victims—especially women, the slight, and the elderly—often feel as if they have narrowly escaped being mugged, assaulted, and robbed, and the sense of violation is not quick to abate. (Recent studies suggest that the fears are not groundless.) Thus, a very small group of frightening panhandlers can ruin a neighborhood or kill a business, robbing citizens of the feeling of security they once felt when walking down the street.

> *"Aggressive begging is . . . uncommon panhandling, a type of harassment bordering on extortion that is practiced by a minority of street people."*

Will aggressive begging laws do any good? Not if the goal is to "throw the bums out" of the local park, or "solve the homeless problem." But they do offer some respite to urbanites who fear being cornered by menacing mendicants. Seattle and Atlanta insist that their laws have helped.

The most surprising feature of public debates over panhandling regulation has been intense opposition from some homeless advocates. Of all people, they should be most aware that high-pressure panhandlers are poisoning public sympathy for the majority of destitute, deinstitutionalized and addicted homeless.

Could some of these advocates have adopted the view that, by making urban streets much more miserable and dangerous, society will be compelled to adopt the "needed" reforms? If that is the case, then we are all victims of an entirely different kind of aggressive begging.

Flag Burning Should Not Receive Free Speech Protection

by Robert H. Bork

About the author: *Robert H. Bork is a former federal court of appeals judge. He is the author of* The Tempting of America: The Political Seduction of the Law.

The Supreme Court's five-to-four decisions allowing the burning of the American flag as a right protected by the First Amendment have set off an emotional debate. Yet the debate reveals that many Americans are confused about the reasoning behind the decisions and about the appropriate response to them.

The majority opinions in *Texas* v. *Johnson* and *United States* v. *Eichman*, both written by Justice William J. Brennan, rest upon one central argument: "If there is a bedrock principle underlying the First Amendment, it is that the government may not prohibit the expression of an idea simply because society finds the idea itself offensive or disagreeable."

Although this statement is quite true, it is irrelevant. In both of the flag-burning cases, no idea of any sort was being suppressed. The flag burners were entirely free to express their "ideas" in a thousand other ways. Gregory Johnson, for example, chanted, "America, the red, white, and blue, we spit on you," while he burned a flag in Dallas. He was not prosecuted for his verbal expression because, under the First Amendment, his right to free speech was protected. Instead, he was prosecuted for a deeply offensive act prohibited by a state and federal statute.

Banning Methods of Expression, Not Ideas

The First Amendment has always permitted our government to ban offensive ways of expressing ideas—though not the ideas themselves. For instance, even after the rulings in *Johnson* and *Eichman*, one would hope that our laws can still punish a televised speech riddled with obscenities, stop a political speech

Robert H. Bork, "Waiving the Flag: Is Our Nation Entitled to One Symbol That Must Remain Undefiled?" *Omni*, October 1990. Copyright © 1990, Omni Publications International, Ltd. Reprinted by permission.

made from a sound truck at 2:00 A.M., or prosecute a protest against sodomy laws where demonstrators engage in the practice in public. The Supreme Court, however, made no attempt to explain why flag burning was not a similarly offensive method of expression. The majority's ruling that flag burning is a form of free speech implies that anybody can express himself with any public behavior at any time, and the community can set no limits on these acts.

Previous Justices Agree

I am not alone in my disagreement with the Court's conclusion. Chief Justice Earl Warren and Associate Justices Hugo Black and Abe Fortas, three of the most liberal Supreme Court judges in our history, stated unequivocally that flag burning was not protected speech and could be punished. In fact, at the time of the *Johnson* decision, the government's power to punish flag burners was so widely accepted that 48 states and the federal government had written statutes or laws prohibiting desecration of the American flag.

Some of us support a constitutional amendment that would allow state and federal legislatures—if they choose—to protect the flag against defilement. Many others have opposed this view. Unfortunately, the public debate is conducted in slogans that drown out sensible discussion.

A War of Slogans

Some opponents of an amendment objected to "chipping away at the First Amendment." A constitutional amendment allowing the government to protect the flag, however, would not diminish the First Amendment. Instead, it would restore the amendment to its condition before the Court made its erroneous rulings.

One opponent of the amendment compared the effort to stop flag desecration to Romania's suppression of speech. But suppressing ideas that a dictator dislikes can hardly be compared to objecting to offensive acts of expression. Others noted that Adolf Hitler made defiling the German flag a crime, suggesting, apparently, that nothing Hitler did should ever find an analogy in any shape or form in our society. Of course, Hitler also attacked unemployment, which apparently means we must drop any social policy directed to reducing unemployment in this country.

> *"To say that the freedom of speech requires that no symbol remain sacrosanct is to say something demeaning about the First Amendment itself."*

Still others said that allowing legislatures to prevent flag desecration is equal to desecrating the Constitution. Warren, Black, and Fortas must have been Constitution desecrators, not because they made up freedoms not mentioned in the Constitution—the usual charge against them—but because they recognized that somewhere there is a limit to freedom. Unlimited freedom would make all law, which by definition restricts freedom, impossible.

A final group of opponents argued that we should not set a precedent of overturning Supreme Court decisions with amendments to the Constitution. The precedent, however, has already been set; in the United States, on numerous occasions, we have adopted amendments to overturn Supreme Court judgments.

Ultimately, the question is whether the nation is entitled to one symbol that must remain undefiled. I think so. To say that the freedom of speech requires that no symbol remain sacrosanct is to say something demeaning about the First Amendment itself.

Song Lyrics Should Not Be Subject to Free Speech Limitations

by *The New Republic*

About the author: The New Republic *is a weekly journal of opinion.*

In culture this year [1992], as in politics, the extremes are touching. The tribunes of the people have joined forces with the conglomerated princes of capitalist darkness to defend the right of Ice-T and Body Count to arouse their listeners with fantasies of cop-killing. Thus Barbara Ehrenreich, oddly conflating two Bob Dylan songs and mistaking "Cop Killer" for rap, writes in Time Warner's *Time* magazine that "you don't need a rap song to tell which way the wind is blowing," that is to say, the fury of the song has a basis in reality; and Gerald M. Levin, president and CEO of Time Warner and, it seems safe to say, something of a stranger to the streets, writes in the *Wall Street Journal* that "this song is rooted in the reality of the streets," and proceeds to call, as a witness for the defense of his corporation, Malcolm X. The comedy is delicious. If ever there was evidence that freedom of expression in this society will be defended in all its precincts, here it is.

Having It a Lot of Ways

The defenders of "Cop Killer," however, are having it a lot of ways. Because of its basis in the wretchedness of South-Central Los Angeles, "Cop Killer" should sound an alarm; and because "Cop Killer" is (in Ehrenreich's words) merely "hyperbole" and "boast" and "gesture," there is no need to be alarmed. Well, which is it? Is the inflammation real or isn't it? Of course, what Ehrenreich has inadvertently described is only the bad faith of a liberal and a rock fan, for whom black rage must be real enough to provide a thrill but not so real that it actually threatens anything. Thus she praises what she calls "the outlaw subcultures of rap and rock," which is about as incorrect and idealized a description of rap and rock as anyone has lately seen.

Nor is that all. How would—how did—some of Ice-T's defenders react, say, to the Willie Horton ad? Did they insist that there was an empirical basis for the white fears of crime upon which the ad preyed? Did they reassure the American electorate that the ad was only hyperbole and gesture, that there was no reason, therefore, to make a fuss? Of course not. They treated the symbol like the real thing. And, in a sense, they were right: not about the liberal refusal to speak candidly about crime, but about the power of symbols in politics and culture. All cultural expressions, after all, are gestures. None of the kisses or the bullets of American popular music, Body Count's included, is real. But symbols are real, which is why they influence thought, which influences behavior.

> *"To defend freedom, you must also defend foulness."*

A Picture of the Inner-City World

No, Ice-T has not killed a cop, and neither has anybody else killed a cop in the name of Ice-T's song. But those who wish that such a song, and more generally American popular culture, be taken seriously had better take it seriously themselves. There is a picture of a world in this song, a picture of the inner-city world and the courses of action that are available to its inhabitants. It makes emotional recommendations. (Consider only the chorus: "COP KILLER, it's better you than me / COP KILLER, fuck police brutality! / COP KILLER, I know your family's grievin' / (FUCK 'EM!) / COP KILLER, but tonight we get even.") When the peddler of rage from the record company writes that "it doesn't incite or glorify violence," he is lying, or at least disqualifying himself from the business of music criticism. The song certainly does incite and glorify violence. If it didn't, it would be only second-rate speed-metal that nobody would buy or discuss.

Censorship Is Not an Answer

We do not believe that the record should be withdrawn from the stores, or that censorship of any kind would improve anything in any way. But the contents of American culture cannot be hidden behind the freedom of American culture. For culture brings news. Consider another song on Ice-T's record, called "Momma's Gotta Die Tonight." Here the singer tells the story of his own disgust at his own mother's hatred of white people: "She taught me hate for race. . . . She taught me bad things, 'Don't trust white people.'" The pure and sorely needed air of tolerance, it would seem—but then "mutha" rejects the singer's white girlfriend, and a rejection of racism gives way to an exaltation of murder. "I found out my mutha was an evil woman. . . . So I got some lighter fluid . . . and I set her on fire! Ha, ha, ha. Burn momma, burn momma, burn momma, burn bitch, burn, burn, burrrrn. Ha, ha, ha. Burn you racist bitch. . . ."

After which our hero grabs a carving knife and cuts her almost dead body into pieces. Is the freedom to make such a song all that needs to be remarked about it, or should we also make mention of its cynicism and its pornography of violence? Of course we must hear the news that culture brings. But then we must engage it, and challenge it, as citizens of an open society do. To defend freedom, you must also defend foulness: and then you must acknowledge that it is foulness that you are defending.

Regulation of the Press Would Be a Tragedy

by Alan Dershowitz

About the author: *Alan Dershowitz is a professor at Harvard Law School and a nationally syndicated columnist.*

The greatest danger to freedom of the press in America today is not the religious right, which has always favored censorship of erotic, blasphemous or other expressions offensive to them. Nor is it the censorial left which has recently taken to advocating censorship of "politically incorrect" speech. It is not even the Supreme Court, with its reactionary plurality that seems increasingly insensitive to liberty. The greatest danger to freedom of the press today is the press itself, especially those arrogant and irresponsible journalists and editors who use the First Amendment not as a shield against censorship, but as a sword for deliberate and reckless falsehoods.

A New Right for the Media

A generation ago the Supreme Court ruled that because the First Amendment needs breathing room, the media must be given a right never before accorded journalists and editors anywhere in the world: the right to be wrong, at least when the subject of the publication is a public figure. Thus, the media could no longer be sued successfully for libel or slander even if they said something defamatory about a public figure, so long as it was an honest mistake—a mistake that was not malicious.

In subsequent cases, the courts so narrowed the definition of what constituted "malice" that the media began to act as if they had a license to lie. It became almost impossible for any public figure—and that concept is broad indeed—to find a forum to set the record straight, to correct errors or to be compensated for losses caused by media irresponsibility. Every so often, a courageous victim of a media mugging decides to fight back. When the victims do fight back, they tend to be assaulted by the media again—this time for endangering the First Amendment.

Alan Dershowitz, "Malice and Arrogance," *The Washington Times*, September 29, 1992. Reprinted by permission of UFS, Inc.

Rarely are the media sufficiently self-critical to look into the mirror and see who is really endangering our vulnerable liberties. If the media were really concerned about preserving the First Amendment—as distinguished from protecting their own often hefty pocketbooks from compensating victims of their own abuse—they would do what every other profession has long since done: namely, establish internal procedures under which unethical members of their own profession could be challenged, disciplined and made to set the record straight.

> *"Unless the media themselves develop internal procedures for disciplining unethical journalists . . . there will be increasing pressures for governmental intervention."*

The arrogant unwillingness of the media to submit to private, internal, non-governmental self-regulation is the surest invitation to governmental intrusion and ultimately, censorship. A lawsuit in California is a case in point. A shoddy journalist named James Mills wrote a best-selling book about drug dealers titled *The Underground Empire*. The *Los Angeles Times* interviewed many of the people involved in events described in the book, and 43 of them said that what was written about them was erroneous. I reviewed the book quite critically, noting obvious inaccuracies and exaggerations.

Unethical Reporting

One of those written about by Mr. Mills was a respected Los Angeles lawyer named Barry Tarlow, who the author claimed was involved in laundering money for drug dealers. Mr. Tarlow sued and—after a five-year effort to try to prove Mr. Mills' allegation—the publisher threw in the towel and apologized to Mr. Tarlow, acknowledging that he had not engaged in "wrongful activity of any kind." In other words, Mr. Mills (or his questionable sources) had made up the whole story. The publisher also agreed to pay Mr. Tarlow a "significant" amount of money in damages. Mr. Tarlow said he would contribute some of the money to Centurion Ministries, a free investigative service for indigent inmates, and use the rest of it to buy himself a house on the ocean in Malibu to help him "erase the unpleasant memories" of the book. He also said: "Hopefully, settlements like this will force irresponsible journalists to live up to their responsibilities under the First Amendment."

"Encouraging" the Media to Be Responsible

It is too bad that it requires five-year lawsuits and significant financial settlements to encourage the media to place truth before salability and to correct errors. But until and unless the media begin to monitor [their] own dishonest and ambitious journalists, it is hard to blame those whose reputations have been unfairly trashed when they decide to fight back in the only way currently available to them—namely by bringing libel suits. Now the world knows that Barry Tarlow is an honest lawyer and that Mr. Mills is a shoddy journalist. In that respect, Mr. Tarlow's win is a victory for the marketplace of ideas.

Now it remains to be seen how the media will deal with Mr. Mills and with the hundreds of shoddy, irresponsible and dishonest journalists who abuse the freedom of the press for their own profit and self-aggrandizement. Unless the media themselves develop internal procedures for disciplining unethical journalists and for correcting errors, there will be increasing pressures for governmental intervention. And that would be a major tragedy for freedom of the press.

Free Speech Is Essential for Democratic Self-Governance

by Rodney A. Smolla

About the author: *Rodney A. Smolla is Arthur B. Hanson Professor of Law and director of the Institute of Bill of Rights Law at the College of William and Mary, Marshall-Wythe School of Law, in Williamsburg, Virginia. He is the author of several books on constitutional law.*

Free speech is an indispensable tool of self-governance in a democratic society. The Supreme Court has stated that "Whatever differences may exist about interpretations of the First Amendment, there is practically universal agreement that a major purpose of that Amendment was to protect the free discussion of governmental affairs." Justice Louis Brandeis wrote that "freedom to think as you will and to speak as you think are means indispensable to the discovery and spread of political truth."

Freedom of Speech and Self-Governance

Freedom of speech is related to self-governance in at least five ways. First, speech is a means of participation, the vehicle through which individuals debate the issues of the day, cast their votes, and actively join in the processes of decision-making that shape the polity. This participatory value, it should be emphasized, is a value focusing on the fulfillment of the individual—free speech serves the individual's right to join the political fray, to stand up and be counted, to be an active player in the democracy, not a passive spectator. The participatory interest served by freedom of speech in a democracy thus grows out of the entitlement of the citizen, not the needs of the state. Political participation is an avenue of individual fulfillment, and the dignity of the individual is enlarged by recognition of the right to participate in collective self-governance.

The second self-governance interest served by free speech is the pursuit of political truth. This interest serves both the collective and the individual, and is a derivative of the broader marketplace-of-ideas rationale. If in the long run the best test of truth is the power of the thought to gain acceptance in the competition of the market, then in the long run the best test of intelligent political policy is its power to gain acceptance at the ballot box.

Majority Rule

The third self-governance interest served by free speech is the facilitation of majority rule. This is related to the pursuit of political truth, but is less grandiose, emphasizing instead the importance of speech as a means of ensuring that collective policy-making represents, to the greatest degree possible, the collective will. As constitutional scholar Alexander Bickel asserted, the value of free speech is that "the country may better be able to adopt the course of action that conforms to the wishes of the greatest number, whether or not it is wise or founded in truth."

A fourth self-governance interest served by free speech is the restraint on tyranny, corruption, and ineptitude. For most of the world's history the state has presumed to play the role of benevolent but firm censor, on the theory that the wise governance of men proceeds from the wise governance of their opinions. But the United States was founded on the more cantankerous revolutionary principles of John Locke, who taught that under the social compact ultimate sovereignty always rests with the people, who never surrender their natural right to protest, or even revolt, when the state exceeds the limits of legitimate authority. Locke cautioned, however, that rebellion, particularly violent rebellion, should be only a last and desperate resort. It is through nonviolent speech that the people may ferret out corruption and discourage tyrannical excesses, keeping government within the metes and bounds of the charter through which the people first brought it into existence.

The fifth self-governance value served by free speech is stability. Ironically, democratic values and openness values are at times in conflict. For while openness is an aid to democracy, the democratic process will on occasion produce majority decisions that squelch the speech of the minority. When this conflict of values occurs, a society will be both more stable and more free in the long run if openness values prevail. This is an extremely difficult principle to accept. Why shouldn't the concept of majority rule always prevail in a democracy, even on questions of freedom of expression? How can protecting a minority viewpoint against the wishes of the majority actually be better for stability and order?

> *"Free speech serves the individual's right . . . to be an active player in the democracy, not a passive spectator."*

No better answer has ever been supplied than the words of Justice Louis Brandeis, who wrote that the framers of the Constitution "knew that order can-

not be secured merely through fear of punishment for its infraction; that it is hazardous to discourage thought, hope and imagination; that fear breeds repression; that repression breeds hate; that hate menaces stable government; that the path of safety lies in the opportunity to discuss freely supposed grievances and proposed remedies; and that the fitting remedy for evil counsels is good ones." If societies are not to explode from festering tensions, there must be valves through which the citizens may blow off steam. Openness fosters resiliency; peaceful protest displaces more violence than it triggers; free debate dissipates more hate than it stirs.

Those Who Doubt

There are, of course, respected scholars who doubt the validity of these rationales. Judge Robert Bork, for example, agrees that political speech deserves special First Amendment protection, but on the very narrowest of grounds. Judge Bork does not accept individual self-fulfillment, even when related to political participation, as an adequate basis for treating speech as a preferred value. As to the capacity of speech to promote political stability, he argues that this benefit merely raises questions of expediency that are for the political branches to resolve. Political speech advocating the overthrow of the government—even in abstract generalities—is not protected, because it cannot contribute to self-governance.

"Peaceful protest displaces more violence than it triggers; free debate dissipates more hate than it stirs."

For Judge Bork, whether it is a good or bad idea to let the citizenry "blow off steam" in the interest of stability is simply a question of peacekeeping strategy for the government, not a right of the citizen. Yet even a scholar with as limited a conception of free speech as Judge Bork is willing to concede that free speech contributes to democratic self-governance in ways that justify placing at least some types of expression on a pedestal of heightened constitutional protection—and while on the bench he at times wrote opinions that granted generous protection to political free expression.

There is, indeed, virtually unanimous endorsement of the proposition that the relationship of free speech to self-governance is a major justification for treating free speech as a preferred constitutional value. The controversy over this rationale centers on whether it should be regarded as the *exclusive* basis for elevated protection for speech.

Some argue that somehow nonpolitical speech topics do not really count—at least not enough to merit any unique constitutional protection. Because political speech is vital to a democratic society, it is treated as the only speech meriting heightened protection. But this is illogical and unconvincing. There are at least four sound reasons to treat self-governance as *a* rationale for specially protected speech, but not as *the exclusive* rationale.

153

First, no one maintains that nonpolitical speech is intrinsically less valuable than political speech. No serious student of free speech has ever been so unimaginative as to argue that nonpolitical topics of human inquiry and expression are not an essential part of what makes life worth living. Those who created the First Amendment may not have left us with any precise definition of "freedom of speech," but they certainly did leave us with marvelous examples of how rich and eclectic intellectual life can be. Theirs were renaissance minds, engaged by science, art, literature, philosophy, morality, religion, architecture, horticulture, law, business, and politics. A culture that treats politics as somehow more vital than art, science, sex, or religion is a culture with an intellectual landscape that is barren, sterile, and gray, probably designed by bureaucrats and tended by lawyers. The Sunday *New York Times* is more than the government and op-ed sections; only the most crimped and niggardly understanding of free expression would treat those sections alone as worthy of the protection of the First Amendment. Chief Justice Earl Warren was fond of explaining that he always read the sports pages first, for it is on the sports pages that man's achievements are recorded; the news pages merely record man's failures.

Free Speech Is an Individual Right

Second, there is no logic *internal* to the self-governance theory that demands exclusivity. Nothing in the self-governance rationale "knocks out" the marketplace of ideas rationale or the self-fulfillment rationale. Nothing in those theories is limited to politics. The collective search for truth and the individual quest for intellectual fulfillment embrace the full life of the mind. Indeed, the argument that the self-governance theory is alone a sufficient justification for heightened protection for speech is linked to an exceedingly narrow view of the self-governance theory itself—the view that it derives from the needs of the state alone. But free speech is also an individual right standing on its own foundation, serving the citizen's interests in participation, truth-seeking, and checking official abuse of power. There is, in sum, nothing *inside* the self-governance theory that disqualifies the marketplace or fulfillment theories, and nothing *outside* those two theories that limits them to self-governance issues.

> *"The relationship of free speech to self-governance is a major justification for treating free speech as a preferred constitutional value."*

Third, even when considered on its own terms, the self-governance theory proves incapable of supporting a principled limitation to conventional "political" speech, because in modern life it is virtually impossible to identify any topic that might not bear some relation to self-governance. Those who advocate limiting First Amendment protection to political speech are usually inclined to soften that position by admitting the need to protect a wider circle of speech to provide a "buffer zone" for political speech, because it is so difficult to extract the political from the nonpolitical. Theorists who advocate relatively narrow protection for "political speech" are, in fact, plagued by a certain "rebound effect" that inevitably accompanies their general willingness to apply a lax "reasonableness" test in measuring the constitutionality of most speech regulation. The more that they emphasize how nonpolitical speech should be subject to the routine "reasonable basis" tests applicable to routine governmental regulation of most of the affairs of life, the more they highlight how virtually all affairs of life are relevant to self-government. They cannot have it both ways. Government has "reasonabled" its way into regulating most aspects of economic and social life; a ubiquitous cover of "reasonable" law envelops modern existence like a *Bleak House* fog. If laws get passed on all aspects of culture, then it is vital that freedom of speech extend to all aspects of law. Even in those rare cases in which law has not yet permeated some nook or cranny of life, free speech is still essential to self-governance, to enable the citizenry to debate intelligently whether to permit the law's entry.

> *"In modern life it is virtually impossible to identify any topic that might not bear some relation to self-governance."*

"Hard-Core" Political Speech

The fate of Alexander Meiklejohn's attempts to hold the line on a narrow conception of political speech is illustrative. Meiklejohn's influential 1948 book *Free Speech and Its Relation to Self-Government* began with a narrow definition of relatively "hard-core" political speech. The view was sharply criticized by, among others, Zechariah Chafee, another enormously important figure in the free speech tradition, and Meiklejohn retreated. In 1961, Meiklejohn conceded that "there are many forms of thought and expression within the range of human communications from which the voter derives knowledge, intelligence, sensitivity to human values: the capacity for sane and objective judgment which, so far as possible, the ballot should express." For Meiklejohn these included "education, in all its phases," the "achievements of philosophy and the sciences in creating knowledge and understanding of men," "literature and the arts," and "public discussions of public issues." This later Meiklejohn view gave away most of the store, and rendered his self-governance theory almost indistinguishable from the marketplace and self-fulfillment rationales.

Fourth, there is a dangerous habit of mind that permeates efforts to treat political speech alone as meriting exalted First Amendment status, a combination of statism and elitism that sends the message: "Only that speech useful to the enterprise of government will be granted special protection by the government, and it will be for the government to define what is useful." One of Alexander Meiklejohn's most famous statements in *Free Speech and Its Relation to Self-Government* was "What is essential is not that everyone shall speak but that everything worth saying shall be said." Meiklejohn could not have been more wrong.

To the individual seeking the catharsis, fulfillment, and participation that comes from free expression, it *is* important that *he* be heard, even if only to second another's views. More profoundly, the state lacks the moral entitlement to presume to dictate what is "worth saying" and when "everything worth saying" has been said. Meiklejohn improperly drew his model of free speech from the town meeting. In a *meeting*, of course, some rules of order are needed, and moderators may need to draw discussions to an end when it appears that all viewpoints have been heard, even though some hands may still be waving, seeking recognition.

First Amendment Principles

But the general marketplace of discourse is *not* a massive town meeting, and government is not empowered to act as a pandemic moderator. Outside special settings in which the "meeting" analogy is appropriate, the Meiklejohn thesis puts the government in precisely the position that First Amendment doctrines should be designed to prohibit. There may, of course, be instances in which speech is not part of the general marketplace of discourse, but rather takes place in unique settings in which lower levels of First Amendment protection should apply. In those settings, which represent situations that are outside normal First Amendment principles, it may often be that what is important

> *"The state lacks the moral entitlement to presume to dictate what is 'worth saying.'"*

is that everything relevant be said, and not that everyone be heard. The First Amendment must be adjusted in a courtroom or a classroom, for example. Judges must have the power to determine what evidence is relevant and what is repetitious, and teachers the power to decide when to draw discussions to a close. Under Meiklejohn's theory, however, the government would retain this power even in the general marketplace of discourse—a power that cannot be reconciled with the values of a truly open culture.

Self-governance . . . is an important justification for free speech, but it is by no means exclusive. The Supreme Court, quite wisely, has declined the invitation to limit First Amendment protection to political speech. While recognizing in many cases that political speech lies at the core of the First Amendment, it has nevertheless insisted that the "guarantees for speech and press are not the preserve of political expression or comment upon public affairs, essential as those are to healthy government." The Court has declared that the free speech and free press guarantees "are not confined to any field of human interest," and that it is "immaterial whether the beliefs sought to be advanced . . . pertain to political, economic, religious or cultural matters."

Begging Should Receive Free Speech Protection

by Helen Hershkoff and Adam S. Cohen

About the authors: *Helen Hershkoff is associate legal director of the American Civil Liberties Union. Adam S. Cohen is staff attorney of the American Civil Liberties Union.*

Three competing but interrelated values have guided courts and commentators in their interpretation of the first amendment: enlightenment, democratic governance, and self-realization. . . . Begging advances each of these values. . . . If the fit between begging and these values seems inexact, the inexactness stems from an insufficient regard for the economic constraints on the ways in which the poor can and do express themselves.

The Enlightenment Value

Perhaps the most time-honored value underlying freedom of expression is the notion that truth emerges from the free exchange of information and ideas. Judge Learned Hand stated that the first amendment "presupposes that the right conclusions are more likely to be gathered out of a multitude of tongues, than through any kind of authoritative selection." The enlightenment value is avowedly instrumentalist: it holds that free expression "is not only an aspect of individual liberty—and thus a good unto itself—but also is essential to the common quest for truth and the vitality of society as a whole" [*Bose Corp. v. Consumers Union of United States*, 1984]. It maintains that free expression helps to resolve society's public questions as well as an individual's private choices.

Begging is speech that adds to both societal and individual enlightenment: it provides information about poverty and the lives of poor people. . . .

The beggar informs the listener that there are people in his community who need help. This information will have different significance to different people. The beggar's words may provide some listeners with an occasion for self-inquiry. Their thoughts may range from guilt over the degree to which they are complicit

From Helen Hershkoff and Adam S. Cohen, "Begging to Differ: The First Amendment and the Right to Beg," *Harvard Law Review* 104 (February 1991): 896-916, © 1991 by The Harvard Law Review Association. Reprinted with permission of the authors and the *Harvard Law Review*.

in the beggar's impoverished state to fear that they themselves may one day be destitute. The beggar's plea may also provide some people with a moral touchstone with which to judge their friends and neighbors. The beggar makes a public demand on those whom she addresses, and people may learn things about others by watching their response—or lack of response—to such entreaties. Finally, the beggar's words may provide some listeners with information on which they will want to act. Many of the world's major religions—and many secular ethicists— hold that there is a duty to give money to people in need. Beggars provide information that enables listeners to fulfill such moral obligations.

The primary argument that begging does not advance enlightenment is that it is a request for money rather than the communication of an idea or information. The truth, of course is that it is both. The Supreme Court has recognized that speech is neither unenlightening nor unprotected simply because the speaker speaks to obtain money. The first amendment fully protects various forms of entertainment, such as movies and television, even if motivated largely by commercial gain. The beggar's speech, like expression sold for profit, remains enlightening despite its pecuniary purpose. . . .

The Democratic Governance Value

A second value underlying the first amendment is the role of expression in promoting democratic governance. As set out by its primary architect, Alexander Meiklejohn, the democratic governance theory holds that the democratic order is akin to a town meeting in which people "meet as political equals" and have a "right and a duty to think [their] own thoughts, to express them, and to listen to the arguments of others." Speech in this model has value because "[t]he welfare of the community requires that those who decide issues shall understand them." All facts and arguments relevant to governance aid such understanding.

Begging, by alerting listeners to the conditions and existence of poverty and deprivation, is speech that helps society's decisionmakers. Every society must decide how and to what extent it will ensure the survival of its members. Begging provides facts about those who believe that they cannot obtain subsistence through the existing social structure. Prohibitions on begging deny decisionmakers the opportunity to make a fully informed choice on this question.

Begging also offers decisionmakers a more theoretical critique of society. Many view the American social order as built on the principle of individualism. Thus, citizens currently have no

> *"The beggar informs the listener that there are people in his community who need help."*

legally recognized right against the state or their fellow citizens for subsistence. Begging challenges both these legal rules and the assumptions underlying them. Understood most simply, the beggar's plea demands that other people ensure her survival. More broadly, the beggar implicitly proposes a communitarian vision in which citizens have a responsibility for each other's survival, a perspective that an informed decisionmaker should consider. . . .

Self-Realization

A third value that underlies the first amendment is individual self-realization. Zechariah Chafee described this value as people's need "to express their opinions on matters vital to them if life is to be worth living." The self-realization value recognizes that speech gives voice to "a [human] spirit that demands self-expression" and provides a medium for fulfilling "the basic human desire for recognition" [Justice Thurgood Marshall].

> *"If the first amendment protects the right to say what is on one's mind, surely begging promotes this self-realization value."*

Our society acknowledges that the human spirit expresses itself in a broad range of ways that we must protect. The Supreme Court has held that the words "Fuck the Draft" affixed to a jacket are protected because of the wearer's need to "express himself." If the first amendment protects the right to say what is on one's mind, surely begging promotes this self-realization value. The beggar speaks to express the thought that is foremost in her mind: that she is destitute and needs help. That the statement may not provide a "dispassionate contribution to intellectual dialogue" is irrelevant from the perspective of this value, which by its terms must accord commensurate respect to even a mere "cry of impulse" [L. Tribe, *American Constitutional Law*]. The principle of self-realization, grounded on "the premise of individual dignity and choice" [*Cohen v. California*, 1971], requires that each individual be allowed to experience the self-respect that comes from free expression. We deny the beggar this most basic level of recognition if we refuse to let her make her plea.

The beggar's words also help her to subsist, and this strengthens the self-realization value of her speech. Commentators have recognized the role of property in delineating an autonomous space between the individual and the government. The beggar's words help her to build a bulwark against the government and to achieve independence. Her attempt to enlist others in her cause is a basic form of self-realizing speech.

Flag Burning Should Receive Free Speech Protection

by Michael Kinsley

About the author: *Michael Kinsley is senior editor of* The New Republic *magazine.*

Aren't you embarrassed? Weary and embarrassed? [In 1990], for the third consecutive summer, we're shouting at one another about the flag. Senator Orrin Hatch says that a nation that doesn't "protect" its flag (from what?) is surely on the decline. The truth is surely the opposite: only a nation feeling insecure about itself and its place in the world would succumb repeatedly to such a frenzy of self-righteousness about the national banner.

But supporters of a constitutional amendment to ban flag burning see it as a way of reviving the anti-liberal Kulturkampf that has been so effective in recent years. And opponents of such an amendment keep struggling because . . . because . . . why? Only William Safire (and it's easy for him, as a conservative) has had the courage to criticize "flag worship" as such. Most opponents are zealous to emphasize their own love for the flag and hatred of flag burners.

A Disingenuous Debate

In fact, the whole debate has become deeply disingenuous. It would be an awfully staunch Democrat who didn't secretly curse the Supreme Court for not avoiding this problem by finding a tiny exception in the First Amendment. And it would be an awfully principled Republican who is not secretly grateful to have this alleged travesty to decry.

And yet some politicians, mostly Democrats, resist the flag amendment. Why? This is a question every supporter of the amendment should be forced to answer. What do they think is the motive of opponents? God knows there is no political advantage to be gained. Is it a matter of insufficient love for the flag?

From Michael Kinsley, "Stars and Snipes," *The New Republic*, July 9 & 16, 1990. Reprinted by permission of *The New Republic*, © 1990, The New Republic, Inc.

If opponents merely didn't care about the flag, didn't love it enough, they would hardly risk their necks opposing a law to protect it. Either opponents of the amendment must actively hate the flag and *want* to see it burned—something supporters like to imply but is too preposterous to say outright—or they are at worst guilty of a mistaken stand on principle: they love freedom too much. Which is it? . . .

Robert Bork, in his book *The Tempting of America*, opines that anti-flag-desecration laws are aimed at proscribing not "the idea expressed" but only "the mode of expression."

The Government's Purpose

The speech/conduct distinction is a staple of First Amendment theological debate. The question usually is how much the government can infringe expressive conduct while serving some legitimate purpose having nothing to do with what is being expressed. For example, can it ban all leafleting in the name of reducing litter? The courts would probably say no. On the other hand, it can forbid the use of bullhorns in the middle of the night.

As constitutional scholar John Hart Ely has explained, every act of communication—even talking, even writing, even semaphore (flags)—is both speech and conduct. What matters is the government's purpose in proscribing the conduct. Is it to curtail expression? In this case, clearly yes, though the past year has seen vast amounts of brainpower expended denying the obvious. You cannot separate the message from its "mode of expression"; it is precisely the extra punch provided by this particular mode of expression that leads people to want to make it unavailable.

The four dissenters in *U.S.* v. *Eichman*, [1990's] Supreme Court flag-burning opinion, miss the point here. They note that burning the flag may convey any number of messages, and they reason: "Thus, the government may . . . protect the symbolic value of the flag without regard to the specific content of the flag burners' speech." But whatever the message may be, it is a message of dissent from that symbolic value. If a flag is burned in secret, that is no threat to the flag's symbolic value. It is only when a flag burner is communicating a message that the flag's symbolic value is in any way affected.

> *"Every act of communication . . . is both speech and conduct."*

George Will argues that all nine justices share "the mistaken belief that 'symbolic expression' is tantamount to speech." There is nothing wrong with "limiting particular forms of expression to protect particular ideas," he writes, because "the Constitution mandates agnosticism only about religious, not political, ideas." The Framers said "speech," not "expression," because "speech is intrinsically connected with reason."

I had a law school professor who used to greet arguments like this with a magnificent shrug and a wry, "Well, I hear the words. . . ." No one doubts that the government can promote civic virtue by engaging in communication of its own. But can it do so by prohibiting communication that it regards as unvirtuous? And if the purpose is protecting the party line, why are we placing our anathema on what Will regards as the *least* powerful forms of communication—mere "symbolic expression"—rather than the most powerful: speech itself? (That's just a rhetorical point—not a suggestion!)

Dissenting in last year's flag case, Chief Justice [William] Rehnquist denied that flag burning communicates anything at all. "Flag burning is the equivalent of an inarticulate grunt or roar." If so, the same is true of flag flying. One message of flag burning is: whatever you mean by flying the flag, I mean the opposite.

Chapter 4

Should Pornography Be Censored?

CURRENT CONTROVERSIES

Debate over Pornography: An Overview

by John Elson

About the author: *John Elson is a regular contributor to* Time *magazine.*

Is pornography essentially an outlet for sexual fantasy, rightly protected by the First Amendment's free speech provisions? Or is it an instruction manual for violent men that shatters women's civil rights by contributing to their harassment, humiliation and subordination? Those questions are at the heart of an often acrimonious debate that has divided feminists and civil libertarians across the U.S.

The argument is currently raging on three fronts:

• In Massachusetts, feminist groups can be found on both sides of the debate over a proposed bill that would allow individuals who can prove that they were assaulted as a result of pornography—defined as a form of sexual discrimination—to recover damages in civil court from publishers and purveyors of the material.

• In Florida, Jacksonville Shipyards is appealing the January 1991 ruling by a federal judge that a welder named Lois Robinson was harassed by male co-workers who put up graphically sexual posters and calendars, some showing women being abused. Among the offensive materials was a poster with a frontal view of a nude woman and the imprinted words USDA CHOICE. One surprising supporter of the appeal: the American Civil Liberties Union, which also opposes the Massachusetts bill.

• In Washington, the Senate Judiciary Committee is considering S 1521, introduced last year by Kentucky Republican Mitch McConnell, which would allow victims of sex crimes to sue the producers, distributors and sellers of obscene material and child pornography if the victims can prove that the material was a "substantial cause" of the injury. Some have informally dubbed McConnell's proposal "the Bundy bill," after serial killer Ted Bundy, who claimed just before his execution that pornography had fueled his violent fantasies.

The co-authors of the Massachusetts bill are the odd couple of American feminism. Michigan law professor Catharine MacKinnon is sleek and stylishly dressed-for-success. Writer Andrea Dworkin (*Pornography: Men Possessing Women* and *Intercourse*), with her tousled hair and overalls-and-T-shirt décor, looks like a radical from the '60s.

The two activists have been campaigning in tandem against pornography since the early '80s; city ordinances they devised for Minneapolis, Indianapolis and Bellingham, Wash., all similar to the Massachusetts bill, were rejected by courts or local officials. Their basic argument is that Supreme Court rulings on obscenity, meaning prurient material that offends community standards, provide no impediment to the increasing violence directed against women. Much of that violence, they argue, has been inspired by pornography, which their bill defines as "the graphic, sexually explicit subordination of women through pictures or words."

"Pornography currently has more protection than women do," MacKinnon told the statehouse committee considering the Massachusetts bill. In corroboration, several witnesses gave chilling testimony of being sexually abused by husbands and boyfriends who admitted that they had been prompted by porn films or magazines. Fighting back tears, Pat Haas, of Brookline, Mass., said she had been beaten by her boyfriend, who forced her to act out scenes from pornography. "He did what was in the movies," says Haas. "If he had seen a snuff film, I wouldn't be here." Under the proposed antipornography civil rights

> *"Supreme Court rulings on obscenity . . . provide no impediment to the increasing violence directed against women."*

bill, victims like Haas could sue the pornographers for being indirectly responsible for the crime.

That burden shifting bothers many civil rights activists who otherwise care deeply about violence against women and children. "We feel this bill is censorship," says Marilyn Fitterman of the New York State chapter of the National Organization for Women. "It takes the onus off the criminal and blames the publishers and artists." Nancy Ryan of the Cambridge women's commission, which opposed a similar measure introduced in that Boston suburb, argues that "the men who did these acts would have done them without pornography." Others contend that the evidence linking pornography to systematic violence is more anecdotal than statistically solid.

The A.C.L.U. opposes the Massachusetts initiative for much the same reason it argued against previous MacKinnon-Dworkin bills. Pornography no doubt causes harm, says Burt Neuborne, the union's former national legal director. But to suppress it, under First Amendment rules, "you have to show, in addition to the harm, that there is no other societal way of dealing with a problem than censorship. Here, the current bills fail."

The internal debate within the A.C.L.U. on the Florida case was, in the words of an insider, "fairly acrimonious." Many women members believe that by filing an amicus curiae brief in support of the shipyard, the organization displayed insensitivity to the intimidating effect that pornography has on women in predominantly male environments. "The workplace is different from the street," contends Mary Ellen Gale, a Whittier College law professor and member of the A.C.L.U.'s national board. "If someone shouts an obscenity on the street, you're not captive and you're not being denied equal opportunity. But it's different when it happens in the workplace. Robinson's ability to do her job was affected."

Other A.C.L.U. officials readily concede that Robinson was sexually harassed by lewd comments of male welders and X-rated scrawling in her work area. But they argue that U.S. District Judge Howell Melton went too far in responding to the complaint. Robyn Blumner, executive director of the Florida A.C.L.U., argues that Melton's sweeping order, which barred male workers from bringing sexually suggestive materials to work, would have applied as readily to a newspaper brassiere ad as to the crude posters that offended Robinson. Beyond that, she says, Melton's ruling that workers cannot even possess the pornographic calendars clearly violates their First Amendment rights. (One quirk of the case: by shipyard practice, employees could not bring newspapers or magazines to work—but the pornography was O.K.)

MacKinnon, Dworkin and the A.C.L.U. all have qualms about the Senate's so-called Bundy bill, although for different reasons. The two feminists contend that since the proposed legislation narrowly bans only "obscenity"—which is not protected by the First Amendment, courts have ruled—this restriction may prove to be legally counterproductive. "If pornography is excessively violent," Dworkin explains, "very often a jury will find that it's not obscene because it's not sexually arousing."

As for the A.C.L.U., it considers the bill a dangerous threat to the First Amendment. So does an Ad Hoc Committee of Feminists for Free Expression, whose members include such noted writers as Betty Friedan, Nora Ephron and Erica Jong. In a Valentine's Day letter to the Judiciary Committee, the group argued that S 1521 is a "logical and legal muddle" that "scapegoats speech as a substitute for action against violence" and "reinforces the 'porn made me do it' excuse for rapists and batterers."

MacKinnon and Dworkin believe theirs is an idea whose time has come at last. As evidence, they can cite last month's unanimous ruling by Canada's Supreme Court—endorsing MacKinnon's argument—that pornography harmful to women can be outlawed even though freedom of expression is infringed. Cass Sunstein, a professor of constitutional law at the University of Chicago, notes that the courts have carved out numerous exceptions to the First Amendment; for example, it does

> *"[Judge] Melton's ruling that workers cannot even possess the pornographic calendars clearly violates their First Amendment rights."*

166

not protect bribes, fraud, threats or conspiracy.

True enough, First Amendment defenders answer, but the MacKinnon-Dworkin approach may be a cure worse than the disease. On dubious evidence, they say, the antiporn bills take aim at a secondary cause of female subordination and ignore the reality that woman-hating psychopaths have more often cited the Bible as inspiration. Beyond that, advocates of the antiporn bills seem blithely indifferent to the crippling cultural impact of legislation that places so much emphasis on the subjective views of crime victims. Porn, like beauty, may be in the beholder's eye. But it is a bad perspective for building good law.

Pornography Debases Women and Should Be Censored

by Andrea Dworkin

About the author: *Andrea Dworkin is the author of* Intercourse, Pornography: Men Possessing Women, *the novel* Mercy, *and other books. She is co-author with Catharine A. MacKinnon of a law recognizing pornography as a violation of the civil rights of women.*

The word *pornography*, derived from the ancient Greek *porne* and *graphos*, means "writing about whores." *Porne* means "whore," specifically and exclusively the lowest class of whore, which in ancient Greece was the brothel slut available to all male citizens. The *porne* was the cheapest (in the literal sense), least regarded, least protected of all women, including slaves. She was, simply and clearly and absolutely, a sexual slave. *Graphos* means "writing, etching or drawing."

Meaning of Pornography

The word *pornography* does not mean "writing about sex" or "depictions of the erotic" or "depictions of sexual acts" or "depictions of nude bodies" or "sexual representations" or any other such euphemism. It means the graphic depiction of women as vile whores. In ancient Greece, not all prostitutes were considered vile: only the *porneia*.

Contemporary pornography strictly and literally conforms to the word's root meaning: the graphic depiction of vile whores, or, in our language, sluts, cows (as in sexual cattle, sexual chattel), cunts. The word has not changed its meaning and the genre is not misnamed. The only change in the meaning of the word is with respect to its second part, *graphos*: now there are cameras—there is still photography, film, video. The methods of graphic depiction have increased in number and in kind: the content is the same; the meaning is the same; the purpose is the same; the status of the women depicted is the same; the sexuality of the women depicted is the same; the value of the women depicted is the same. With the technologically advanced methods of graphic depiction, real women are required for the depiction as such to exist.

Degrading to Women

The word *pornography* does not have any other meaning than the one cited here, the graphic depiction of the lowest whores. Whores exist to serve men sexually. Whores exist only within a framework of male sexual domination. Indeed, outside that framework the notion of whores would be absurd and the usage of women as whores would be impossible. The word *whore* is incomprehensible unless one is immersed in the lexicon of male domination. Men have created the group, the type, the concept, the epithet, the insult, the industry, the trade, the commodity, the reality of woman as whore. Woman as whore exists within the objective and real system of male sexual domination. The pornography itself is objective and real and central to the male sexual system. The valuation of women's sexuality in pornography is objective and real because women are so regarded and so valued. The force depicted in pornography is objective and real because force is so used against women. The debasing of women depicted in pornography and intrinsic to it is objective and real in that women are so debased. The uses of women depicted in pornography are objective and real because women are so used. The women used in pornography are used in pornography. The definition of women articulated systematically and consistently in pornography is objective and real in that real women exist within and must live with constant reference to the boundaries of this definition. The fact that pornography is widely believed to be "sexual representations" or "depictions of sex" emphasizes only that the valuation of women as low whores is widespread and that the sexuality of women is perceived as low and whorish in and of itself. The fact that pornography is widely believed to be "depictions of the erotic" means only that the debasing of women is held to be the real pleasure of sex. As Kate Millet wrote, women's sexuality is reduced to the one essential: "cunt . . . our essence, our offense" (Kate Millet, *The Prostitution Papers*). The idea that pornography is "dirty" originates in the conviction that the sexuality of women is dirty and is actually portrayed in pornography; that women's bodies (especially women's genitals) are dirty and lewd in themselves. Pornography does not, as some claim, refute the idea that female sexuality is dirty; instead, pornography embodies and exploits this idea; pornography sells and promotes it.

> *"Woman as whore exists within the objective and real system of male sexual domination."*

In the United States, the pornography industry is larger than the record and film industries combined. In a time of widespread economic impoverishment, it is growing; more and more male consumers are eager to spend more and more money on pornography—on depictions of women as vile whores. Pornography is now carried by cable television; it is now being marketed for home use in video machines. The technology itself demands the creation of more and more *porneia* to meet the market opened up by the technology. Real women are tied up, stretched, hanged, fucked, gang-banged, whipped, beaten, and begging for more. In the photographs

> *"The power of men in pornography is imperial power, the power of the sovereigns who are cruel and arrogant."*

and films, real women are used as *porneia* and real women are depicted as *porneia*. To profit, pimps must supply the *porneia* as the technology widens the market for the visual consumption of women being brutalized and loving it. One picture is worth a thousand words. The number of pictures required to meet the demands of the marketplace determines the number of *porneia* required to meet the demands of graphic depiction. The numbers grow as the technology and its accessibility grow. The technology by its very nature encourages more and more passive acquiescence to the graphic depictions. Passivity makes the already credulous consumer more credulous. He comes to the pornography a believer; he goes away from it a missionary. The technology itself legitimizes the uses of women conveyed by it.

In the male system, women are sex; sex is the whore. The whore is *porne*, the lowest whore, the whore who belongs to *all* male citizens: the slut, the cunt. Buying her is buying pornography. Having her is having pornography. Seeing her is seeing pornography. Seeing her sex, especially her genitals, is seeing pornography. Seeing her in sex is seeing the whore in sex. Using her is using pornography. Wanting her means wanting pornography. Being her means being pornography.

In the system of male sexual domination explicated in pornography, there is no way out, no redemption; not through desire, not through reproduction.

The woman's sex is appropriated, her body is possessed, she is used and she is despised; the pornography does it and the pornography proves it.

The power of men in pornography is imperial power, the power of the sovereigns who are cruel and arrogant, who keep taking and conquering for the pleasure of power and the power of pleasure.

Women are the land, as Marcuse wrote. He did not write the rest: men are the army; penises and their symbolic representations are the weapons; terror is the means; violence is the so-called sex. And inside this system, women are *porneia*, in our real live bodies the graphic depictions of whores, used as whores are used, valued as whores are valued.

True Freedom

We will know that we are free when the pornography no longer exists. As long as it does exist, we must understand that we are the women in it; used by the same power, subject to the same valuation, as the vile whores who beg for more.

The boys are betting on our compliance, our ignorance, our fear. We have always refused to face the worst that men have done to us. The boys count on it. The boys are betting that we cannot face the horror of their sexual system and survive. The boys are betting that their depictions of us as whores will beat us down and stop our hearts. The boys are betting that their penises and fists and knives and fucks and rapes will turn us into what they say we are—the compliant women of sex, the voracious cunts of pornography, the masochistic sluts who resist because we really want more. The boys are betting. The boys are wrong.

The First Amendment Does Not Protect Pornography

by Patty McEntee

About the author: *Patty McEntee is a member of Morality In Media, Inc., a nonprofit, interfaith, national organization working to keep pornography from being protected by the First Amendment.*

On a typical day in New York City, my senses are assaulted by pornographic material almost continuously. On my way to work, I pass newstands with racks of porn magazines, one more explicit than the next. I pick up a newspaper and flip past advertisements for dial-a-porn "services," erotic dancing clubs and video stores with "adult" sections. Small cards advertising dial-a-porn are occasionally scattered all over the sidewalk or placed on car windshields. When I turn on the television, I may come across a talk show host respectfully interviewing porn movie "actresses" or the producers of the homemade porn movies that are now on the shelves of my local video store. Every so often, the mailman delivers an unsolicited envelope of full-color ads for the latest porn videos that are now available through the mail.

Available in Neighborhoods

While not all this material is available in every neighborhood, hi-tech advances have made it almost impossible to shield oneself completely from the pornography industry and its products. What's more, newscasts regularly interview distributors who claim it is their right to display and promote the sale of these items. But whose rights are at stake here? Most Americans get only one side of the story and are repeatedly fed the clichés and distortions of the very people profiting from pornography. So, let's take a look at "censorship," the First Amendment, pornography and obscenity.

If I refuse to shop in my neighborhood stationery store because it sells pornographic magazines, am I a "censor"? If Morality In Media (MIM) encourages citizens to urge their district attorney to enforce their state's obscenity law, is it

From Patty McEntee, "Is Pornography a Matter of Free Expression?" *America*, August 10, 1991. Reprinted by permission of Patty McEntee Knap.

guilty of "censorship"? Although it may surprise some people, the answer is no. The word censorship has been misused ad nauseam. Censorship is *prior* restraint *by government* of freedom of speech or the press.

Although civil libertarians may not like to say so, the First Amendment is not without limits. Obscenity, slander, libel, perjury, inciting a riot and false advertising are not within the area of constitutionally protected speech or freedom of the press.

> *"The First Amendment is not without limits."*

"Pornography" is a generic term that includes both hardcore and softcore porn. "Obscenity" is the legal term for "hardcore" pornography, and obscenity is not protected by the First Amendment. Another legal term is "indecency," and it is prohibited in broadcasting (radio and television). The Federal Communications Commission (F.C.C.) has defined indecency as "language or material that depicts or describes, in terms patently offensive as measured by contemporary community standards for the broadcast medium, sexual or excretory activities or organs."

The F.C.C. has also imposed fines on those who broadcast indecency. This 24-hour ban on indecency was, however, challenged in the Federal Court of Appeals in Washington, D.C., by the American Civil Liberties Union, People for the American Way, the television networks and a group ironically calling itself "Action for Children's Television." Morality In Media believes, on the contrary, that the potential flow of indecent broadcasts into the nation's living rooms is a great threat to the country's moral well-being. If the 24-hour indecency ban is struck down, television depictions of oral sex, sodomy, orgies, sadomasochism and bestiality could become commonplace by the turn of the century.

Supreme Court Rulings

According to the U.S. Supreme Court, materials or performances are "obscene" if: a) taken as a whole, they appeal to the prurient interest; b) depict or describe in a patently offensive manner sexual conduct specifically defined, or c) taken as a whole, lack serious literary, artistic, political or scientific value. Obscenity may apply to magazines, videos, dial-a-porn, cableporn or live performances.

Throughout our history, the Supreme Court, no matter whether characterized as conservative, moderate or liberal, has held that obscenity is not protected by the First Amendment. In 1973, the Court stated: "We hold that there are legitimate state interests at stake in stemming the tide of commercialized obscenity. . . . These include the interest of the public in the quality of life and the total community environment, . . . and, possibly, the public safety itself. . . . There is a 'right of the nation and the states to maintain a decent society.'. . . The sum of experience, including that of the past two decades, affords an ample basis for legislatures to conclude that a sensitive, key relationship of human existence, central to family

173

life, community welfare and the development of the human personality, can be debased and distorted by crass commercial exploitation of sex."

In recent years, Federal law enforcement against illegal pornography (obscenity) has increased substantially. Major law enforcement efforts are still needed, however, at the state or local (district attorney) level. Nor are these the only effective measures that can be taken. Meetings with store owners, picketing, public seminars to educate the community and counseling groups for pornography addicts and their wives are also useful. These efforts may be labeled "censorship" by those who don't know what censorship is or who want to confuse the public. But does not our freedom as persons and citizens include the right to try to influence others for good, the right to rebel against total decadence and the right to preserve our cherished Judeo-Christian values? Is it not our *right* to protect our children from sexual abuse and exploitation? Have we not the *right* to try to create safer and more decent communities for these children? It sometimes seems, however, that the right to raise children has taken a back seat to the so-called "right" to distribute hardcore pornography despite a local community's protests.

Studies indicate that porn addicts are 40 percent more likely to commit a sex crime than non-addicts, but these are not the only damages that pornography inflicts on our society. Men addicted to porn lose faith in marriage and commitment and are more likely to have extramarital affairs or to visit prostitutes. They think convicted rapists should be given lighter sentences and they persuade themselves that sexual perversions are more common than is the fact ("Everyone's doing it"). Not surprisingly, the marriages of these men often end in divorce.

[Former] attorney general Richard Thornburgh said that enforcement of pornography laws would be one of his top five priorities, but the battle continues. Pornography is still a business that makes from $9 billion to $10 billion annually in the United States. It is the third largest profit maker for organized crime after drugs and gambling. As federal judge Jose Gonzales remarked in the obscenity trial of the 2 Live Crew rap group: "This is a case between two ancient enemies: 'anything goes' and 'enough already!'"

That conviction of "enough already" is now widespread. Common sense perceives that pornography is related to sex crimes, promiscuity and the devaluation of committed marriages and family life. Citizens everywhere are tired of the pornographic assault. Since the obscenity law is grounded in contemporary community standards, it is vital that communities loudly and clearly protest against the invasion of their homes and neighborhoods by illegal pornography. If they do not, their silence may be misinterpreted as acceptance.

> *"The Supreme Court . . . has held that obscenity is not protected by the First Amendment."*

Pornography Contributes to Violence Against Women

by Ron Thorne-Finch

About the author: *Ron Thorne-Finch is a therapist at Klinic, Inc., a community health center in Winnipeg, Manitoba, Canada. He is the author of* Ending the Silence: The Origins and Treatment of Male Violence Against Women, *from which the following viewpoint is excerpted.*

The pornography and censorship debate has become something of a stalemate. Pro-censorship activists have continued to try to restrict the sale and distribution of pornography. The major effort by anti-censorship feminists has been to encourage significant changes in social values by asking numerous questions about the consumption of pornography. For example, if a man spends his lunch hour watching a film in which a female office worker, apparently in unbridled lust, suddenly rips off her clothes and those of her male co-workers in order to hold an orgy on the office floor, is this not going to affect how he views the women in his office upon his return from the theatre? Is he going to see them in a different way? Will the women appear less like skilled, knowledgeable professionals and more like sexual commodities? How successfully will he separate the film 'fantasy' from reality? How many men, having viewed the same film, will want to *make* that fantasy their reality? In short, how does pornography affect the way in which men relate to women? This question has motivated a cadre of researchers to look for answers. Their findings, while not yet complete, confirm three major fears of feminists.

Desensitization to Violence Against Women

Numerous researchers are showing, through laboratory investigations, that media portrayals of aggression against women generally result in more negative attitudes toward, and increased aggression against, women. Daniel Linz, Edward Donnerstein, and Steven Penrod, for example, have shown that "men who viewed five movies depicting violence against women came to have fewer negative emotional reactions to the films, to perceive them as significantly less violent, and to consider them significantly less degrading to women."

Neil Malamuth was one of the first researchers to point to the connection between viewing filmed pornographic violence and increased levels of aggression against women. He had males view either aggressive or non-aggressive pictorials from *Penthouse* magazine that had been judged to be equally sexually arousing. The aggressive stimulus pictures implied that the woman was sexually aroused by rape. The non-aggressive pictures depicted mutually consenting sex. In order to reduce inhibition against aggression, half of the subjects were told that it was acceptable to behave as aggressively as desired. After the stimuli, subjects were insulted by a female confederate and allowed to give her electric shocks if they chose. The males who viewed the violent pornography and received the disinhibitory message delivered significantly more shocks than those who had not.

The work of other researchers has supported these results. Edward Donnerstein, for example, had his male subjects either angered or treated in a neutral manner, then exposed to either a non-aggressive pornographic film, an aggressive pornographic film, or a neutral film. Upon viewing the films, subjects were given the opportunity to aggress against a male confederate of the experimenter; others were paired with a female confederate. The combination of exposure to aggressive pornography, a high level of pre-exposure anger, and pairing with a female confederate led to the highest level of aggression. Also of significance, even non-angered male subjects exposed to violent pornography showed substantially higher levels of aggressive behaviour when paired with a female confederate.

Pornography Reduces Women's Self-Esteem

There also is growing research verification for what many have argued for years, namely, that pornography devalues women not only in men's eyes but also in their own. Suzin Mayerson and Dalmas Taylor investigated the effects of reading pornography on women's self-esteem and their attitudes about rape and interpersonal violence and how these effects were mediated by a woman's degree of sex-role stereotyping (SRS). They had ninety-six undergraduate females, rated at various levels of SRS, read one of three sexually explicit stories portraying different combinations of a woman's consent to (or absence of consent to), and arousal by (or absence of arousal by), forceful sexual activity. They found that differences attributable to the consent and arousal manipulations were minimal. Yet, compared to not reading a story, reading it generally led to changes in self-esteem and greater acceptance of rape myths and interpersonal violence. Individuals indicating high SRS generally reported lower self-esteem and more tolerance of rape and other violence. This is

"Pornography devalues women not only in men's eyes but also in their own."

particularly disturbing in that we know that women with high SRS or women whose self-esteem is weakened are significantly less likely than other women to report assaults or seek help.

An Instructive Study

To compound the pornography problem, there has recently emerged the argument that its effects on men may in fact be short-lived. After examining individual subjects' self-reported likelihood to rape (LR), Neil Malamuth and Joseph Ceniti have speculated that, depending on the degree, LR may be an important factor in buffering the effects of pornography. Males who had a high LR score did rate high on their likelihood to act violently against women. But the results did not indicate that repeated exposure to violent or non-violent pornography had a significant effect on laboratory aggression in the longer term. Malamuth and Ceniti's work has important parallels with that of L. Berkowitz on media effects. All three warn that one should not trivialize the significance of an apparently short-lived effect from viewing violence. While short-lived, it is sufficient to stimulate the viewer's existing behavioural tendencies. Berkowitz alleges that there may be "retrieval cues," found in our environment, which will reactivate an earlier message portrayed in the media and again strengthen the potential expression of behavioural inclinations. The Malamuth and Ceniti study, likewise, revealed that the effects of pornography may not end completely after a short time, as they may mix with previously held views through the presence of a retrieval cue. The absence of a retrieval cue of some sort may well prevent the violence from being exhibited; once it appears, however, the effects may be displayed.

> *"By the time males encounter pornography . . . they have already internalized many of society's negative values about women."*

This idea that violent pornography, though not directly causing men to be violent, may in fact reinforce previously held views is supported by a growing body of researchers. They argue that by the time males encounter pornography, even as adolescents, they have already internalized many of society's negative values about women. Yet even if we were to definitively determine that pornography only reinforces, instead of creating, values dangerous to women, or that its effects may only be short-lived, there is still substantial reason to be concerned. The extensive availability of pornography and the annual volume of sales make it appear that a large portion of our adult male population are pornography addicts. Because pornography is always available in some form, be it on videotape or on paper, the effects, however short-lived, can be produced frequently and repeatedly. The *cumulative* effects, meanwhile, may be more long-lasting. Furthermore, even if pornography does not create, but only reinforces, negative values, what we reinforce in this generation, we are establishing for the next. Even if pornography reinforces only one man's views against women, that man plays an important role in the creation of his son's and daughter's views about women.

Feminists argued that the display of sex in combination with violence, and not sex itself, was the problem. The emerging evidence indicates that their concerns were well-founded. It is the level of violence in a society rather than sexual explicitness that affects women's safety; research indi-

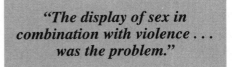

"The display of sex in combination with violence . . . was the problem."

cates that it is erroneous to assume high sexual explicitness ensures high levels of violence.

Ted Palys, a criminologist at Simon Fraser University [in British Columbia], wanted to determine if the advent of home video technology was increasing the market and, consequently, the availability of sexual, aggressive, and sexually aggressive material. The experiment involved the selection of 58 videos that were classified in the video outlets as 'Adult' (or single-X) and 92 that were labelled triple-X. While all the videos were gathered from various outlets in and around Vancouver, Canada, 89 per cent of the videos had been produced in the United States, 4 per cent in Canada, and 7 per cent in Europe. As anticipated, the triple-X videos depicted considerably more sexually explicit content than the adult videos. Quite unexpectedly, however, the adult videos "contained significantly more aggressive and sexually aggressive content, and depicted this violence with significantly greater severity."

Palys's results also helped dispel a popular notion that videos had become more violent. He found no significant increase in aggressive images between 1979 and 1983 for either the triple-X or adult videos; indeed, he noted that the triple-X videos had become less sexually violent.

This information signals our need to be aware of the effect of images of violence against women in pornography and in the media generally. It is these images which encourage and reinforce male violence against women, particularly sexual assault. Sexually violent media images typically are versions of rape scenes which are a fusion of violence with sexual content. Many of these images, by portraying women as wanting and enjoying the violence, reflect the third detrimental effect of pornography: it perpetuates various myths that are supportive of sexual assault.

Several Sexual Assault Myths

Myth 1: Men rape because of uncontrollable sexual urges. This belief portrays male sexuality as an autonomous instinct and, like all the myths, absolves the man of all responsibility for his actions. It implies that the woman is responsible for making sure that she does not precipitate a sexual assault through any actions or dress that could sexually arouse the male. In reality, sex drive is a learned behaviour, part of sexual socialization; in our society, boys learn that to satisfy their sex drive, they have a right to use—or abuse—any woman at any time. Yet, if sex drive is so instinctual, studies would not show that 71 per cent of sexual assaults are planned in advance, or that only 11 per cent are between strangers.

This myth also subtly coerces women into feeling they have to participate in sex when they do not want to, for fear of physical effects (for example, that once a man is sexually aroused it can harm his sexual organs if he does not ejaculate) and/or of emotional consequences (it is better to submit than to get him angry or upset). This situation is often referred to as 'grey rape.'

Blaming the Victim

Myth 2: It is not really possible to rape a non-consenting adult female (i.e., no woman can really be raped against her will). Implicit in this myth is the belief that there is in fact no such thing as sexual assault; a woman must consent to sexual intercourse for it to occur. This ignores the reality that fear physically and psychologically impedes, if not completely paralyses, a woman's ability to resist and thereby prevent assault. Not only do 82 per cent of the sexual assaults in Canada involve verbal threats or threats with a weapon, but also women are in general socialized to be passive and not fight back.

This myth removes the responsibility from the man by implying that if the woman really wants to, she can stop the assault. It is this myth that often impairs a woman's recovery from the post-assault feelings of self-doubt, guilt, shame, and blame. Unless the woman has been severely beaten and bruised, police, hospital workers, clinicians, friends, family, and the victim herself will often believe, at some level, that she did not adequately resist and thus, in effect, consented to the attack. There is a preposterous double standard at work here. If, for example, a person is robbed of a wallet, the violation is validated regardless of whether he or she was physically beaten. (Muggings usually happen without severe visible physical trauma to the victim.) Sexual assaults, however, must result in blood, bruises, and broken bones to be authentic; otherwise there is an assumption that the woman was 'just wanting it.'

Myth 3: 'Nice girls' do not get sexually assaulted. This myth gives the false impression that if a woman conforms to the current, socially prescribed notion of nice-girl behaviour, she will be immune to sexual assault. It is predicated on the assumption that there is an absolute way of judging what is 'nice' and what is 'loose' or 'bad.' Yet even if there were some collectively agreed-upon distinctions, one

> *"Boys learn that to satisfy their sex drive, they have a right to use—or abuse—any woman at any time."*

must ask why 'loose' women should be more deserving of sexual assault than any others. It is a no-win situation for women. Society, on the one hand, says women are supposed to be attractive and alluring, yet, on the other, blames them for their provocative appearance if they are sexually assaulted.

The fact is all women are vulnerable to sexual assault; virtue is no guarantee of freedom from it. And in any case, a woman's consent—not her socially evaluated level of virtue—should be the only criterion for a sexual interaction.

> *"Sexual assaults . . . must result in blood, bruises, and broken bones . . . ; otherwise there is an assumption that the woman was 'just wanting it.'"*

Myth 4: Women ask to be raped . . . and probably enjoy it. Once again, the woman is held responsible for behaviour that a man or men may interpret as an invitation for sexual assault. If she does not avoid certain behaviours, she takes the consequences. One problem is that virtually any action by a female could be construed as 'asking for it.' Not surprisingly, many males in our society feel that women who step beyond certain unspoken limits (e.g., by walking alone at night) are subconsciously asking to be sexually assaulted. Belief in this myth undoubtedly puts tremendous constraints on women's activities and behaviour. It is an important form of social control. However, even if our society could codify the unspoken limits, and women did conform to them, they still would not be safe from sexual assault; it happens just as often to women asleep at home or opening their doors to allow in service personnel.

Maligning the Mentally Ill

Myth 5: Most rapists are mentally ill. This myth as well removes responsibility for the assault from the man. It says that the man who sexually assaults is mentally disturbed, is not rational, and is therefore not responsible for his actions. Yet numerous studies disprove this, showing that fewer than 5 per cent of all men who sexually assault were psychotic at the time of the assault. So, if indeed the vast majority of sexual assaults are committed by normal males, this myth has two serious effects. First, it wrongly blames a segment of our population that already is largely maligned and ostracized. The myth says that rapists are mentally ill—and therefore, it is assumed, all mentally ill males are rapists. This works to isolate many individuals who, as it is, are struggling for a place in society—to say nothing of dealing with mental illness itself. Second, the 'most rapists are mentally ill' myth encourages women to trust all other 'normal' males. This myth often gets combined with the 'nice girls don't get raped' myth: the woman assaulted by an acquaintance might conclude that by somehow failing to be 'nice' she was responsible—because, after all, he was such a nice 'normal' guy.

Pornography Should Not Be Censored

by Ellen Willis

About the author: *Ellen Willis has been a militant voice for women's libera-tion in the mass media. This essay, written in 1979, was one of the earliest pub-lic feminist critiques of the growing anti-pornography movement.*

For women, life is an ongoing good cop-bad cop routine. The good cops are marriage, motherhood, and that courtly old gentleman, chivalry. Just cooperate, they say (crossing their fingers), and we'll go easy on you. You'll never have to earn a living or open a door. We'll even get you some romantic love. But you'd better not get stubborn, or you'll have to deal with our friend rape, and he's a real terror; we just can't control him.

The Power to Terrorize

Pornography often functions as a bad cop. If rape warns that without the pro-tection of one man we are fair game for all, the hard-core pornographic image suggests that the alternative to being a wife is being a whore. As women be-come more "criminal," the cops call for nastier reinforcements; the proliferation of lurid, violent porn (symbolic rape) is a form of backlash. But one can be a solid citizen and still be shocked (naively or hypocritically) by police brutality. However widely condoned, rape is illegal. However loudly people proclaim that porn is as wholesome as granola, the essence of its appeal is that emotionally it remains taboo. It is from their very contempt for the rules that bad cops derive their power to terrorize (and the covert approbation of solid citizens who would love to break the rules themselves). The line between bad cop and outlaw is tenuous. Both rape and pornography reflect a male outlaw mentality that rejects the conventions of romance and insists, bluntly, that women are cunts. The cru-cial difference between the conservative's moral indignation at rape, or at *Hus-tler*, and the feminist's political outrage is the latter's understanding that the problem is not bad cops or outlaws but cops and the law.

Unfortunately, the current women's campaign against pornography seems determined to blur this difference. Feminist criticism of sexist and misogynist pornography is nothing new; porn is an obvious target insofar as it contributes to larger patterns of oppression—the reduction of the female body to a commodity (the paradigm being prostitution), the sexual intimidation that makes women regard the public streets as enemy territory (the paradigm being rape), sexist images, and propaganda in general. But what is happening now is different. By playing games with the English language, anti-porn activists are managing to rationalize as feminism a single-issue movement divorced from any larger political context and rooted in conservative moral assumptions that are all the more dangerous for being unacknowledged.

> *"Anti-porn activists are managing to rationalize as feminism a single-issue movement divorced from any larger political context."*

A Political Crusade

When I first heard there was a group called Women Against Pornography, I twitched. Could I define myself as Against Pornography? Not really. In itself, pornography—which, my dictionary and I agree, means any image or description intended or used to arouse sexual desire—does not strike me as the proper object of a political crusade. As the most cursory observation suggests, there are many varieties of porn, some pernicious, some more or less benign. About the only generalization one can make is that pornography is the return of the repressed, of feelings and fantasies driven underground by a culture that atomizes sexuality, defining love as a noble affair of the heart and mind, lust as a base animal urge centered in unmentionable organs. Prurience—the state of mind I associate with pornography—implies a sense of sex as forbidden, secretive pleasure, isolated from any emotional or social context. I imagine that in utopia, porn would wither away along with the state, heroin, and Coca-Cola. At present, however, the sexual impulses that pornography appeals to are part of virtually everyone's psychology. For obvious political and cultural reasons nearly all porn is sexist in that it is the product of a male imagination and aimed at a male market; women are less likely to be consciously interested in pornography, or to indulge that interest, or to find porn that turns them on. But anyone who thinks women are simply indifferent to pornography has never watched a bunch of adolescent girls pass around a trashy novel. Over the years I've enjoyed various pieces of pornography—some of them of the sleazy Forty-second Street paperback sort—and so have most women I know. Fantasy, after all, is more flexible than reality, and women have learned, as a matter of survival, to be adept at shaping male fantasies to their own purposes. If feminists define pornography, per se, as the enemy, the result will be to make a lot of women ashamed of their sexual feelings and afraid to be honest about them. And the last thing women need is more sexual shame, guilt, and hypocrisy—this time served up as feminism.

So why ignore qualitative distinctions and in effect condemn all pornography as equally bad? WAP organizers answer—or finesse—this question by redefining pornography. They maintain that pornography is not really about sex but about violence against women. Or, in a more colorful formulation, "Pornography is the theory, rape is the practice." Part of the argument is that pornography causes violence; much is made of the fact that Charles Manson and David Berkowitz had porn collections. This is the sort of inverted logic that presumes marijuana to be dangerous because most heroin addicts started with it. It is men's hostility toward women—combined with their power to express that hostility and for the most part get away with it—that causes sexual violence. Pornography that gives sadistic fantasies concrete shape—and, in today's atmosphere, social legitimacy—may well encourage suggestible men to act them out. But if *Hustler* were to vanish from the shelves tomorrow, I doubt that rape or wife-beating statistics would decline.

Porn *vs.* Erotica

Even more problematic is the idea that pornography depicts violence rather than sex. Since porn is by definition overtly sexual, while most of it is not overtly violent, this equation requires some fancy explaining. The conference WAP held in September 1979 was in part devoted to this task. Robin Morgan and Gloria Steinem addressed it by attempting to distinguish pornography from erotica. According to this argument, erotica (whose etymological root is "eros," or sexual love) expresses an integrated sexuality based on mutual affection and desire between equals; pornography (which comes from another Greek root—"porne," meaning prostitute) reflects a dehumanized sexuality based on male domination and exploitation of women. The distinction sounds promising, but it doesn't hold up. The accepted meaning of erotica is literature or pictures with sexual themes; it may or may not serve the essentially utilitarian function of pornography. Because it is less specific, less suggestive of actual sexual activity, "erotica" is regularly used as a euphemism for "classy porn." Pornography expressed in literary language or expensive photography and consumed by the upper middle class is "erotica"; the cheap stuff, which can't pretend to any purpose but getting people off, is smut. The erotica-versus-porn approach evades the (embarrassing?) question of how porn is *used*. It endorses the portrayal of sex as we might like it to be and condemns the portrayal of sex as it too often is, whether in action or only in fantasy. But if pornography is to arouse, it must appeal to the feelings we have, not those that by some utopian standard we ought to have. Sex in this culture has been so deeply politicized that it is impossible to make clear-cut distinctions be-

> "*In itself, pornography . . . does not strike me as the proper object of a political crusade.*"

tween "authentic" sexual impulses and those conditioned by patriarchy. Between, say, *Ulysses* at one end and *Snuff* at the other, erotica/pornography conveys all sorts of mixed messages that elicit complicated and private responses. In practice, attempts to sort out good erotica from bad porn inevitably come down to "What turns me on is erotic; what turns you on is pornographic."

It would be clearer and more logical simply to acknowledge that some sexual images are offensive and some are not. But logic and clarity are irrelevant—or rather, inimical—to the underlying aim of the anti-porners, which is to vent the emotions traditionally associated with the word "pornography." As I've suggested, there is a social and psychic link between pornography and rape. In terms of patriarchal morality both are expressions of male lust, which is presumed to be innately vicious, and offenses to the putative sexual innocence of "good" women. But feminists supposedly begin with different assumptions—that men's confusion of sexual desire with predatory aggression reflects a sexist system, not male biology; that there are no good (chaste) or bad (lustful) women, just women who are, like men, sexual beings. From this standpoint, to lump pornography with rape is dangerously simplistic. Rape is a violent physical assault. Pornography can be a psychic assault, both in its content and in its public intrusions on our attention, but for women as for men it can also be a source of erotic pleasure. A woman who is raped is a victim; a woman who enjoys pornography (even if that means enjoying a rape fantasy) is in a sense a rebel, insisting on an aspect of her sexuality that has been defined as a male preserve. Insofar as pornography glorifies male supremacy and sexual alienation, it is deeply reactionary. But in rejecting sexual repression and hypocrisy—which have inflicted even more damage on women than on men—it expresses a radical impulse.

Sexual Attitudes Revealed

That this impulse still needs defending, even among feminists, is evident from the sexual attitudes that have surfaced in the anti-porn movement. In the movement's rhetoric pornography is a code word for vicious male lust. To the objection that some women get off on porn, the standard reply is that this only shows how thoroughly women have been brainwashed by male values—though a WAP leaflet goes so far as to suggest that women who claim to like pornography are lying to avoid male opprobrium. (Note the good-girl-versus-bad-girl theme, reappearing as healthy-versus-sick, or honest-versus-devious; for "brainwashed" read "seduced.") And the view of sex that most often emerges from talk about "erotica" is as sentimental and euphemistic as the word itself: lovemaking should be beautiful, romantic, soft, nice, and devoid of messiness, vulgarity,

*"If **Hustler** were to vanish from the shelves tomorrow, I doubt that rape or wife-beating statistics would decline."*

impulses to power, or indeed aggression of any sort. Above all, the emphasis should be on *relationships*, not (yuck) *organs*. This goody-goody concept of eroticism is not feminist but feminine. It is precisely sex as an aggressive, unla-

dylike activity, an expression of violent and unpretty emotion, an exercise of erotic power, and a specifically genital experience that has been taboo for women. Nor are we supposed to admit that we, too, have sadistic impulses, that our sexual fan-

> *"It would be clearer and more logical simply to acknowledge that some sexual images are offensive and some are not."*

tasies may reflect forbidden urges to turn the tables and get revenge on men. (When a woman is aroused by a rape fantasy, is she perhaps identifying with the rapist as well as the victim?)

Feminine Self-Righteousness

At the WAP conference lesbian separatists argued that pornography reflects patriarchal sexual relations; patriarchal sexual relations are based on male power backed by force; ergo, pornography is violent. This dubious syllogism, which could as easily be applied to romantic novels, reduces the whole issue to hopeless mush. If all manifestations of patriarchal sexuality are violent, then opposition to violence cannot explain why pornography (rather than romantic novels) should be singled out as a target. Besides, such reductionism allows women no basis for distinguishing between consensual heterosexuality and rape. But this is precisely its point; as a number of women at the conference put it, "In a patriarchy, all sex with men is pornographic." Of course, to attack pornography, and at the same time equate it with heterosexual sex, is implicitly to condemn not only women who like pornography, but women who sleep with men. This is familiar ground. The argument that straight women collaborate with the enemy has often been, among other things, a relatively polite way of saying that they consort with the beast. At the conference I couldn't help feeling that proponents of the separatist line were talking like the modern equivalents of women who, in an era when straightforward prudery was socially acceptable, joined convents to escape men's rude sexual demands. It seemed to me that their revulsion against heterosexuality was serving as the thinnest of covers for disgust with sex itself. In any case, sanitized feminine sexuality, whether straight or gay, is as limited as the predatory masculine kind and as central to women's oppression; a major function of misogynist pornography is to scare us into embracing it. As a further incentive, the good cops stand ready to assure us that we are indeed morally superior to men, that in our sweetness and nonviolence (read passivity and powerlessness) is our strength.

Women are understandably tempted to believe this comforting myth. Self-righteousness has always been a feminine weapon, a permissible way to make men feel bad. Ironically, it is socially acceptable for women to display fierce aggression in their crusades against male vice, which serve as an outlet for female anger without threatening male power. The temperance movement, which made alcohol the symbol of male violence, did not improve the position of women; substituting porn for demon rum won't work either. One reason it won't is that it bolsters the good girl-bad girl split. Overtly or by implication it isolates women who like porn or "pornographic" sex or who work in the sex industry. WAP has refused to take a position on prostitution, yet its activities—particularly its support for cleaning up Times Square—will affect prostitutes' lives. Prostitution raises its own set of complicated questions. But it is clearly not in women's interest to pit "good" feminists against "bad" whores (or topless dancers, or models for skin magazines).

Women Against Pornography

So far, the issue that has dominated public debate on the anti-porn campaign is its potential threat to free speech. Here too the movement's arguments have been full of contradictions. Susan Brownmiller and other WAP organizers claim not to advocate censorship and dismiss the civil liberties issue as a red herring dragged in men who don't want to face the fact that pornography oppresses women. Yet at the same time, WAP endorses the Supreme Court's contention that obscenity is not protected speech, a doctrine I—and most civil libertarians—regard as a clear infringement of First Amendment rights. Brownmiller insists that the First Amendment was designed to protect political dissent, not expressions of woman-hating violence. But to make such a distinction is to defeat the amendment's purpose, since it implicitly cedes to the government the right to define "political." (Has there ever been a government willing to admit that its opponents are anything more than anti-social troublemakers?) Anyway, it makes no sense to oppose pornography on the grounds that it's sexist propaganda, then turn around and argue that it's not political. Nor will libertarians be reassured by WAP's statement that "We want to change the definition of obscenity so that it focuses on violence, not sex." Whatever their focus, obscenity laws deny the right of free expression to those who transgress official standards of propriety—and personally, I don't find WAP's standards significantly less oppressive than [Supreme Court chief justice] Warren Burger's. Not that it matters, since WAP's fantasies about influencing the definition of obscenity are appallingly naive. The basic purpose of obscenity laws is and always has been to reinforce cultural taboos on sexuality and suppress feminism, homosexuality, and other forms of sexual dissidence. No pornographer has ever been punished for being a woman-hater, but not too long ago information about female sexuality, contraception, and abortion was assumed to be obscene. In a male supremacist society the only obscenity law that will not be used against women is no law at all.

> *"To lump pornography with rape is dangerously simplistic."*

As an alternative to an outright ban on pornography, Brownmiller and others have advocated restricting its display. There is a plausible case to be made for the idea that anti-woman images displayed so prominently that they are impossible to avoid are coercive, a form of active harassment that oversteps the bounds of free speech. But aside from the evasion involved in simply equating pornography with misogyny or sexual sadism, there are no legal or logical grounds for treating sexist material any differently from (for example) racist or anti-Semitic propaganda; and equitable law would have to prohibit any kind of public defamation. And the very thought of such a sweeping law has to make anyone with an imagination nervous. Could Catholics claim they were being harassed by nasty depictions of the pope? Could Russian refugees argue that the display of Communist literature was a form of psychological torture? Would pro-abortion material be taken off the shelves on the grounds that it defamed the unborn? I'd rather not find out.

Surface Respectability

At the moment the First Amendment issue remains hypothetical; the movement has concentrated on raising the issue of pornography through demonstrations and other public actions. This is certainly a legitimate strategy. Still, I find myself more and more disturbed by the tenor of anti-pornography actions and the sort of consciousness they promote; increasingly their focus has shifted from rational feminist criticism of specific targets to generalized, demagogic moral outrage. Picketing an anti-woman movie, defacing an exploitative billboard, or boycotting a record company to protest its misogynist album covers conveys one kind of message, mass marches Against Pornography quite another. Similarly, there is a difference between telling the neighborhood news dealer why it pisses us off to have *Penthouse* shoved in our faces and choosing as a prime target every right-thinking politician's symbol of big-city sin, Times Square.

In contrast to the abortion rights movement, which is struggling against a tidal wave of energy from the other direction, the anti-porn campaign is respectable. It gets approving press and cooperation from the New York City government, which has its own stake (promoting tourism, making the Clinton area safe for gentrification) in cleaning up Times Square. It has begun to attract women whose perspective on other matters is in no way feminist ("I'm anti-abortion," a participant in WAP's march on Times Square told a reporter, "but this is something I can get into"). Despite the insistence of

> *"It makes no sense to oppose pornography on the grounds that it's sexist propaganda."*

WAP organizers that they support sexual freedom, their line appeals to the anti-sexual emotions that feed the backlash. Whether they know it or not, they are doing the good cops' dirty work.

Censoring Pornography Endangers Feminism

by Wendy McElroy

About the author: *Wendy McElroy is a fellow of the Independent Institute, which conducts economic, legal, and historic research on domestic and international policies in civil liberties and other areas. She is the author of* Freedom, Feminism and the State.

Pornography has been a traditional battleground between conservatives, who advocate family values, and liberals, who champion freedom of expression. The political makeup of contemporary feminism is overwhelmingly liberal; the more extreme feminists—called "radical" feminists—are socialist. But since the mid-1980s, there has been a startling development. Feminists have been standing alongside conservatives to demand legislation against pornography. Anti-pornography feminists have even joined hands with religious fundamentalists in a common cause.

Consequences of Fighting Pornography

This alliance makes some feminists nervous. Lisa Duggan, in her essay *False Promises*, expressed concern about future consequences:

> One is tempted to ask in astonishment, how can this be happening? . . . But in fact this new development is not as surprising as it at first seems. Pornography has come to be seen as a central cause of women's oppression by a significant number of feminists. . . . This analysis takes feminism very close—indeed far too close—to measures that will ultimately support conservative, anti-sex, pro-censorship forces in American society for it is with these forces that women have formed alliances.

Radical feminists dismiss the dangers of this alliance. They discount the possibility that the legislation they seek could backlash against the feminist movement. For instance, Catharine MacKinnon wrote:

> The question becomes not whether one trusts the law to behave in a feminist

Wendy McElroy, "The Unholy Alliance," *Liberty*, February 1993. Reprinted with permission of *Liberty*.

way. We do not trust medicine, yet we insist it respond to women's needs. We do not trust theology, but we claim spirituality as more than a male preserve. We do not abdicate the control of technology because it was not invented by women. . . . If women are to restrict our demands for change to spheres we can trust, spheres we already control, there will not be any.

An Unlikely Alliance

The unlikely alliance between feminists and conservatives, and the split within feminism itself, has led to strange spectacles. For example, when an anti-pornography ordinance was proposed in Indianapolis, the law was supported by the Moral Majority . . . even though it had been drafted by radical feminists. Within the local feminist community, however, the ordinance found no support.

The current anti-pornography crusade within feminism is something new on the political scene. It is new in at least two important ways: (1) it signals a break in feminism from its liberal insistence on freedom of speech; and (2) it offers a revolutionary definition of pornography. The battle over pornography has shifted to new ground.

Pornography is the *bête noire* of radical feminism. To them, pornography is gender violence and a violation of the civil rights of women. It victimizes not merely women who work in the in-dustry or who are exposed to maga-zines and films; pornography dam-ages *all* women because it con-tributes to the general degradation of women that is prevalent in our society. Indeed, some theorists go so far as to claim that pornography is the source of society's unhealthy attitude toward women. Pornography is considered to be so damaging that it is linked, in a cause-and-effect relationship, to violent crimes such as rape. Thus, eliminating this form of expression is viewed as self-defense, not censorship.

> "*Pornography and feminism have much in common.*"

The legal theorist Catharine MacKinnon has been a key voice in the anti-pornography campaign. In her book, *Feminism Unmodified*, MacKinnon de-fined the object of attack: "Pornography, in the feminist view, is a form of forced sex, a practice of sexual politics, an institution of gender inequality." MacKinnon claimed that pornography was not a form of expression; porno-graphic material was—in and of itself—an act of violence:

> Pornography not only teaches the reality of male dominance. It is one way its reality is imposed as well as experienced. It is a way of seeing and treating women. Male power makes authoritative a way of seeing and treating women, so that when a man looks at a pornographic picture—pornographic meaning that the woman is defined as to be acted upon, a sexual object, a sexual thing— the *viewing* is an *act*, an act of male supremacy. [emphasis in the original.]

The wholesale condemnation of pornography is a departure for feminism. Since its revival in the early 1960s the movement has been dominated by so-

cialists and liberals; both these traditions advocated freedom of speech. Moreover, pornography tended to be viewed as part of a larger trend toward sexual
liberation—a liberation that feminists applauded because it ushered in such
things as birth control and the unveil-
ing of women's sexuality.

Lisa Duggan typified this attitude
in acknowledging the possible benefits pornography offered to women:

> *"If pornography is an act of violence, then the First Amendment is irrelevant."*

> The existence of pornography
> has served to flout conventional sexual mores, to ridicule sexual hypocrisy and
> to underscore the importance of sexual needs. Pornography carries many mes-
> sages other than woman-hating; it advocates sexual adventure, sex outside of
> marriage, sex for pleasure, casual sex, illegal sex, anonymous sex, public sex,
> voyeuristic sex. Some of these ideas appeal to women reading or seeing pornog-
> raphy, who may interpret some images as legitimating their own sense of sexual
> urgency or desire to be sexually aggressive.

Pornography and feminism have much in common. Both deal with women as
sexual beings and both attempt to bring this sexuality out into the open.
Pornography and feminism also share a history of being targeted by obscenity
laws. In particular, the Comstock laws of the 1870s were used not only against
pornographic material but also against birth control information. Feminist material—especially lesbian material—has always suffered under laws that regulate sexual expression.

Redefining Pornography

Nevertheless, by the late 1970s sexual liberation was being viewed with suspicion. Pornography was being redefined as an enemy of women. In her book,
Our Blood, radical feminist Andrea Dworkin explained:

> In pornography, sadism is the means by which men establish their dominance.
> Sadism is the authentic exercise of power which confirms manhood; and the
> first characteristic of manhood is that its existence is based on the negation of
> the female—manhood can only be certified by abject female degradation, a
> degradation never abject enough until the victim's body and will have both
> been destroyed. . . . The heart of darkness is this—the sexual sadism actualizes
> male identity. . . . The common erotic project of destroying women makes it
> possible for men to unite into a brotherhood; this project is the only firm and
> trustworthy groundwork for cooperation among males and all male bonding is
> based on it.

Sex itself seemed to be identified as sexism. Dworkin continued:

> Romantic love, in pornography as in life, is the mythic celebration of female
> negation. For a woman, love is defined as her willingness to submit to her own
> annihilation.

But the feminist attack on pornography was not merely another cry for censorship. It was more sophisticated than that. Feminists were and are using a strategy that has proved successful with other issues, such as affirmative action. Pornography is being defined as a violation of women's civil rights. Thus, instead of advocating criminal proceedings against pornographers, feminists restrict themselves to civil suits. This approach avoids sticky constitutional questions; in particular, it avoids the First Amendment. It also turns the entire discussion of pornography on its head. Conventional arguments for and against pornography simply do not apply.

Traditional obscenity laws have focused on the connection between pornography and moral harm. One of the standard tests of obscenity came from Supreme Court justice William J. Brennan Jr. in his ruling on *Memoirs vs Massachusetts:*

> (a) the dominant theme of the material taken as a whole appeals to the prurient interest in sex; (b) the material is patently offensive because it affronts contemporary community standards relating to the description or representation of sexual matters; and (c) the material is utterly without redeeming social value.

Anti-pornography feminists dwell on the connection between pornography and political harm—namely, the oppression of women. Consider MacKinnon's presentation of how pornography differs from obscenity:

> Obscenity law is concerned with morality, specifically morals from the male point of view, meaning the standpoint of male dominance. The feminist critique of pornography is a politics, specifically politics from women's point of view, meaning the standpoint of the subordination of women to men. Morality here means good and evil; politics means power and powerlessness. Obscenity is a moral idea; pornography is a political practice. Obscenity is abstract; pornography is concrete. The two concepts represent two entirely different things.

City by City

In the mid-'80s, radical feminists launched a campaign to pass anti-pornography ordinances on a city-by-city basis. By localizing the issue, they by-passed the problem of obtaining a national consensus, which had proven so difficult with the E.R.A. [Equal Rights Amendment]. The first ordinance—drafted by MacKinnon and Dworkin—served as the model

> *"After the anti-pornography crusade, who will take a woman's consent seriously?"*

for future ones. This was the Minneapolis Ordinance of 1983. In addressing the Minneapolis City Council, MacKinnon declared:

> We are proposing a statutory scheme that will situate pornography as a central practice in the subordination of women. . . . The understanding and the evidence which we will present to you today to support defining pornography as a practice of discrimination on the basis of sex is a new idea . . . in particular we want to show how the concept of pornography conditions and determines the way in which men actually treat women . . . and we will show that it is central to the way in which women remain second-class citizens.

191

Under the ordinance's provisions, a woman who had worked in pornography—a *Playboy* centerfold, for example—could bring a civil lawsuit against her employers for having coerced her into a "pornographic performance." Laws and remedies already existed for fraud or for contracts signed under duress. The purpose of the ordinance was to make "coercion" into a civil matter:

> The bigotry and contempt it promotes, with the acts of aggression it fosters, harm women's opportunities for equality of rights in employment, education, property rights, public accommodations and public services; create public harassment and private denigration; promote injury and degradation such as rape, battery and prostitution and inhibit just enforcement of laws against these acts; contribute significantly to restricting women from full exercise of citizenship.

The definition of coercion was all important. The ordinance was clear. Coercion was deemed to be present even if the woman was of age, she fully understood the nature of the performance, she signed a contract and release, there were witnesses, she was under no threat, and she was fully paid. None of these factors provided evidence of consent.

Consent Was Not Possible

In essence, consent was not possible. In principle, the woman could not be treated as a consenting adult. By definition, coercion was always present in a pornographic act. MacKinnon later explained that "in the context of unequal power (between the sexes), one needs to think about the meaning of consent—whether it is a meaningful concept at all" (Toronto *Star*, 2/17/92). Gloria Steinem, in her introduction to Linda Lovelace's exposé *Out of Bondage*, agreed: "The question is free will: Are the subjects of pornography there by choice, or by coercion, *economic* or physical?" [emphasis added].

> *"Even in feminist terms, there are compelling arguments for freedom of speech."*

In other words, if the woman needed or wanted the money offered, this would constitute economic coercion. The politics of society made it impossible for women to fully consent to a pornographic act. Women who thought they had agreed were mistaken. Such women had been so damaged by a male-dominated culture that they were not able to give true consent. Lisa Duggan observed:

> Advocates of the ordinance effectively assume that women have been so conditioned by the pornographic world view that if their own experiences of the sexual acts . . . are not subordinating, then they must simply be victims of false consciousness.

Several years ago, anti-pornography feminists attempted to pass an ordinance in Los Angeles. I was among the feminists who went down to City Hall to argue against the ordinance. The arguments I decided *not* to use are almost as revealing as the ones I settled on.

I decided not to argue that pornography is undefinable and, therefore, not appropriate for a legal system that requires a clear point of enforcement. The Ordinance had defined what it meant by pornography in excruciating—if subjective—detail. To focus on definitions would be to divert the debate into the bogs of what constitutes "dehumanization" or "exploitation." I simply accepted the rule of thumb offered by Supreme Court justice Potter Stewart in his ruling on *Jacobellis vs Ohio*: "I know it when I see it." I assumed that everyone was talking about the same thing.

The First Amendment

I also abandoned appeals to the First Amendment. Anti-pornography feminists had a tangled web of counterarguments, which would require more time to answer than I would be allotted. MacKinnon's arguments are typical:

> The First Amendment essentially presumes some level of social equality among people and hence essentially equal social access to the means of expression. In a context of inequality between the sexes, we cannot presume that that is accurate. The First Amendment also presumes that for the mind to be free to fulfill itself, speech must be free and open. . . . Pornography amounts to terrorism and promotes not freedom but silence. Rather, it promotes freedom for men and enslavement and silence for women.

If pornography is an act of violence, then the First Amendment is irrelevant.

I also avoided a discussion of privacy rights. Supreme Court justice Thurgood Marshall (*Stanley vs Georgia*, 1969) had maintained:

> If the First Amendment means anything, it means that a state has no business telling a man, sitting alone in his own house, what books he may read or what films he must watch.

But, again, if pornography was violence, the issue of committing it in private was beside the point.

The only way to challenge the new attack effectively is to answer radical feminists in their own terms. The key questions have become: are all women coerced into pornography? and how does pornography relate to violence against women? Everything seemed to return to the basic contention of feminists: pornography is an act of violence. It is an act committed upon and against unconsenting women.

> *"It is the state—not free speech—that has been the oppressor of women."*

To begin with, I divided women into two categories: women who were directly involved with pornography—either in production or consumption; and women who had no direct exposure. The first category was the litmus test. If women are degraded by pornography, surely the women closest to it would be the most deeply affected. At the heart of this question was the problem of pinning down subjective terms such as "degrading." I considered the most important of these subjective evaluations to come from those women who were directly involved in pornography. It was not possible to ask each woman whether she was degraded by producing or consuming pornography. This left only one objective way to judge the matter. Namely, did women freely choose to work in or consume pornography?

> *"No 'healthy' woman would consent to the humiliation of pornography."*

The answer is clear: pornographic models and actresses signed contracts. Women who produced pornography, such as Ms. Hefner at *Playboy*, did so willingly. Women shopkeepers who stocked pornography chose to fill in the order forms. Those who consumed pornography paid money to do so.

But, radical feminists insisted, no "healthy" woman would consent to the humiliation of pornography. Therefore, women who made this choice were so psychologically damaged by a male-dominated culture that they were incapable of true consent. In Minneapolis, the ordinance argued that women, like children, needed special protection under the law:

> Children are incapable of consenting to engage in pornographic conduct, even absent physical coercion, and therefore require special protection. By the same token, the physical and psychological well-being of women ought to be afforded comparable protection, for the coercive environment in which most pornographic models work vitiates any notion that they consent or "choose" to perform in pornography.

Pause with me for a moment. Consider how insulting this is to women who have made an "unacceptable" choice with their bodies—that is, women who work in pornography. Anti-pornography feminists label these women as "psychologically sick" because they have made non-feminist choices. These women are called "victims" of their culture.

Only Those Who Agree Are "Enlightened"

But radical feminists were raised in the same culture. Presumably, these "enlightened" women wish us to believe that their choices are based on reason and knowledge; somehow, they have risen above the culture in which they were raised. They are unwilling, however, to grant such a courteous assumption to any woman who disagrees with them.

Radical feminists are adamant: Women involved in the production of pornography cannot be held legally responsible for their actions because they are psychologically impaired by cultural influence. Their arguments need not be taken seriously. Their contracts need not be respected. They are psychologically impaired. If a woman enjoys consuming pornography, it is not because she comes from another background, has a different emotional makeup or has reasoned from different facts. No: it is because she is mentally incompetent. Like any three-year-old, she is unable to give informed consent regarding her own body.

The touchstone principle of feminism used to be, "a woman's body, a woman's right." Regarding date rape, feminists still declare, "No means no." The logical corollary of this is "Yes means yes." Now, modern feminists are declaring that "yes" means nothing. It is difficult to believe that any form of pornography could be more degrading to women than this attitude.

As to whether cultural pressure has influenced women's decisions—of course it has. The culture we live in impacts on every choice we make. But to say that women who participate in pornography cannot make a choice because of cultural pressure is to eliminate the possibility of choice in any realm. Because every choice of every person is made in the presence of cultural pressure . . . including the choice to become a feminist.

Anti-Porn Ordinances

The anti-pornography ordinances were intended to protect women from the consequences of their own actions. But what legal implications does this have for women's contracts?—a right for which past generations fought hard. In the 19th century, women battled to become the legal equals of men, to have their consent taken seriously in the form of contracts and to have control of their own bodies legally recognized. After the anti-pornography crusade, who will take a woman's consent seriously? When the 15th Amendment was proposed in a form that enfranchised black men while ignoring women, the pioneering feminist Susan B. Anthony protested:

> *"To deprive women of the right to make their own contracts is to place them . . . with lunatics, idiots and criminals."*

> We have stood with the black man in the Constitution over a half a century. . . . Enfranchise him and we are left outside with lunatics, idiots and criminals.

To deprive women of the right to make their own contracts is to place them, once again, outside the Constitution with lunatics, idiots and criminals. Radical feminists are reducing a woman's consent to a legal triviality. Women are being granted the protection of no longer being taken seriously when they sign contracts. This is not a step toward the dignity or freedom of women.

But what of the women who do not choose to be involved in pornography? What of the women who are offended by it? The simplistic answer is that they should not buy or consume it. Moreover, they should use any and all peaceful means to persuade others that pornography is not a proper form of expression.

But the argument runs . . . whether or not women are directly exposed to pornography, they are still victimized. Pornography is the first step of a slippery slope that leads to explicit violence against women, such as rape. Thus, *every* woman is a victim, because every woman is in danger.

This argument assumes: (1) that pornography impacts on men's behavior, (2) that the impact can be measured objectively, and (3) that it can be correlated with sexual violence.

Pornography probably does impact on people's behavior. But it is next to impossible to objectively measure that impact. Human psychology is extremely complex, especially in the area of sexual response. Moreover, the standard of measurement and the conclusions drawn from data usually depend on the bias of the researchers or of those who commission the research.

Toronto Task Force

For example, in 1983, the Metropolitan Toronto Task Force on Violence Against Women commissioned Thelma McCormack to study pornography's connection with sexual aggression. Her research did not support the assumption that there is one. Indeed, McCormack's study indicated that the effect of pornography might be cathartic. It might reduce the incidence of rape. McCormack anticipated a hostile response to her findings. She wrote:

> There has been a dissatisfaction with the catharsis hypothesis. This probably reflects a political impatience . . . the catharsis hypothesis offers no support for collective efforts to resolve problems; it also offers no support for those who want to intervene to change the person.

Then, McCormack summarized her findings:

> The studies of pornography suggest that the use of pornography has become widespread and that it stimulates sexual activity and sexual fantasy but does not alter established sexual practices. In spite of the more permissive social environments of today, people are still ambivalent about pornography: they believe it is harmful to others, not themselves.

Her report, *Making Sense of Research on Pornography*, was discarded. The study was reassigned to David Scott, a non-feminist committed to anti-pornography. Scott found a clear connection between pornography and sexual aggression. Students, journalists and researchers who tried to obtain a copy of McCormack's paper were told that it was unavailable.

Statistics almost always contain assumptions and biases. Sometimes the bias is an honest one. For example, a researcher who believes that sexual aggression is a learned behavior will naturally ask different questions than someone who believes aggression is an instinct. Other forms of bias are not so honest. For example, when a reporter for the Boston *Phoenix* asked the radical feminist Susan Brownmiller to supply some evidence for her assertions,

> *"McCormack's study indicated that the effect of pornography might be cathartic."*

she snapped back: "The statistics will come. We supply the ideology; it's for other people to come up with the statistics."

But, for the sake of argument, let's assume that a correlation exists between pornography and rape. What would such a correlation prove? If a society with more pornography tended to have more rape, what would this say?

A correlation is not a cause-and-effect relationship. It is a logical fallacy to assume that if A is correlated with B, then A causes B. Both might be caused by a totally separate factor, C. For example, there is a high correlation between the number of doctors in a city and the amount of alcohol consumed there. One does not cause the other. Both result from a third factor: the size of the city's population.

Pornography and Rape

Similarly, a correlation between pornography and rape may indicate nothing more than a common cause for both. Namely, that we live in a sexually re-pressed society. To further repress

> *"A correlation between pornography and rape may indicate nothing more than a common cause for both."*

sex by restricting pornography might well increase the incidence of rape. Opening up the area of pornography might well diffuse sexual violence by making it more understandable. In her book *Sexual Personae* Camille Paglia contended that women have difficulty in understanding rape be-cause it involves what she called a "blood-lust . . . joy." Paglia wrote:

> Women may be less prone to such fantasies because they physically lack the equipment for sexual violence. They do not know the temptation of forcibly invading the sanctuary of another body. Our knowledge of these fantasies is expanded by pornography, which is why pornography should be tolerated.

Even in feminist terms, there are compelling arguments for freedom of speech. Feminist Ann Gronau explained:

> Knowledge gives us the power to progress, and without access to information, such as our history, we cannot engage in the necessary process of redefinition and reevaluation. Censorship removes the evidence and hinders the acquisition of knowledge. I believe that this hurts feminism a great deal, for being able to document our oppression has been, and continues to be, of inestimable value in battling sexism. It was only when pioneering thinkers began to systemati-cally study the great and small documents of social history that they discov-ered the complicated religious, psychological and medical theories that had been employed through the centuries to prove the "inevitability" of male dom-inance. Until this evidence was produced, sexism, as a word or a concept, did not exist.

There is great irony in the spectacle of radical feminists aligning with their two greatest ideological enemies: conservatives and the patriarchal state. In us-ing ordinances, anti-pornography feminists are legitimizing a system they themselves condemn as patriarchy. It is a strange leap of faith. After all, once a law is on the books, it is the state bureaucracy, not NOW [National Organiza-tion for Women], who will enforce it. In *Our Blood*, Andrea Dworkin excoriates patriarchal bureaucracy:

> Under patriarchy, no woman is safe to live her life, or to love, or to mother children. Under patriarchy, every woman is a victim, past, present and future. Under patriarchy, every woman's daughter is a victim, past, present, and future. Under patriarchy, every woman's son is her potential betrayer and also the inevitable rapist or exploiter of another woman.

Now feminists are appealing to this same state as a protector.

The State Is the Culprit

The final irony is that it is the state—not free speech—that has been the oppressor of women. It was the state, not pornography, that burned women as witches. It was 18th-century law, not pornography, that defined women as chattel. 19th-century laws allowed men to commit wayward women to insane asylums, to claim their wives' earnings, and to beat them with impunity. 20th-century laws refuse to recognize rape within marriage and sentence the sexes differently for the same crime. It is the state, not pornography, that has raised barriers against women. It is censorship, not freedom, that will keep the walls intact.

One of the most important questions confronting feminism at the turn of this century is whether or not women's liberation can embrace sexual liberation. Can the freedom of women and freedom of speech become fellow travellers once more?

The feminist Myrna Kostash answered this question well by paraphrasing Camus: "Freedom to publish and read does not necessarily assure a society of justice and peace, but without these freedoms it has no assurance at all."

Censoring Pornography
Is a Danger to Society

by F. M. Christensen

About the author: *F. M. Christensen is associate professor of philosophy at the University of Alberta, Canada. A Ph.D. from Indiana University, he has done extensive research in the behavioral sciences.*

The fundamental motive for criminalizing sexual materials is nothing more than feeling offense that such things should exist. (The legal term "obscene," be it remembered, refers to what is highly offensive, not to what is harmful.) Centuries of horrible religious war and persecution finally made Western societies realize that merely disliking the activities of others is not a morally acceptable reason to interfere in their lives. This understanding is sometimes called "the harm principle," the principle that only actual or probable harm or hurt by others justifies harming or hurting them. Further, the harm must be publicly verifiable, involving physical or psychological pain or disability, not the metaphysical damage to the soul that the warring religionists alleged. Unfortunately, the lesson has not yet been fully learned. . . .

No Justification for Antiporn Laws

There is no more justification for antipornography laws than for "Jim Crow" laws, which harmed and coerced people for the color of their skin—and which were also rationalized, in their time, as promoting both moral values and the physical safety of society. In addition, there is ample evidence of the evils produced by sexual repressiveness; by fostering antisexual attitudes, such laws do yet more harm than that of restricting liberty and punishing unjustly. There is far better reason to punish those who propagate sexual aversion than those who promote sexual pleasure. Beyond all this are the other evils laws like this are known to spawn; for example, the high profits produced by black or gray markets attract criminals and lead to such vices as blackmail, exploitation of workers, and the bribing of judges and police. Laws against sexual explicitness are not only terribly unjust to individuals but terribly unwise for society as a whole.

Those who want to ban pornography have often sought ways to excuse the laws without reasonable evidence of harm. One of the arguments runs like this: "We don't know it's harmful, but we also don't know it's not; since it might be, and since so much is at stake, we can't take the chance." It is true that even a low likelihood of bad consequences can justify preventing a given type of action, at least if the harm is potentially great enough. But in this case that fact is of no avail, for there is as much or more evidence against even a low probability of serious consequences than in support of such. Indeed, there is about as much reason to believe pornography prevents harm as that it causes it. So the argument can just be turned around: "We don't know it doesn't prevent harm; since it might, and since much is at stake, we must allow it." Beyond this, the principle of not punishing unjustly stands supreme—we *do* know that being fined or put in prison hurts people. Hence we are morally obligated to be very sure that what someone does is apt to have ill effects before we apply any legal sanctions.

Appealing to Democracy

Another argument in this same "There may be no harm, but . . ." category appeals to the concept of democracy. "If a majority of people find something offensive—whether or not they are justified in feeling that way—surely they have a moral right to keep it out of their society." Again the reasoning is fallacious. In fact, it becomes something of an embarrassment when it turns out, as it has done repeatedly of late, that the majority believe sexual explicitness per se should not be banned. As is so often the case, the laws in question are promoted and maintained by the inertia of tradition and powerful minorities, not the majority. The fundamental point here, however, is that not even a majority is morally justified in harming those who have done or threatened no harm. Indeed, there is something especially pernicious about the power of the many being used to oppress a minority or an individual. Would it be right if the majority in this society decided to imprison, say, those who practice Judaism or Christian fundamentalism? Majority rule without the legal standard of the harm principle to protect individuals is not just; it is mob rule. Those who argue for the importance of "shared values" to a society often do not seem to regard justice, much less tolerance, as being among those values.

> *"Those who want to ban pornography have often sought ways to excuse the laws without reasonable evidence of harm."*

This is why the "community standards" criterion of U.S. and Canadian obscenity law is a miscarriage of justice. A plainer admission that nothing but popular prejudice underlies the statutes could hardly be asked. For it tacitly acknowledges what was true all along, that those particular standards have no objective moral basis that can be stated but are subject solely to the arbitrary and variable forces of socialization. This criterion has not been used to carve out exceptions to other basic rights—for example, to support laws against other things many have found obscene, such as interracial marriage. That reveals pretty clearly how much it is really worth. In fact, as the latter comparison also reveals, a history of prejudice against a certain type of behavior provides an excellent reason for giving it *special* legal protection. At least this is so if it involves an important area of human life—which sexuality, like religion, certainly is. Traditional laws prohibiting nonharmful sexual behavior violate the most fundamental moral rights, those of privacy and personal dignity. Majority rule is required for enterprises that are unavoidably cooperative, such as our highly interdependent economic system. But behavior that is not intrinsically harmful, and which influences others only as they choose to emulate it, should be protected as a private matter.

An issue closely related to that of majority rule involves the aesthetic intolerance that is central to judgments of what is "obscene." Historically, the suppression of sexual materials has involved a large element of class conflict. For the entertainment of the lower classes is typically sweaty and boisterous, their tastes unsubtle (i.e., explicit) and "unrefined," according to the ruling classes (upper or middle). In other words, "erotica" is what the latter enjoy, while "pornography" is what the former like. If the story ended there, it would be of small concern. But the law has been used to enforce these matters of taste. And the law always falls more heavily on the lower classes; it is often an instrument of class oppression. Even if such differences do not divide along class lines, however, the political oppression remains. In recent times, aesthetic standards have entered the

> *"The 'community standards' criterion of U.S. and Canadian obscenity law is a miscarriage of justice."*

criminal law overtly, by way of the judicial dictum that "artistic merit" can decide whether or not a sexual representation is legal. Whether a person is to be locked up in prison hinges on something as trivial and subjective as bad taste, as morally irrelevant as aesthetic judgment.

What Should Be Protected?

All this brings us to the question of what kinds of things should be protected by a governmental constitution or bill of rights. That is much too complex an issue in philosophy of law to deal with at length here; the more general issue of what ought to be legal or illegal is the important one for our purposes. However, since the "community standards" criterion has arisen in the context of judicial interpretation of constitutional law, one further point should be made. The main purpose for having a special system of legal rights to restrain government bodies, in a democracy, is to protect minorities and individuals from abuse of power by the majority; what is popular certainly does not need much protection. Hence appealing to that criterion to interpret the right of free expression is a clear violation of that original intent: it says some sort of majority can after all override a legal right that was meant to be above majority rule. In the process of trying to find an objective measure for the subjective notion of obscenity, what the average person finds offensive, the justices have undermined the very purpose of constitutional law.

"Traditional laws prohibiting nonharmful sexual behavior violate the most fundamental moral rights, those of privacy and personal dignity."

It is sometimes claimed the only freedom of expression that should be constitutionally assured is that of political speech, narrowly construed, on the grounds that such speech has a special importance in the democratic process. This view has its value-priorities backward. Democracy (i.e., majority rule) is justified by freedom, not the other way around; exercise of power by the majority is good only because, and to the extent that, it promotes people's control over their own lives. Beyond this, the fact that the voters get to be heard only once every few years means they have little control over most of the decisions of government and its massive bureaucracy. Individual members of a majority also need protection against the vast power of the state. Finally, even granting the special importance of political expression, that category surely must be construed broadly, so as to cover not only who should be elected but how life in the nation should be lived. After all, the freedom to influence others and be influenced by others is essential to making informed decisions, in all the aspects of life that government might touch and that voting might influence. . . .

Degrading Portrayals

Let us now turn to that other special legal issue, sexual portrayals that are genuinely or allegedly degrading to someone. In an important way, the case for censoring depictions or descriptions that are genuinely debasing is stronger than that for violent ones. (Certain types of violence are themselves degrading, of course.) For though there is still considerable doubt about the effects of exposure to the latter, little such doubt remains concerning the former. At least this is true when identifiable individuals or groups are recipients of the debasement. For we know something about the harmful effects of an atmosphere of racist messages, effects on the attitudes and behavior of both the victims and others. Not the least of the evils of debasing messages is the immediate psychological pain of those being degraded: *hatred hurts*. It can be more damaging than a physical assault—it can easily lead to physical violence, in fact, to others or to oneself. Self-dignity is a fundamental human need, as vital as food and water, and to be robbed of it is devastating.

Just as with violence, however, the legal proposals standardly made on this subject in recent years are blatantly selective, since they usually mention only sexual degradation and degradation of women. One of these proposed laws was actually passed in two or three different localities. Under its provisions, portrayals of female nudity or of women inviting intercourse could be legally punishable, while those of the gang rape and murder of a male would not. (The law was struck down by the courts, not on grounds of violating equal protection of the law, but on those of threatening freedom of expression.) An ironic aspect of these proposals warrants mention. It is likely that the sole reason for the existence of genuinely degrading sexual materials is the way this culture traditionally degrades sex itself. Raised with the teaching that their natural sexual feelings are "animalistic," "degrading," "objectifying," or worse, to those toward whom they are directed, vulnerable individuals turn consciously or unconsciously to various defense mechanisms to escape the self-hatred that would otherwise result—and fantasies of sexual degradation are evidently one of those mechanisms. This applies much more strongly to males, who, because of their greater tendency to be attracted to the genitals of the opposite sex, are the target of that hateful rhetoric. This being so, a sane law—not to mention a just one—against degradation would also be applied to writings and portrayals exhibiting the original kind of degradation. A law that would punish people involved with, say, that infamous cover on *Hustler*, but not those guilty of the antimale bigotry that leads to such defensive reactions, would be as unjust as any other law that punished acts of self-defense but not the original assault.

> *"Many are only too happy to attach the label 'degrading' to behavior they actually consider bad on other grounds."*

The irony goes deeper yet, however. Some of the people most actively involved in the campaign to eradicate sexual portrayals they consider degrading to women are the most vicious in their sexism against men; they can only be described as hatemongers. One of the most extreme of these women has been very influential in government antipornography efforts. She regards any sort of vaginal penetration as equivalent to rape, and makes statements such as "Men especially love murder." She calls the killing of women "the prime sexual act for men in reality and/or in imagination." Without the knowledge that he could kill his partner with impunity, she insists, a man would not enjoy sex. In spite of all this, she managed to induce the city councils of Indianapolis and Minneapolis to pass her proposed censorship law, and she later contributed heavily to the conclusions of the Meese Commission. Dozens of charges that are equally hateful (if not equally insane), in books by scores of extremist feminists, are to be found in most bookstores and libraries and are required reading in many college women's-studies programs. If anyone is to be locked up for sexually degrading anyone, it is clear where we should start.

Influence of Antidegradation Laws on Behavior

Yet it is not clear that there *should* be laws against degrading communications, that the very real harm they can cause would not be outweighed by the harmful effects of the laws themselves. One serious difficulty is the vagueness and subjectivity of the concept of degradation. Part of the problem here is in making clear to individuals just what the law does and does not allow. The continuing scandal of the existing obscenity laws is that the terms they use, such as "patently offensive" (United States) and "undue exploitation of sex" (Canada), are hopelessly unclear. All laws are vague to some degree, but in this case the degree is extreme. Moreover, experience has shown that the community-standards test does not solve this problem; no one ever knows what the "average person's" standard will be judged to be in a given case, or whether it might continue to be so judged tomorrow. To the question, "What type of thing *is* obscene, anyway?" the usual answer has been, "You'll find out in court." Imagine what it would be like, someone has suggested, for speeding laws to be handled this way: that is, for the law to read simply "Don't drive too fast," leaving it up to the judge or jury to decide whether you have done so.

A Chilling Effect

Part of what is evil about this is the "chilling effect" it has on behavior in general. Such laws can be used to prevent things that would never actually be prosecuted, or at least not convicted in court, out of concern that they just *might* be punished. Beyond that, such legal uncertainty is a terrible injustice because of the fear it can generate in people's lives. To make this point as vivid as possible, the reader should ask how safe she or he would feel living in a society where the law said, in effect, "Anyone who says or produces anything that is degrading will be put in prison." Another thing that is wrong about vague laws is the ease with which they can be manipulated. Regarding degradation in particular, many are only too happy to attach the label "degrading" to behavior they actually consider bad on other grounds. That description has been promiscuously applied to all sorts of things involving sex, from being outside a committed relationship, to being only for fun rather than affectionate, to being too enthusiastic. With equal ease, it could be charged that socialism or capitalism, atheism or religion, is degrading to some or all people. It seems clear enough why we do not have *general* laws against degradation—and

> "The legal suppression of sexual materials has gotten worse at an accelerating rate."

clearer still why it would be so unjust to police for this offense only one special category of expression, the sexual one.

In fact, special prohibitions regarding sexual degradation are a far *greater* threat to justice than would be those directed at other sorts of degradation. The reason is that in this society, all sorts of sexual behavior that are not debasing are commonly regarded as being so. Indeed, most of what those calling for such laws want banned is perfectly innocuous. In a society where for one person to do something she enjoys can be seen as degrading to all other persons of the same gender, where the general level of sexual anxiety is so high that extremists can manipulate the system with false charges, and where so many people think a feeling of revulsion in their gut is all the justification they need to lock another human being in a cage, laws against "degrading" portrayals of sex can only make an already grossly unjust situation even worse. Until such time as we as a society are able to tell the difference between what is and what is not debasing with regard to sex, such laws are a grave threat to that very human dignity they would ostensibly defend.

The Present Peril

Unjust and irrational though it is, the legal suppression of sexual materials has gotten worse at an accelerating rate [during the 1980s]. The main reason for this is increased activity on the part of extremist feminism and the right wing, and of certain others who share their sexual views. They have achieved great political power by getting well organized. Beyond that are two major reasons why they are able to wield such great influence in this special matter.

First, there is the high level of ignorance and misinformation about sexuality that characterizes the general public. They can so easily be misled by further misinformation under these conditions. A case in point is the investigation by the Commission on Pornography appointed by the U.S. attorney general. The staff, the chairman, and a majority of the commissioners were

> *"In circumstances of high emotion, such as those sexophobia involves, . . . protection of rights is most needed."*

on record in advance as strong opponents of sexual materials, while none of the others were known as proponents of erotic materials, or even as defenders of the status quo concerning obscenity laws. Their mandate was to make recommendations "concerning more effective ways in which the spread of pornography could be contained," which *assumes* it is evil and all but instructs them to declare it so. The obvious purpose of appointing the commission in the first place was not to explore the issues objectively but to indict pornography. This is borne out by the highly biased way in which their hearings were conducted, under conditions well suited to elicit gross exaggerations and outright falsehoods from the large numbers of antipornography zealots called to testify.

The second reason for the strong influence of the campaign against pornography is the shame and anxiety most people in this culture already feel regarding sexuality and its portrayal. These make it easy for those with positive sexual attitudes to be intimidated; if they speak out, they'll be labeled immoral and suspected of being closet perverts of some sort. This is especially true of politicians, who are notoriously afraid of being seen as "soft on smut." (Their votes can be bought wholesale by powerful lobbies such as the tobacco industry and gun-control opponents, in spite of the millions the products at issue have maimed and killed). This fear is relieved only in the privacy of the voting booth, where majorities from conservative Utah to conservative Maine have cast their ballots against sexual censorship. Even that could change, however; for if such fear continues to assure that only one side is heard, a majority will eventually be converted.

A Wave of Legal Repression

Under these influences, a wave of legal oppression has already been created, and in some places it has become a virtual witchhunt. The vagueness of the obscenity laws has been a particularly powerful weapon in this, deliberately used to coerce behavior far beyond what would be upheld in court. Since storekeepers can seldom know whether they have broken the law until a judge or jury decides, they are frightened into removing from their shelves everything even remotely sexual. Government attorneys and police chiefs, often working hand-in-glove with private censorship groups, have large amounts of taxpayers' money with which to harass and prosecute store owners and employees, and they have been doing so with a vengeance. The U.S. government's sweeping censorship legislation is meant to promote country-wide prosecutions of the sale of sexual materials. (One tactic has been the seizure of all money and property of the accused, on grounds that one item may later be judged obscene, so that he or she has no funds for a legal defense.) With all the highly conservative judges appointed to the Supreme Court and lower courts in the United States in recent years, even the incomplete constitutional protection existing previously is threatened with being swept away.

As if unjust laws were not bad enough, in many places there have been gross violations of supposedly protected legal rights. From all across the land have come reports of police harassment and brutality, blatant entrapment, intimidation of defense witnesses, and judicial misconduct. After all, "bad guys" do not deserve the protection of law and order. With official attitudes of such kinds, extremists are encouraged to acts of violence of their own; there have been firebombings of adult bookstores and the like in many places while these campaigns were going on (conveniently blamed on "organized crime"). It is precisely in circumstances of high emotion, such as those sexophobia involves, that protection of rights is most needed; without a strong stand against racial prejudice by an earlier Supreme Court, the United States today would very likely still be segregated. If silent citizens do not start speaking up, however, the sexual McCarthyism will continue.

Censoring Pornography
Is a Danger to Freedom

by Fred Small

About the author: *Fred Small is a singer/songwriter and environmental activist who lives in Cambridge, Massachusetts. He is a former practicing attorney.*

Writing about pornography I shoulder two burdens: guilt and fear. Each clouds reason and impedes communication. I feel guilty about patriarchy, about the injuries women have for centuries suffered at the hands of men and the oppression against which they struggle today. While I have actively supported their struggle, I have also unwittingly participated in their oppression. This knowledge is painful. I worry about making more mistakes, causing more hurt.

And I am afraid of controversy, afraid of criticism and denunciation by sisters and brothers who share my critique of patriarchy and my commitment to equality. I fear their anger. When Andrea Dworkin says that "any defense of pornography is war" against women, I am discouraged from contemplative and free-ranging discussion. Pornography is so complicated and so vast a subject. My thinking on it has changed more than once and will change again. Dare I cast my thoughts in unchangeable print?

The pain of pornography is not equally shared. As a man, I am not hurt and enraged by pornography in the same way as women. Some will feel I have nothing to contribute, no moral ground to stand on. But I am concerned enough about the dangers of censorship and about my priorities for activism that I offer my thoughts.

I oppose censorship because I believe it threatens our freedom to express unpopular ideas, to create subversive images, to make radical culture. I think that the legislative restrictions proposed for pornography are so vague that they could and would be used against feminist publications. Even if worded more precisely, these restrictions would set a precedent for governmental repression dangerous to us all.

My views on pornography itself are less strongly held. They are tentative, ad-

From "Pornography and Censorship" by Fred Small, *Changing Men*, no. 15, Fall 1985. © 1985, Fred Small. Reprinted by permission of the author.

mitting of error, colored by personal experience and inexperience. As an artist I strive to create a new culture that fully respects all women and men as human beings. Pornography has no place in such a culture. I denounce pornography as I denounce all sexist propaganda. But I suspect that pornography is not the central problem of patriarchy, that it is more symptom than disease. I suspect it may account for less direct harm than is sometimes attributed to it. I suspect that strategies other than antiporn activism may be more effective against sexism and violence. Pornography may not be the best target for our rage.

Censorship: Too Blunt and Dangerous an Instrument

Misogynist violence in this country has imposed a state of siege against women. Responding to these intolerable conditions, women and men in Minneapolis proposed an ordinance in 1983 that would permit individuals to sue to prevent the production or sale of pornography as a civil rights violation. Slightly modified, the Minneapolis ordinance has been offered as model legislation against pornography. Initially appealing, this legislation threatens grave dangers.

While proponents of the ordinance argue that its meaning is plain, many people—including widely respected feminist leaders—find its language vague and confusing. It defines pornography as "the graphic sexually explicit subordination of women through pictures and/or words" that satisfies *any one* of nine criteria. These include the presentation of women "dehumanized as sexual objects" or "in postures of sexual submission" or "as whores by nature" or "being penetrated by objects" or "in scenarios of degradation," or the exhibition of "women's body parts . . . such that women are reduced to those parts."

These terms do not mean what you or I or Catharine MacKinnon or Andrea Dworkin thinks they should mean. *They mean whatever a commissioner or judge or jury or the Supreme Court of the United States thinks they should mean in the political and social climate of the moment.*

Is fellatio "subordination"? Is genital exposure? Is wearing high heels? Is a short story about lesbians making love a "scenario of degradation"? Is the missionary position a "posture of sexual submission"? Does the word "objects" include a speculum demonstrated in a woman's self-help health manual or a dildo described in a lesbian sex guide? Does a documentary on prostitution depict women as "whores by nature"? Does an illustration teaching

> *"I suspect that pornography is not the central problem of patriarchy."*

women how to examine their breasts "reduce" women to their "parts"? Don't ask me. Ask a juror in Attapulgus, Georgia, or Brigham City, Utah, or New York, New York. Ask [Chief Justice] William Rehnquist.

Advocates of this legislation may believe that they command its destiny, that it will be used forever in the spirit of its creation. Historically, however, censorship is invoked not against the powerful and ideologically dominant, but against the weak, the outlaw, the radical. Ordinance coauthor Dworkin concedes—indeed, she asserts proudly—that this ordinance will be applied against materials produced by and for the gay and lesbian community. She even concedes that it could be used against her own writing on pornography. She is willing to take that chance. I am not. A time when *Our Bodies, Our Selves* is being removed from library shelves under pressure from the Right is no time to devise a new rationale for censorship.

Writers, photographers, artists, models, producers, directors, actors, publishers, clerical workers, magazine distributors, news dealers, and art exhibitors are all potential defendants under this legislation. They can't be sure how its language will be interpreted, either—and they can't afford to find out. Many will refrain from producing, selling, or exhibiting legally protected materials because of the possibility of a ruinous adverse ruling or because the costs of defending a lawsuit would be prohibitive.

The Problem with Censorship

Proponents of the ordinance emphasize that its enforcement provisions are civil, not criminal. But civil law can have the same impact as criminal law. When individuals sue for damages or to enjoin publication, the power of the state is invoked. A judge or jury looks at the material and decides if it is "pornography." If the judge issues an injunction, and the defendant refuses to comply, he or she can be sent to jail. The result is censorship: the materials are forbidden, banned by state decree.

> "The result is censorship: the materials are forbidden, banned by state decree."

Censorship advocates argue that if pornography contributes to violence against women, then censorship is *ipso facto* justified. Research in this area is very new. The studies some find conclusive others find ambiguous or flawed. But even if we assume for the sake of argument that pornography does influence violence against women, censorship is still not the answer. It is too dangerous, and it will not work.

The lethal effects of alcohol on the victims of crimes (including rape and drunk driving) committed under its influence, on alcoholics, and on people close to them are unarguable. But when prohibition was tried it failed utterly, and succeeded only in romanticizing liquor further, feeding organized crime, and breeding public cynicism. Likewise, prostitution is an abhorrent way for human beings to relate to one another. It systematically exploits and brutalizes women and girls forced by economic oppression to engage in it. But its illegality in forty-nine states has done nothing to protect women or to improve sexual relations. Banning porn will not make it unavailable, just illegal—thereby enhancing its allure.

If the state can ban pornography because it "causes" violence against women, it can also ban *The Wretched of the Earth* because it causes revolution, *Gay Community News* because it causes homosexuality, *Steal This Book* because it causes thievery, and *The Feminine Mystique* because it causes divorce. When speech is abridged in order to prevent crime, the precedent is set for censoring any book, magazine, or film documentary that encourages civil disobedience or draft resistance, suggests herbal remedies unapproved by the F.D.A. [Food and Drug Administration], explains home birth techniques, or approves gay or lesbian sex. Despite its shortcomings, failures, and misapplications, the First Amendment does protect ideas worth protecting. Carving out special exceptions to it will return to haunt us.

> *"When speech is abridged in order to prevent crime, the precedent is set for censoring any book, magazine, or film documentary."*

Pornography is a concrete, stationary target for our rage against misogynist violence, a horrifying and seemingly intractable problem. It is an issue on which feminists and our old foes, the religious Right, can at last agree, and thus united, win. It is just a start, goes the argument, but at least it's winnable.

But a start to what? After the porn shop is closed down, the Moral Majority's next target will not be the businessmen's club that excludes women or the sweatshop that exploits them; it will be the gay bookstore, another purveyor of "perversion." I am in favor of building coalitions with those who disagree with us on other issues, but people who rail against pornography, abortion, sex education, and gay rights in the same breath are too dangerous to dignify with alliance or embolden with victory. We in the men's movement are all sexual outlaws: sissies, gays, bisexuals, egalitarians, nudists, abortionists, sodomists, pacifists. Let us not arm those who would destroy us.

Pornography: A Picture of the Pain

Revolting as pornography can be, it does not exist in a cultural vacuum. I perceive it as just one band in a continuous spectrum of sexist media. Other media, it seems to me, are equally destructive and more pervasive.

The critics of pornography are right. Pornography is relentlessly sexist, displaying women as objects for men's sexual gratification. It wrenches sex from any human context of affection, understanding, or commitment. It depicts intercourse without reference to either contraception or conception. It generally presents a viciously narrow and rigid physical stereotype of women: young, slim-waisted, large-busted, with virtually no body hair. Often it associates sex with violence. It is patriarchal, produced by a multimillion-dollar, male-dominated industry in which women are exploited and frequently mistreated.

In each of these particulars pornography seems indistinguishable from American mass media as a whole. Advertising (including TV, radio, print, billboard, and shop window display), movies, television, music videos, recorded music (including album cover art), magazines, and written fiction inculcate the same values and perpetuate the same stereotypes. Sexism and violence are epidemic in our society. Sexism and violence run in a seamless continuum from *The New Yorker* to *Esquire* to *Playboy* to *Hustler*. The sole unique feature of pornography is that its sexism and violence involve women, and frequently men, with their genitalia graphically displayed.

Personally, I am no more offended by sexism and violence unclothed than clothed. I am no more offended by *Playboy* than by *Bride's* magazine, no more by *Gallery* than by the mercenary magazine *Soldier of Fortune*, no more by *Behind the Green Door* than by *Porky's*, no more by an s/m video than by *The Texas Chainsaw Massacre*. One of the top-grossing films of all time was also one of the most sexist and violent: *Indiana Jones and the Temple of Doom*, targeted at and enthusiastically promoted to a juvenile audience. The "classic" *Gone with the Wind* panders vicious racist and sexist stereotypes while it celebrates rape.

Among so many media abuses, why does pornography strike us as patently, uniquely offensive? Nearly all of us, women and men, are survivors of deep hurt and humiliation around sexuality and nudity. As children we were reprimanded if we touched our genitals, punished if we engaged in sex play, yelled at if we wandered outside naked. Our questions about sex provoked adult discomfort, hostility, and sometimes violence. Many of us were victims of sexual abuse. Nudity is still taboo in public and in most households. Sex remains largely forbidden, mysteri-

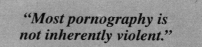

"Most pornography is not inherently violent."

ous, charged with cloudy memories of pain and powerlessness. No wonder the depiction of women and men in a sexual context brings intense response, whether revulsion or stimulation. Both may be a distorted measure of reality.

My own observations of pornography do not rise to the level of scientific research. Feminism has taught us, however, that personal experience may be at least as true as what passes for science. My observations suggest that most pornography is not inherently violent, and that explicitly violent pornography is not as ubiquitous as some have alleged. . . .

The Road to a Just Society: No Shortcuts

If censorship is too blunt and dangerous an instrument to use against pornography, and if the role of pornography in real world violence is not clear cut, how do we fight sexual exploitation and violence?

The remedy to bad speech is not less speech, but more. The messages of pornography are insidious in part because they are virtually the only messages most men get about sex. In the absence of free and open discussion of sexuality, porn speaks to men without rebuttal. It is frequently the only sex "education" boys receive. It flourishes in the darkness. It thrives on taboo. In a society that encouraged inquisitive, guilt-free discussion of sex from childhood on, pornography would be an absurd irrelevancy. In the long term, the only effective strategy against porn and the values it represents is to build that society.

We need to bring sex out in the open, into the light. We need universal, relaxed, nonreproachful, nonhomophobic sex education. We need stories, drawings, photographs, poems, songs, street theater, movies, advertisements, and TV shows about the ways real sex with real people can be. We need to see each other naked, casually and nonsexually, at the beach and in our backyards, to know what real people look like, to preempt prurience. We need to think about and heal the hurts in our lives that have left us with sexual compulsions, addictions, and obsessions.

> *"The remedy to bad speech is not less speech, but more."*

We need to continue the long struggle against sexism and violence. There are no shortcuts. We need more shelters for battered women and effective police response to domestic violence. We need to counsel men to stop abusing women and women not to tolerate it. We need a massive education campaign against rape—in schools, at workplaces, on the airwaves. We need boycotts of products advertised with sexist imagery. We need nonsexist textbooks and sports programs. We need to encourage children to feel proud and powerful. We need to elect feminist women and antisexist men to public office. We need to organize working women. We need gay rights. We need to involve men fully in raising and loving our children.

We must crack down on crime in the porn industry. Assault, battery, rape, and coercion occur in that industry like any other and should be prosecuted. The production of child pornography is virtually always child abuse and should be prosecuted. Publication and distribution of pornography that is made possible by unlawful coercion or violence against a "model" should be enjoined as a violation of her or his privacy rights. We can regulate the time, place, and manner of pornography sale and display so as not to offend the unwary. We can use picket lines to challenge the consumers of pornography to reexamine the way they think about women and about themselves.

A century ago, many feminists turned their energies away from women's rights toward moral purity. Alcohol became a scapegoat for innumerable social ills. It was widely believed that booze, by loosening men's inhibitions, brought out their inherently degraded nature. The result of this historic shift was the temperance movement, short-lived prohibition, and slowed gains for women. Let us not repeat this mistake with pornography out of frustration with the pace of our progress against the injustice that surrounds us.

Our society is misogynist and violent. Pornography is a sign of the times. Killing the messenger, however tempting, will not change the bad news. Sex and sexuality are complicated and poorly understood. The history of sexual legislation is frightening. It is the wrong course. We need more speech about sex, not less. Let us continue to talk in a way that cherishes the humanity in all of us.

Pornography Should Receive Free Speech Protection

by Wendy Kaminer

About the author: *Wendy Kaminer is a lawyer and a public-policy fellow at Radcliffe College. She is the author of* I'm Dysfunctional, You're Dysfunctional: The Recovery Movement and Other Self-Help Fashions.

Despite efforts to redevelop it, New York's Forty-second Street retains its underground appeal, especially for consumers of pornography. What city officials call "sex-related uses"—triple-X video (formerly book) stores, peep shows, and topless bars—have declined in number since their heyday in the 1970s, and much of the block between Seventh and Eighth avenues is boarded up, a hostage to development. New sex businesses—yuppie topless bars and downscale lap-dancing joints (don't ask)—are prospering elsewhere in Manhattan. But Peepland (MULTI-VIDEO BOOTHS! NUDE DANCING GIRLS!) still reigns, and Show World, a glitzy sex emporium, still anchors the west end of the block, right around the corner from the *New York Times*.

Touring Forty-second Street

In the late 1970s I led groups of suburban women on tours through Show World and other Forty-second Street hot spots, exposing them, in the interests of consciousness-raising, to pornography's various genres: Nazi porn, nurse porn, lesbian porn, bondage porn—none of it terribly imaginative. The women didn't exactly hold hands as they ventured down the street with me, but they did stick close together; traveling en masse, they were not so conspicuous as individuals. With only a little less discomfort than resolve, they dutifully viewed the pornography.

This was in the early days of the feminist anti-porn movement, when legislative strategies against pornography were mere gleams in the eye of the feminist

Wendy Kaminer, "Feminists Against the First Amendment," *The Atlantic*, November 1992. Reprinted by permission of the author. (Some subheadings have been added by Greenhaven Press).

writer Andrea Dworkin, when it seemed possible to raise consciousness about pornography without arousing demands for censorship. That period of innocence did not last long. By 1981 the New Right had mounted a nationwide censorship campaign to purge schools and public libraries of sex education and other secular-humanist forms of "pornography." Sex education was "filth and perversion," Jerry Falwell announced in a fund-raising letter that included, under the label "Adults Only. Sexually Explicit Material," excerpts from a college health text. By the mid-1980s right-wing advocates of traditional family values had co-opted feminist anti-porn protests—or, at least, they'd co-opted feminist rhetoric. The feminist attorney and law professor Catharine MacKinnon characterized pornography as the active subordination of women, and Phyllis Schlafly wrote, "Pornography really should be defined as the degradation of women. Nearly all porn involves the use of women in subordinate, degrading poses for the sexual, exploitative, and even sadistic and violent pleasures of men." Just like a feminist, Schlafly worried about how pornography might "affect a man who is already prone to violence against women." President Ronald Reagan deplored the link between pornography and violence against women.

> *"The alliance between feminists and the far right was not ideological but political."*

Pornography as Sex Discrimination

Of course, while feminists blamed patriarchy for pornography, moral majoritarians blamed feminism and other humanist rebellions. The alliance between feminists and the far right was not ideological but political. In 1984 anti-porn legislation devised by Andrea Dworkin and Catharine MacKinnon, defining pornography as a violation of women's civil rights, was introduced in the Indianapolis city council by an anti-ERA [Equal Rights Amendment] activist, passed with the support of the right, and signed into law by the Republican mayor, William Hudnut.

With the introduction of this bill, a new legislative front opened in the war against pornography, alienating civil-libertarian feminists from their more censorious sisters, while appealing to populist concerns about declining moral values. By calling for the censorship of pornography, some radical feminists found their way into the cultural mainstream—and onto the margins of First Amendment law.

The legislation adopted in Indianapolis offered a novel approach to prohibiting pornography which had all the force of a semantic distinction: pornography was not simply speech, Catharine MacKinnon suggested, but active sex discrimination, and was therefore not protected by the First Amendment. (In her 1989 book *Toward a Feminist Theory of the State*, MacKinnon characterized pornography as "a form of forced sex.") Regarding pornography as action, defining it broadly as any verbal or visual sexually explicit material (violent or not) that subordinates women, presuming that the mere existence of pornography oppresses women, the Indianapolis ordinance gave any woman offended by any arguably pornographic material the right to seek an order prohibiting it, along with damages for the harm it presumably caused. In other words, any woman customer browsing in a bookstore or patrolling one, glancing at a newsstand or a triple-X video store, was a potential plaintiff in a sex-discrimination suit. Given all the literature, films, and videos on the mass market that could be said to subordinate women, this ordinance would have created lots of new business for lawyers—but it did not stand. Within a year of its enactment the Dworkin-MacKinnon law was declared unconstitutional by a federal appeals court, in a decision affirmed by the U.S. Supreme Court.

The feminist anti-porn movement retreated from the legislative arena and passed out of public view in the late 1980s, only to re-emerge with renewed strength on college campuses. College professors following fashions in poststructuralism asserted that legal principles, like those protecting speech, were mere rhetorical power plays: without any objective, universal merit, prevailing legal ideals were simply those privileged by the mostly white male ruling class. The dominant poststructural dogma of the late 1980s denied the First Amendment the transcendent value that the liberal belief in a marketplace of ideas has always awarded it.

Massachusetts Mischief

This unlikely convergence of First Amendment critiques from multiculturalists, poststructuralists, and advocates of traditional family values, recently combined with high-profile rape and harassment cases and women's abiding concern with sexual violence, buoyed the feminist anti-porn movement. In 1992 it re-emerged on the national and local scene with renewed legislative clout. The presumption that pornography oppresses women and is a direct cause of sexual violence is the basis for bills introduced in the U.S. Senate and the Massachusetts legislature. In June 1992 the Senate Judiciary Committee passed the Pornography Victims' Compensation Act, which would make producers, distributors, exhibitors, and retailers convicted of disseminating material adjudged obscene liable for damages to victims of crimes who could claim that the material caused their victimization. The Massachusetts legislature held hearings on a much broader anti-porn bill, closely modeled on the

> *"College professors . . . asserted that legal principles, like those protecting speech, were mere rhetorical power plays."*

Indianapolis ordinance. Disarmingly titled "An Act to Protect the Civil Rights of Women and Children," the Massachusetts bill would not only make purveyors of pornography liable for crimes committed by their customers; it would also allow any woman, whether or not she has been the victim of a crime, to sue the producers, distributors, exhibitors, or retailers of any sexually explicit visual material that subordinates women. (The exclusion of verbal "pornography" from the anti-trafficking provision would protect the likes of Norman Mailer, whom many feminists consider a pornographer, so long as his works are not adapted for the screen.) What this bill envisions is that the First Amendment would protect only that speech considered sexually correct.

Unclear Connections

The feminist case against pornography is based on the presumption that the link between pornography and sexual violence is clear, simple, and inexorable. The argument is familiar: censorship campaigns always blame unwanted speech for unwanted behavior: Jerry Falwell once claimed that sex education causes teenage pregnancy, just as feminists claim that pornography causes rape. One objection to this assertion is that it gives rapists and batterers an excuse for their crimes, and perhaps even a "pornography made me do it" defense.

The claim that pornography causes rape greatly oversimplifies the problem of sexual violence. We can hardly say that were it not for pornography, there would be no rape or battering. As feminists opposed to anti-porn legislation have pointed out, countries in which commercial pornography is illegal—Saudi Arabia, for example— are hardly safe havens for women.

> *"Countries in which commercial pornography is illegal—Saudi Arabia, for example—are hardly safe havens for women."*

This is not to deny that there probably is some link between violence in the media and violence in real life, but it is complicated, variable, and difficult to measure. Not all hate speech is an incantation; not all men are held spellbound by pornography. Poststructural feminists who celebrate subjectivism should be among the first to admit that different people respond to the same images differently. All we can confidently claim is that the way women are imagined is likely to have a cumulative effect on the way they're treated, but that does not mean any single image is the clear and simple cause of any single act.

The Dworkin-MacKinnon bill, however, did more than assume that pornography causes sex discrimination and other crimes against women. It said that pornography *is* violence and discrimination: the active subordination of women (and it assumed that we can all agree on what constitutes subordination). MacKinnon and her followers deny that prohibiting pornography is censorship, because they effectively deny that pornography is speech—and that is simply Orwellian. The line between speech and behavior is sometimes blurred: dancing nude down a public street is one way of expressing yourself which may also be a form of disorderly conduct. But if pornography is sex discrimination, then an editorial criticizing the President is treason.

Most feminists concerned about pornography are probably not intent on suppressing political speech, but the legislation they support, like the Massachusetts anti-porn bill, is so broad, and its definition of pornography so subjective, that it would be likely to jeopardize sex educators and artists more than it would hard-core pornographers, who are used to operating outside the law. Feminist legislation makes no exception for "pornography" in which some might find redeeming social value; it could, for example, apply in the case of a woman disfigured by a man who had seen too many paintings by Willem de Kooning. "If a woman is subjected," Catharine MacKinnon writes, "why should it matter that the work has other value?"

With this exclusive focus on prohibiting material that reflects incorrect attitudes toward women, anti-porn feminists don't deny the chilling effect of censorship; they embrace it. Any speech that subordinates women—any pornography—is yelling "Fire!" in a crowded theater, they say, falling back on a legal canard. But that's true only if, just as all crowds are deemed potential mobs, all men are deemed potential abusers whose violent impulses are bound to be sparked by pornography. It needs to be said, by feminists, that efforts to censor pornography reflect a profound disdain for men. Catharine MacKinnon has written that "pornography works as a behavioral conditioner, reinforcer and stimulus, not as idea or advocacy. It is more like saying 'kill' to a trained guard dog—and also the training process itself." That's more a theory of sexuality than of speech: pornography is action because all men are dogs on short leashes.

This bleak view of male sexuality condemns heterosexuality for women as an exercise in wish fulfillment (if only men weren't all dogs) or false consciousness (such as male-identified thinking). True feminism, according to MacKinnon, unlike liberal feminism, "sees sexuality as a social sphere of male power of which forced sex is paradigmatic." With varying degrees of clarity, MacKinnon and Dworkin suggest that in a context of pervasive, institutionalized inequality, there can be no consensual sex between men and women: we can never honestly distinguish rape from intercourse.

An Esoteric Debate

A modified version of this message may well have particular appeal to some college women today, who make up an important constituency for the anti-porn movement. In their late teens and early twenties, these women are still learning to cope with sexuality, in a violent and unquestionably misogynistic world. Feminism on campus tends to focus on issues of sexuality, not of economic equity. Anxiety about date rape is intense, along with anxiety about harassment and hate speech. Understanding and appreciation of the First

"Anti-porn feminists don't deny the chilling effect of censorship; they embrace it."

Amendment is a lot less evident, and concern about employment discrimination seems somewhat remote. It's not hard to understand why: college women, in general, haven't experienced overt repression of opinions and ideas, or many problems in the workplace, but from childhood they've known what it is to fear rape. In the age of AIDS, the fear can be crippling.

> *"Anti-stalking laws could protect many more women than raids on pornographic video stores are ever likely to."*

Off campus the anti-porn feminist critique of male sexuality and heterosexuality for women has little appeal, but it is not widely known. MacKinnon's theoretical writings are impenetrable to readers who lack familiarity with poststructural jargon and the patience to decode sentences like this: "If objectivity is the epistemological stance of which women's sexual objectification is the social process, its imposition the paradigm of power in the male form, then the state will appear most relentless in imposing the male point of view when it comes closest to achieving its highest formal criterion of distanced aperspectivity." Dworkin is a much more accessible polemicist, but she is also much less visible outside feminist circles. Tailored, with an air of middle-class respectability and the authority of a law professor, MacKinnon looks far less scary to mainstream Americans than her theories about sexuality, which drive the anti-porn movement, might sound.

Concerns and Perceptions of an Educated Elite

If anti-pornography crusades on the right reflect grassroots concern about changing sexual mores and the decline of the traditional family, anti-pornography crusades on the feminist left reflect the concerns and perceptions of an educated elite. In the battle for the moral high ground, anti-porn feminists claim to represent the interests of a racially diverse mixture of poor and working-class women who work in the pornography industry—and they probably do represent a few. But many sex-industry workers actively oppose anti-porn legislation (some feminists would say they've been brainwashed by patriarchy or actually coerced), and it's not at all clear that women who are abused in the making of pornography would be helped by forcing it deeper underground; working conditions in an illegal business are virtually impossible to police. It's hard to know how many other alleged victims of pornography feel represented by the anti-porn movement, and I know of no demographic study of the movement's active members.

Leaders of the feminist anti-porn movement, however, do seem more likely to emerge from academia and the professions than from the streets or battered-women's shelters. Debra Robbin, a former director of the New Bedford Women's Center, one of the first shelters in Massachusetts, doesn't believe that "women on the front lines," working with victims of sexual violence, will "put much energy into a fight against pornography." Activists don't have time: "They can barely leave their communities to go to the statehouses to fight for more funding." The poor and working-class women they serve would say, "Yeah, pornography is terrible, but I don't have food on my table." Carolin Ramsey, the executive director of the Massachusetts Coalition of Battered Women Service Groups, says that the pornography debate "doesn't have a lot to do with everyday life for me and the women I'm serving." She explains, "Violence in the home and the streets that directly threatens our lives and our families is more pressing than a movie. Keeping my kids away from drugs is more important than keeping them away from literature."

What Is the Issue?

Ramsey is sympathetic to anti-porn feminists ("there's room in the movement for all of us"), and she believes that "violence in the media contributes to violence in real life." Still, she considers the pornography debate "esoteric" and "intellectual" and feels under no particular pressure from her constituents to take a stand against pornography.

If censoring pornography is the central feminist issue for Catharine MacKinnon, it is a peripheral issue for activists like Robbin and Ramsey. Robbin in particular does not believe that eliminating pornography would appreciably lessen the incidence of sexual abuse. David Adams, a co-founder and the executive director of Emerge, a Boston counseling center for male batterers, believes that only a minority of his clients (perhaps 10 to 20 percent) use hard-core pornography. He estimates

> *"The history of anti-porn campaigns in this country is partly a history of campaigns against reproductive choice."*

that half may have substance-abuse problems, and adds that alcohol seems more directly involved in abuse than pornography. Adams agrees with feminists that pornography is degrading to women but does not support legislation regulating it, because "the legislation couldn't work and would only open the door to censorship."

What might work instead? Emerge conducts programs in Boston and Cambridge public schools on violence, aimed at both victims and perpetrators. "There's a lot of violence in teen relationships," Adams observes. Debra Robbin wishes that women in the anti-porn movement would "channel their energies into funding battered-women's shelters and rape-crisis centers."

Reforming the criminal-justice system is also a priority for many women concerned about sexual violence. Anti-stalking laws could protect many more women than raids on pornographic video stores are ever likely to; so could the efficient processing of cases against men who abuse women.

Sensationalism as an Organizing Tool

Why do some women channel their energies into a fight against pornography? Anti-porn legislation has the appeal of a quick fix, as Robbin notes. And, she adds, "there's notoriety to be gained from protesting pornography." The "harder work"—promoting awareness and understanding of sexual violence, changing the way children are socialized, and helping women victims of violence—is less sensationalist and less visible.

Sensationalism, however, is an organizing tool for anti-porn feminists. If questions about the effects of pornography seem intellectual to some women involved in social-service work, the popular campaign against pornography is aggressively anti-intellectual. Although advocates of First Amendment freedoms are stuck with intellectual defenses of the marketplace of ideas, anti-porn feminists whip up support for their cause with pornographic slide shows comprising hard-core pictures of women being tortured, raped, and generally degraded. Many feminists are equally critical of the soft-core porn movies available at local video stores and on cable TV, arguing that the violence in pornography is often covert (and they include mainstream advertising images in their slide shows). But hard-core violence is what works on the crowd. Feminist rhetoric often plays on women's worst fears about men: "Pornography tells us that there but for the grace of God go us," Gail Dines, a sociology professor at Wheelock College, exclaimed during her recent slide show at Harvard, as she presented photographs of women being brutalized.

> *"Pornography is probably the most divisive issue feminists have faced."*

Dines's porn show was SRO [standing room only], its audience some three hundred undergraduates who winced and gasped at the awful slides and cheered when Dines pointed to a pornographic picture of a woman and said, "When I walk down the street, what they know about me is what they know about her!" She warned her mostly female audience that pornographers have "aggressively targeted college men." She seemed preoccupied with masturbation. Part of the problem of pornography, she suggested, is that men use it to masturbate, and "women weren't put on this world to facilitate masturbation." She advised a student concerned about the presence of *Playboy* in the college library that library collections of pornography aren't particularly worrisome, because men are not likely to masturbate in libraries.

Questionable Horror Stories

In addition to condemnations of male sexuality, Dines offered questionable horror stories about pornography's atrocities, like this: Rape vans are roaming the streets of New York. Women are dragged into the vans and raped on camera; when their attackers sell the rape videos in commercial outlets, the women have no legal recourse.

A story like this is impossible to disprove (how do you prove a negative?), but it should probably not be taken at face value, as many students in Dines's audience seemed to take it. William Daly, the director of New York City's Office of

Midtown Enforcement, which is responsible for monitoring the sex industry in New York, has never heard of rape vans; almost anything is possible on Forty-second Street, but he is skeptical that rape vans are a problem. Part of Dines's story, however, is simply untrue: under New York State privacy law, says Nan Hunter, a professor of law at Brooklyn Law School, women could seek damages for the sale of the rape videos, and also an injunction against their distribution.

It would be difficult even to raise questions about the accuracy of the rape-van story, however, in the highly emotional atmosphere of a slide show; you'd be accused of "not believing the women." Just as slides of bloody fetuses pre-empt rational debate about abortion, pornographic slide shows pre-empt argumentative questions and rational consideration of First Amendment freedoms, the probable effect of efforts to censor pornography, and the actual relationship between pornography and violence.

A Pornographic Culture?

Does pornography cause violence against women, as some feminists claim? Maybe, in some cases, under some circumstances involving explicitly violent material. Readers interested in the social-science debate should see both the report of the Attorney General's Commission on Pornography, which found a link between pornography and violence against women, and the feminist writer Marcia Pally's "Sense and Censorship," published by Americans for Constitutional Freedom and the Freedom to Read Foundation. In addition to the equivocal social-science data, however, we have the testimony of

> *"The more broadly pornography is defined, . . . the harder it is to control."*

women who claim to have been brutalized by male consumers of pornography. Anti-porn feminists generally characterize pornography as a "how to" literature on abusing women, which men are apparently helpless to resist. But evidence of this is mainly anecdotal: At a hearing on the anti-porn bill in the Massachusetts legislature, several women told awful, lurid tales of sexual abuse, said to have been inspired by pornography. Like a TV talk show, the Attorney General's commission presented testimony from pornography's alleged victims, which may or may not have been true. It's difficult to cross-examine a sobbing self-proclaimed victim; you either take her testimony at face value or you don't.

Still, many people don't need reliable, empirical evidence about a link between pornography and behavior to believe that one exists. When feminists talk about pornography, after all, they mean a wide range of mainstream media images—Calvin Klein ads, Brian De Palma films, and the endless stream of TV shows about serial rapist stranglers and housewives who moonlight as hookers. How could we not be affected by the routine barrage of images linking sex and violence and lingerie? The more broadly pornography is defined, the more compelling are assertions about its inevitable effect on behavior, but the harder it is to control. How do we isolate the effects of any particular piece of pornography if we live in a pornographic culture?

Narrowly drawn anti-porn legislation, which legislators are most likely to pass and judges most likely to uphold, would not begin to address the larger cultural problem of pornography. Feminists themselves usually claim publicly that they're intent on prohibiting only hard-core pornography, although on its face their legislation applies to a much broader range of material. But if you accept the feminist critique of sexism in the media, hard-core porn plays a relatively minor role in shaping attitudes and behavior. If feminists are right about pornography, it is a broad social problem, not a discrete legal one—that is, pornography is not a problem the law can readily solve, unless perhaps we suspend the First Amendment entirely and give feminists the power to police the mainstream media, the workplace, and the schools.

The likelihood that feminists would not be the ones to police Forty-second Street should anti-porn legislation pass is one reason that many feminists oppose the anti-porn campaign. If society is as sexist as Andrea Dworkin and Catharine MacKinnon claim, it is not about to adopt a feminist agenda when it sets out to censor pornography. The history of anti-porn campaigns in this country is partly a history of campaigns against reproductive choice and changing roles for men and women. The first federal obscenity legislation, known as the Comstock Law, passed in 1873, prohibited the mailing of not only dirty pictures but also contraceptives and information about abortion. Early in this century Margaret Sanger and the sex educator Mary Ware Dennett were prosecuted for obscenity violations. Recently the New Right campaign against socially undesirable literature has focused on sex education in public schools. Anti-porn activists on the right consider feminism and homosexuality (which they link) to be threats to traditional family life (which, in fact, they are). In Canada a landmark Supreme Court ruling which adopted a feminist argument against pornography was first used to prohibit distribution of a small lesbian magazine, which a politically correct feminist would be careful to label erotica.

Dangers of the Anti-Porn Movement

Gay and lesbian groups, as well as advocates of sex education and the usual array of feminist and nonfeminist civil libertarians, actively oppose anti-pornography legislation. Some state chapters of the National Organization for Women—New York, California, and Vermont—have taken strong anti-censorship stands, but at the national level NOW has not taken a position in the pornography debate. Its president, Patricia Ireland, would like to see pornography become socially unacceptable, "like smoking," but is wary of taking legal action against it, partly because she's wary of "giving people like

> *"Censorship campaigns . . . promise panaceas for profound social pathologies."*

Jesse Helms the power to decide what we read and see." But for major, national feminist organizations, like NOW and the NOW Legal Defense and Education Fund, the pornography debate is a minefield to be carefully avoided. Pornography is probably the most divisive issue feminists have faced since the first advocates of the ERA, in the 1920s, squared off against advocates of protective labor legislation for women. Feminists for and against anti-porn legislation are almost as bitterly divided as pro-choice activists and members of Operation Rescue.

Panaceas for Profound Social Pathologies

Renewed concern about abortion rights may drain energy from the anti-porn movement. Feminists may awaken to the danger that anti-pornography laws will be used against sex educators and advocates of choice. (The imposition of a gag rule on family-planning clinics may have made some feminists more protective of the First Amendment.) Politicians courting women voters may find that anti-porn legislation alienates more feminists than it pleases. Still, censorship campaigns will always have considerable appeal. Like campaigns to reinstate the death penalty, they promise panaceas for profound social pathologies. They make their case by exploiting the wrenching anecdotal testimony of victims: politicians pushing the death penalty hold press conferences flanked by mothers of murdered children, just as feminists against pornography spotlight raped and battered women.

Rational argument is no match for highly emotional testimony. But it may be wishful thinking to believe that penalizing the production and distribution of hard-core pornography would have much effect on sexual violence. It would probably have little effect even on pornography, given the black market. It would, however, complicate campaigns to distribute information about AIDS, let alone condoms, in the public schools. It would distract us from the harder, less popular work of reforming sexual stereotypes and roles, and addressing actual instead of metaphorical instruments of violence. The promise of the anti-porn movement is the promise of a world in which almost no one can buy pornography and almost anyone can buy a gun.

Bibliography

Books

Ellen Alderman and Caroline Kennedy	*In Our Defense: The Bill of Rights in Action*. New York: Avon Books, 1991.
Lee C. Bollinger	*Images of a Free Press*. Chicago: University of Chicago Press, 1992.
Kevin Boyle, ed.	*Article 19: Information, Freedom, and Censorship*. New York: Random House, 1988.
Clifford E. Christians, John P. Ferre, and P. Mark Fackler	*Good News: Social Ethics and the Press*. New York: Oxford University Press, 1993.
Joan DelFattore	*What Johnny Shouldn't Read: Textbook Censorship in America*. New Haven: Yale University Press, 1992.
Barbara Dill and Martin London	*At What Price? Privacy, Libel, and Freedom of the Press*. Washington, DC: Brookings Books, 1993.
Steven C. Dubin	*Arresting Images: Impolitic Art and Uncivil Actions*. New York: Routledge, 1992.
Jonathan W. Emord	*Freedom, Technology, and the First Amendment*. San Francisco: Pacific Research Institute for Public Policy, 1991.
Patrick Garry	*An American Paradox: Censorship in a Nation of Free Speech*. Westport, CT: Praeger Publishers, 1993.
Michael G. Gartner	*Advertising and the First Amendment*. New York: Priority Press, 1989.
Carol Gorman	*Pornography*. New York: Franklin Watts, 1988.
Mark A. Graber	*Transforming Free Speech: The Ambiguous Legacy of Civil Libertarianism*. Berkeley: University of California Press, 1991.
Edward de Grazia	*Girls Lean Back Everywhere: The Law of Obscenity and the Assault on Genius*. New York: Random House, 1992.
Gordon Hawkins	*Pornography in a Free Society*. New York: Cambridge University Press, 1988.
Anthony Lewis	*Make No Law: The Sullivan Case and the First Amendment*. New York: Random House, 1991.

Dave Marsh	*Fifty Ways to Fight Censorship*. New York: Thunder's Mouth Press, 1991.
Jonathan Rauch	*Kindly Inquisitors: The New Attacks on Free Thought*. Chicago: University of Chicago Press, 1993.
Cass R. Sunstein	*The Partial Constitution*. Cambridge, MA: Harvard University Press, 1993.
Rivian Taylor	*Contrary to Popular Opinion*. New York: Pharos Books, 1992.
R. George Wright	*The Future of Free Speech Law*. New York: Quorum Books, 1990.

Periodicals

Andrew Altman	"Liberalism and Campus Hate Speech: A Philosophical Examination," *Ethics*, January 1993.
The American Legion Magazine	"Stand By Our Flag: Special Section," June 1990.
Elizabeth Anderson	"Racism Versus Academic Freedom," *Against the Current*, May/June 1991. Available from Center for Changes, 7012 Michigan Ave., Detroit, MI 48210.
William F. Buckley	"Sorting Out the 'Rights' of College Students," *Conservative Chronicle*, March 27, 1991.
Paul G. Chevigny	"Begging and the First Amendment: Young v. New York City Transit Authority," *Brooklyn Law Review* 57 (Summer 1991): 525-45.
James S. Coleman	"A Quiet Threat to Academic Freedom," *National Review*, March 18, 1991.
Congressional Digest	Entire issue on federal funding of the arts, January 1991.
Arthur C. Danto	"Art for Activism's Sake," *Utne Reader*, November/December 1991.
Irah H. Donner	"Young v. New York City Transit Authority: The First Amendment Protects Flag Burners, Nazis, Professional Solicitors, and Commercial Advertisers: Did Our Framers Forget About the Poor?" *Transportation Practitioners Journal*, 1992. Available from 1725 K St. NW, Suite 301, Washington, DC 20006-1401.
Barbara Dority	"The War on Rock and Rap Music," *The Humanist*, September/October 1990.
Samuel Francis	"Degradation Is the Evil Core of Obscenity," *Insight*, May 25, 1992.
Jewelle Gomez	"Arts: The Economics of Censorship," *Ms.*, May/June 1992.
Philip D. Harvey	"Federal Censorship and the 'War on Pornography,'" *SIECUS Report*, February/March 1992. Available from 130 W. 42d St., Suite 2500, New York, NY 10036.

Bibliography

Orrin G. Hatch "The Arts in America: Who Should Judge the Merits?" *USA Today*, July 1991.

Joan M. Henderson "The Destructive Impact of Rap Lyrics," *Conservative Review*, October 1992.

Leanne Katz "Same Old Censorship," *Crossroads*, March 1993.

Bill Kauffman "Art and Politics Don't Mix," *USA Today*, July 1991.

Gara LaMarche "The U.S. 'Hate Speech' Debate," *Peace & Democracy News*, Winter 1992-93.

John Leo "A Sensible Judgment on Hate," *U.S. News & World Report*, July 6, 1992.

Barry Lynn "Don't Force Us to Pray," *The American Legion Magazine*, July 1993.

Jean Otto "Freedom to Speak and Write: We Have Met the Future," *Vital Speeches of the Day*, January 1, 1992.

David Rieff "The Case Against Sensitivity," *Esquire*, November 1990.

Joe Saltzman "Our Too Polite Media," *USA Today*, November 1990.

Phyllis Schlafly "Censorship Is OK When Practiced by Liberals," *Conservative Chronicle*, October 14, 1992.

Joan Wallach Scott "The Campaign Against Political Correctness: What's Really at Stake?" *Change*, November/December 1991.

Barry Siegel "Fighting Words," *Los Angeles Times Magazine*, March 28, 1993.

Tim Stafford "Campus Christians and the New Thought Police," *Christianity Today*, February 10, 1992.

Cliff Stearns and Ted Weiss "Should Congress Stop Funding the National Endowment for the Arts?" *The American Legion Magazine*, November 1992.

Nadine Strossen "The Controversy over Politically Correct Speech," *USA Today*, November 1992.

Jacob Sullum "Penises and Politics," *Reason*, October 1991.

Charles Thorne "The Orwellian University," *Liberty*, July 1990. Available from Dept. B36, PO Box 1181, Port Townsend, WA 98368.

James M. Wall "When Free Speech Is Offensive," *The Christian Century*, December 11, 1991.

Charles M. Whelan "Not Flagburners but the Court," *America*, July 7, 1990.

George F. Will "Curdled Politics on Campus," *Newsweek*, May 6, 1991.

Organizations to Contact

The editors have compiled the following list of organizations that are concerned with the issues debated in this book. All have publications or information available for interested readers. For best results, allow as much time as possible for the organizations to respond. The descriptions below are derived from materials provided by the organizations. This list was compiled at the date of publication. Names, addresses, and phone numbers of organizations are subject to change.

Accuracy in Media (AIM)
4455 Connecticut Ave. NW, Suite 330
Washington, DC 20008
(202) 364-4401

AIM is a conservative watchdog organization. It researches public complaints on errors of fact made by the news media and requests that the errors be corrected publicly. It publishes the bimonthly *AIM Report* and a weekly syndicated newspaper column.

American Civil Liberties Union (ACLU)
132 W. 43d St.
New York, NY 10036
(212) 944-9800

The ACLU champions the rights set forth in the Declaration of Independence and the Constitution. It opposes censoring any form of speech. The ACLU publishes the quarterly newsletter *Civil Liberties Alert* and several handbooks, public policy reports, project reports, civil liberties books, and pamphlets on the Freedom of Information Act.

American Coalition for Traditional Values (ACTV)
100 S. Anaheim Blvd., Suite 350
Anaheim, CA 92805
(714) 520-0300

ACTV is led by evangelical Christian leaders who are united to restore traditional moral and spiritual values to American schools, media institutions, and government. It supports parental input into library materials accessible to children and opposes pornography. The coalition produces videos and publishes the annual *TV Report*.

American Library Association (ALA)
50 E. Huron St.
Chicago, IL 60611
(312) 944-6780

The ALA supports intellectual freedom and free access to libraries and library materials through its Office for Intellectual Freedom. ALA's sister organization, the Freedom to Read Foundation, provides legal defense in important First Amendment cases involving libraries' rights to acquire and make available materials representing all points of view. The ALA publishes the *Newsletter on Intellectual Freedom*, pamphlets, articles, posters, and the Banned Books Week Resource Kit, updated annually.

Eagle Forum
Box 618
Alton, IL 62002
(618) 462-5415

The forum is a Christian group that promotes morality and traditional family values as revealed through the Bible. It opposes the depiction of sex and violence in media outlets such as television, films, magazines, and rock music lyrics. The forum publishes the monthly *Phyllis Schlafly Report* and the periodic Eagle Forum *Newsletter*.

First Amendment Congress
1445 Market St., Suite 320
Denver, CO 80202
(303) 820-5688

The congress believes that a free press is not the special prerogative of print and broadcast journalists but a basic right that assures a responsive government. It works to establish a dialogue between the press and people across the country, to encourage better education in schools about the rights and responsibilities of citizenship, and to obtain broader support from the public against all attempts by government to restrict the citizen's right to information. It publishes the *First Amendment Congress-Newsletter*, brochures, booklets, and educational materials.

Fund for Free Expression
485 Fifth Ave.
New York, NY 10017
(212) 972-8400

This organization is a collection of journalists, writers, editors, publishers, and concerned citizens who work to preserve freedom of expression throughout the world. It serves as the U.S. sponsor for the British publication *Index on Censorship*, which reports on violations of free expression. Its publications include *Off Limits: Censorship and Corruption* and *Restricted Subjects: Freedom of Expression*.

The Heritage Foundation
214 Massachusetts Ave. NE
Washington, DC 20002
(202) 546-4400

The foundation is a public policy institute dedicated to the principles of free competitive enterprise, limited government, individual liberty, and a strong national defense. It believes national security concerns justify limiting the media. The foundation publishes a weekly bulletin, *Backgrounder*; a monthly magazine, *National Security Record*; and many other books and research papers. It has published as part of its lecture series a paper entitled *Why National Security Concerns and the First Amendment Are Not Compatible*.

Morality in Media, Inc. (MIM)
475 Riverside Dr.
New York, NY 10115
(212) 870-3222

MIM believes pornography corrupts children and degrades both men and women. It has worked since 1962 to alert citizens to the dangers of pornography and to demand that the courts enforce obscenity laws. It also works toward maintaining decent moral standards in television. MIM publishes the bimonthly *Morality in Media Newsletter* and the bimonthly *Obscenity Law Bulletin*.

National Coalition Against Censorship (NCAC)
275 Seventh Ave., 20th Floor
New York, NY 10001
(212) 807-6222

NCAC is an alliance of organizations committed to defending freedom of thought, inquiry, and expression by engaging in public education and advocacy on national and local levels. It believes that censorship of violent materials is dangerous because it represses intellectual and artistic freedom. Its publications include *Censorship News* and *Report on Book Censorship Litigation in Public Schools*.

National Coalition Against Pornography (N-CAP)
800 Compton Rd., Suite 9224
Cincinnati, OH 45231
(513) 521-6227

N-CAP is an organization of business, religious, and civic leaders who work to eliminate pornography. It believes that there is a link between pornography and violence. It encourages citizens to support the enforcement of obscenity laws and to close down pornography outlets in their neighborhoods. N-CAP's publications include *Final Report of the Attorney General's Commission on Pornography*, *The Mind Polluters*, and *Pornography: A Human Tragedy*.

Parents' Alliance to Protect Our Children
44 E. Tacoma Ave.
Latrobe, PA 15650
(412) 459-9076

The alliance supports traditional family values and advocates censorship in cases where it believes these values are being undermined. It supports the inclusion of Christian teachings in textbooks and the labeling of records that contain offensive lyrics. It publishes position papers such as "Censorship and Education" and "Ratings-Labels on Recordings and Videos."

People for the American Way (PFAW)
2000 M St. NW, Suite 400
Washington, DC 20036
(202) 467-4999

PFAW is committed to reaffirming the traditional American values of pluralism, diversity, and freedom of expression and religion. It is engaged in a mass media campaign to create a climate of tolerance and respect for diverse people, religions, and values. It distributes educational materials, leaflets, and brochures and publishes the annual *Attacks on the Freedom to Learn*.

World Press Freedom Committee
c/o The Newspaper Center
11660 Sunrise Valley Dr.
Reston, VA 22091
(703) 648-1000

The committee monitors freedom of the press on an international level. It speaks out against "those who seek to deny truth in news and those who abuse newsmen." It has numerous articles on censorship available, including "A Missing Agenda" and "A Free Press Means Better Development."

Index

Index